Shakespeare's Language

In *Shakespeare's Language*, Keith Johnson offers an overview of the rich and dynamic history of the reception and study of Shakespeare's language from his death right up to the present. Tracing a chronological history of Shakespeare's language, Keith Johnson also picks up on classic and contemporary themes, such as:

- lexical and digital studies
- original pronunciation
- rhetoric
- grammar.

The historical approach provides a comprehensive overview, plotting the attitudes towards Shakespeare's language, as well as a history of its study. This approach reveals how different cultural and literary trends have moulded these attitudes and reflects changing linguistic climates; the book also includes a chapter that looks to the future. *Shakespeare's Language* is therefore not only an essential guide to the language of Shakespeare, but it offers crucial insights to broader approaches to language as a whole.

Keith Johnson is Emeritus Professor of Linguistics and Language Education at the University of Lancaster, UK. He is the author of *The History of Early English* (2016) and *Shakespeare's English* (2013).

Shakespeare's Language
Perspectives Past and Present

Keith Johnson

LONDON AND NEW YORK

First published 2019
by Routledge
2 Park Square, Milton Park, Abingdon, Oxon OX14 4RN

and by Routledge
52 Vanderbilt Avenue, New York, NY 10017

Routledge is an imprint of the Taylor & Francis Group, an informa business

© 2019 Keith Johnson

The right of Keith Johnson to be identified as author of this work has been asserted by him in accordance with sections 77 and 78 of the Copyright, Designs and Patents Act 1988.

All rights reserved. No part of this book may be reprinted or reproduced or utilised in any form or by any electronic, mechanical, or other means, now known or hereafter invented, including photocopying and recording, or in any information storage or retrieval system, without permission in writing from the publishers.

Trademark notice: Product or corporate names may be trademarks or registered trademarks, and are used only for identification and explanation without intent to infringe.

British Library Cataloguing-in-Publication Data
A catalogue record for this book is available from the British Library

Library of Congress Cataloging-in-Publication Data
Names: Johnson, Keith, 1944– author.
Title: Shakespeare's language : perspectives past and present / Keith Johnson.
Description: Abingdon, Oxon ; New York, NY : Routledge, 2019. |
Includes bibliographical references and index.
Identifiers: LCCN 2018027277 (print) | LCCN 2018035263 (ebook) |
ISBN 9781315303079 (Master) | ISBN 9781315303062 (Adobe Reader) |
ISBN 9781315303055 (ePub) | ISBN 9781315303048 (MobiPocket) |
ISBN 9781138236172 | ISBN 9781138236172 (hardback : alk. paper) |
ISBN 9781138236189 (paperback : alk. paper) | ISBN 9781315303079 (ebk)
Subjects: LCSH: Shakespeare, William, 1564–1616–Language. |
Shakespeare, William, 1564–1616–Literary style.
Classification: LCC PR3072 (ebook) |
LCC PR3072 .J645 2019 (print) | DDC 822.3/3–dc23
LC record available at https://lccn.loc.gov/2018027277

ISBN: 978-1-138-23617-2 (hbk)
ISBN: 978-1-138-23618-9 (pbk)
ISBN: 978-1-315-30307-9 (ebk)

Typeset in Bembo
by Out of House Publishing

For H and H

Contents

List of figures x
List of tables xi
Preface xiii

PART I
Till 1950 1

1 **The seventeenth century: 'true sublimity ... but puffy style'** 3
   1.1 *Fickle fortune in an eventful century* 3
   1.2 *Changing tastes: Bacon and the Royal Society* 4
   1.3 *Criticisms and, sometimes, reverence* 7
   1.4 *Shakespeare adaptations* 11
   1.5 *From adaptation to restoration* 18

2 **'Retrieving original purity': the eighteenth century** 20
   2.1. *Mouldy bread* 20
   2.2 *Shakespeare's 'meridian blaze'* ... 21
   2.3 *... and his 'dark spots'* 23
   2.4 *What the dark spots were* 24
   2.5 *Editing Shakespeare* 27
   2.6 *Word lists* 29
   2.7 *Attempts to systematize* 32
   2.8 *Seventeenth-century plays and eighteenth-century books* 38

3 **Measuring and classifying: the nineteenth century** 42
   3.1 *A problematic relationship with the truth* 42
   3.2 *Two societies, for Shakespeare and Shakspeare* 43
   3.3 *Editions, long, short, and sometimes expurgated* 46
   3.4 *Abbott and an educational grammar* 48
   3.5 *Two concordances, one lexicon, and a very large dictionary* 51

4 Making Shakespeare difficult: the early twentieth century — 56
4.1 *Ambiguity and the plain man* 56
4.2 *Excavating images* 58
4.3 *Lexical excavations* 64
4.4 *Shakespeare language studies and modern linguistics* 66

PART II
1950 on — 69

5 From oxcart to computer: lexical studies — 71
5.1 *Expressions of* zeitgeist 71
5.2 *Counting Shakespeare's words* 72
5.3 *Shakespeare's word formations* 79
5.4 *More 'interdisciplinariness': metaphor* 82
5.5 *Dictionaries, concordances, glossaries* 83
5.6 *Attribution studies* 87
5.7 *Shakespeare's language in the pecking order* 87

6 'A richness of variant forms': grammar — 90
6.1 *Do and NICE* 90
6.2 *Two new Abbotts: Blake and Hope* 94
6.3 *A fascinating wealth of detail* 97
6.4 *Grammar with a sociolinguistic dimension* 99
6.5 *How to do things with grammar* 101
6.6 *Towards pragmatics* 102

7 Shakespearean 'rules of use': pragmatics — 104
7.1 *Speech acts, and some Shakespeare examples* 104
7.2 *Politeness and impoliteness* 107
7.3 *Thou and you* 109
7.4 *Implicature, and 'flouting maxims'* 114
7.5 *Pragmatic noise* 117

8 Original pronunciation: 'pronounced out of Ireland'? — 119
8.1 *Puns: amusing ... and revelatory?* 119
8.2 *Why study OP* 121
8.3 *Thirty years of OP* 122
8.4 *How we know: 'internal' evidence for OP* 122
8.5 *How we know: 'external' evidence for OP* 126

8.6 *Some Shakespearean sounds* 128
  8.7 *OP performances* 129
  8.8 *Crystal's 2016* Dictionary 130

9 **'Multifarious liberty and gay individualism':
  Shakespeare in print** 133
  9.1 *Variation in spelling and punctuation* 133
  9.2 *Spelling, and graphology* 134
  9.3 *Punctuation* 141
  9.4 *Punctuation's 'new age'* 151

10 **Verse and prose: changing a 'sorry bed'** 153
  10.1 *IPs: Procrustes' 'sorry bed'?* 153
  10.2 *'Miscellaneousness' in blank verse* 155
  10.3 *'Fitting round': the 'art of congruence'* 159
  10.4 *Other verse forms* 164
  10.5 *Prose* 167

11 **Rhetoric: 'maggot ostentation'?** 174
  11.1 *Rhetoric's bad press* 174
  11.2 *Some rhetorical history* 175
  11.3 *Ciceronian style* 176
  11.4 *Beyond Cicero* 178
  11.5 *Figures of speech* 182
  11.6 *A rich variety of tools* 191

12 **Where the future lies** 195
  12.1 *Turning over stones* 195
  12.2 *Lexis and pronunciation* 195
  12.3 *The theatre, speech acts, and cognitive stylistics* 198
  12.4 *Envoi* 199

  References 201
  Index 211

Figures

5.1	Quotation numbers per decade in *OED data*	77
6.1	Survey of uses of *do*	92
6.2	Occurrences of *do* in affirmative statements	92
6.3	Regional distribution of *do* in affirmative statements	93
6.4	The replacement of the third-person singular suffix –*th* by –*s*. Percentages of –*s*.	100
8.1	The entry for the word *hour* in Crystal (2016)	131
10.1	Percentage distribution of prose in Shakespeare's plays	169

Tables

1.1	Some important seventeenth-century Shakespeare adaptations	12
1.2	D'Avenant's adaptation of a Lady Macbeth speech	13
1.3	Categories of changes to Shakespeare's texts	14
2.1	Some eighteenth-century Shakespeare editions	27
2.2	Upton's 14 Shakespearean 'language rules'	32
2.3	Hurd's classification of Shakespeare's word formation strategies	35
3.1	Metrical features of *Love's Labour's Lost* and *The Winter's Tale*	44
3.2	Fleay's chronology of Shakespeare's plays	44
4.1	Empson's seven types of ambiguity, with Shakespearean examples	59
5.1	Uses of *ah*	86
6.1	Chapters dealing with grammar in Salmon and Burness (1987)	97
6.2	'Small words'	98
6.3	Third-person singular indicative suffix -*s* vs. – *th*. Percentages of -*s*	100
7.1	Use of thou/you in relation to status	111
8.1	Some Shakespearean puns	123
10.1	Some of Wright's departures and deviations from standard IP lines	156
10.2	Vickers' image categories	168
11.1	Figures of Speech covered in Adamson et al. (2007)	189

Preface

This book began life as a chapter I was asked to write by Jill Levenson and Robert Ormsby for their *The Shakespearean World* volume, which appeared in 2017. The chapter was intended to show how Shakespeare's language had been viewed from age to age, and to plot the development of Shakespearean language studies. As I was writing the chapter, it became clear just how much material there was to cover; one short chapter could simply not do justice to such a huge field.

But could a book? When I started writing it, I was hopeful of providing reasonably comprehensive coverage of the field. But you only have to glance at Brian Vickers' six-volume collection of Shakespeare criticism – *Shakespeare: The Critical Heritage* – to realize just how comprehensive comprehensiveness is. Admittedly the volumes cover much more than just language, but they also only go up to the beginning of the nineteenth century, and are in all over 3,000 pages long. Then there is the fact that this book focuses almost exclusively on the British and American worlds. Practically no mention is made of the mass of Shakespeare criticism – some related to his language – that has appeared in Europe and elsewhere. All in all, the book must be presented as having a selective focus. I hope readers will appreciate what it does cover, rather than was it does not.

The aims of the book are those of the original chapter – to plot changing views and the development of Shakespeare language studies. In the pursuit of these aims, a good deal of Shakespeare's language gets described, and this may be considered a third, less central aim. Again, the descriptions are very far from being comprehensive – the book is not at all intended as a comprehensive account of Shakespeare's language, though hopefully readers may find descriptions of aspects of his language they are unfamiliar with.

The book is divided into two parts. The first covers the seventeenth, eighteenth, nineteenth, and early twentieth centuries. Part II concentrates on the period from about 1950 up till the present day, with each chapter covering a different linguistic area. Chapter 4, Section 4 discusses the rationale for this structure in a little more detail.

Some conventions:

- I have tried in the text to refer backwards and forwards as much as possible to discussions of related issues. Chapter and section numbers are used where this happens: so Chapter 4, Section 4 would be written as 4.4, and Chapter 11, Section 3 would be 11.3;
- Acts, scenes and line numbers from the plays follow those found in Crystal and Crystal's online *Shakespeare's Words* site: www.shakespeareswords.com;
- Whenever the First Folio is referred to, the version used is Hinman (1996).

As ever, most thanks are due to Helen for all her useful comments on issues both big and small. She has the talent for noticing major omissions in a chapter, at the same time as picking up a typo on page 6, line 3. Thanks too to the anonymous reviewers of the initial proposal, whose comments helped shape the book. I am grateful also to those who offered views on the future of Shakespeare language studies for Chapter 12, as well as to Polly Dodson and Zoë Meyer at Routledge for their help in facilitating the proposal and seeing it through to publication. I am grateful also to Claire Bell for her useful work.

Part I
Till 1950

1 The seventeenth century
'True sublimity ... but puffy style'

1.1 Fickle fortune in an eventful century

William Cartwright, a dramatist and poet, died in 1643. He is virtually forgotten today, but was a popular figure in his lifetime. King Charles I himself was a fan, and apparently wore clothes of mourning on the day of Cartright's death. A collection of his poems was published in 1657. It was prefaced by no fewer than 57 commendatory verses singing the man's praises.

As far as we know, no monarch wore mourning on the 23rd April 27 years earlier, when Shakespeare died. And when the First Folio of his works appeared in 1623, it contained just two commendatory verses. Cartright outshines Shakespeare. But fortune is a fickle goddess. Four hundred years after Shakespeare's death, there were huge celebrations world-wide. It is safe to assume that in 2143, Cartwright's four-hundredth will not be celebrated in the same way, or indeed at all.

Just two commendatory verses for Shakespeare's death, and not that much comment during his lifetime either. As far as his language style is concerned – our concern in this book – there were a few reverent voices, and they often made reference to 'honey': Shakespeare was 'mellifluous and honey-tongued,' his verse was 'hony-flowing,' his characters spoke with 'sugred tongues' – that kind of thing.[1] His language does in fact get a brief mention in one of those two First Folio commendatory verses, when Ben Jonson talks of Shakespeare's 'well turned, and true filed lines.' But Shakespeare's language provoked little discussion then. Now, four hundred years later, things are very different. There is today hardly a Shakespearean linguistic stone that remains unturned.

This book is about the afterlife of Shakespeare's language – how it has been regarded and how studied – since his death 16 years into the seventeenth century. Some historical context will help set the scene for a century in which linguistic attitudes underwent seismic changes. Shakespeare was just 38 when, in the first years of the century, Elizabeth I died and James I became king. It was a moment of unification, because James was also King of Scotland. But the century very quickly turned turbulent for England, and unity was in short supply. Shakespeare had been dead for only 25 years when civil war broke out, the country divided between parliamentarians (eventually led by Oliver Cromwell) and supporters of the king. That was in 1642. The next 18 years were very stormy ones. King Charles was executed in 1649, and England became a 'commonwealth' or 'republic,' headed by Cromwell. Then Cromwell died (of natural causes, in 1658), and Charles II returned from exile to be the new king. This 'Restoration' happened in 1660. The rest of the century was marginally quieter, though the religious conflicts between Protestant groups and Catholics rumbled on. The Stuart dynasty continued to provide sovereigns until the next century. In 1714, George of Hanover was brought over from Germany as king. He, the first Hanoverian, was a foreigner and spoke no English. But at least he was a Protestant.

The fate of the English theatre followed these political events closely. At the beginning of the century it was flourishing. But when the Civil War started, the Puritan parliament passed an act banning theatrical performances. Since England was, the act read, 'threatened with a Cloud of Blood by a Civil War,' it was necessary to 'call for all possible Means to appease and avert the Wrath of God.' 'It is therefore thought fit and ordained …,' the act continued, 'that, while these sad causes and set times of humiliation do continue, public stage plays shall cease.'[2] Theatres closed, and only returned when the new king was in place. Fortunately Charles II was an enthusiastic theatre-goer, and he soon granted patents for the production of plays by two companies. The popularity of the theatre increased thereafter as the century progressed, though it was a very different kind of theatre from the one Shakespeare had worked in.

1.2 Changing tastes: Bacon and the Royal Society

After all that talk about honey, it may come as a surprise to read what John Dryden – one of the most eminent seventeenth-century literary figures – has to say about Shakespeare's language. 'His whole stile,' Dryden writes, 'is so pester'd with Figurative expressions, that it is as affected as it is obscure.'[3] We will later see that others could be even more damning. These are not just the outpourings of irate, hypercritical men. They reveal real reservations about how Shakespeare wrote. What had happened to change 'honey-tongued' and 'mellifluous' into 'affected' and 'obscure'?

How might Shakespeare's language be described? It depends of course on who is doing the describing, and what stage of Shakespeare's career is being described. As for his earlier works, candidate adjectives might be 'rich,' 'copious,' 'exuberant,' 'figurative,' possibly even 'outlandish.' You might be tempted to add 'coarse,' given Shakespeare's mastery of invective. To an extent all these are characteristics of the Early Modern English (EModE) period in which Shakespeare was writing, and to many, these characteristics were linguistic virtues. They signalled robust, energetic creativity.

But with the new (seventeenth) century, tastes were changing, and some earlier linguistic virtues were beginning to be regarded as linguistic vices. Partly responsible was the 'scientific revolution' which was taking place in Europe. Chief among the scientific revolutionaries was a close contemporary of

Shakespeare, Francis Bacon. A philosopher, statesman and scientist, he is sometimes called the 'father of empiricism.' His death says something about how he lived. According to the biographer, John Aubrey (in his *Brief Lives*), Bacon was travelling with the king's physician to Highgate. As frequently happened, Bacon's thoughts were on an empirical, scientific problem: in this case whether snow could be used to preserve meat. To find out, he promptly bought a hen and stuffed it with snow. Unfortunately the snow so chilled Bacon that soon after he died, probably from pneumonia. An ironically appropriate end for an empirical thinker.

Of Bacon's various writings, the ones on scientific method were particularly influential. In *The Advancement of Learning* (1605) he argued that traditional methods of scientific enquiry were unsound. He described the new 'Baconian Method' in his *Novum Organum* ('New Method'), which appeared in 1620. The method is based on inductive thinking – using the observation of specific instances to work out general laws. His approach to scientific enquiry was an important stimulus to the growth of interest in science in seventeenth-century England. When the dust of the Civil War had settled, and England once more had a king, thoughts turned to how – in the words of the English scholar and theologian, Thomas Sprat – 'to render our country, a land of experimental knowledge.'[4] It was proposed that a Royal Society should be established to achieve this aim. Charles II supported the idea, and the inaugural meeting was held just six months after the Restoration. The Society played an important role in the scientific life of the nation, as indeed it still does today. Among the major seventeenth-century figures involved in the enterprise were Isaac Newton, and two men of science who became members of the Society's council: Robert Boyle (one of the founders of modern chemistry) and the natural philosopher, Robert Hooke.

What has all this to do with language? The answer is 'quite a lot,' because (the argument went) if science is to be managed properly, it is important that the language in which it is expressed – what Sprat calls 'the manner of discourse' – should be appropriate. For this reason, language 'reform' was right at the centre of the Society's aims.

Reform really was needed. For Sprat and other like-minded people, English really was in no fit state to provide an appropriate vehicle for scientific expression. The run-up to Civil War, and the War itself, was a time when freedom in almost everything, including language use, was tolerated. The air was filled with controversy, public disputations were lively, and censorship of expression was almost non-existent. Numerous religious and secular groups with exotic names had sprung up. There were the Levellers, the Ranters, the Diggers – all with their own particular versions of non-conformity. Then there were those with other exotic beliefs: in witchcraft, alchemy, astrology. A word sometimes used to characterize such groups was 'Enthusiasts' – people 'under the influence of prophetic frenzy' (the definition is from the *Oxford English Dictionary:* the *OED*). Being 'enthusiastic' in this sense was something highly antipathetic to the emerging scientific ethos. The Enthusiasts' linguistic habits were as excessive as their beliefs. During the Civil War period, Thomas Sprat noted, English 'received many fantastical terms, which were introduced by our religious sects, and many outlandish phrases which ... writers and translators brought in.'[5] Another member of the Society, the writer and philosopher Joseph Glanvill, points his finger at the clergy: 'empty and fantastical preachers,' he calls them, with their 'Metaphors,' 'Fanatick Phrases' and 'Fanciful schemes of speech.'[6]

The language of the previous century was no better. Those very adjectives we suggested earlier to characterize some of Shakespeare's writing – 'rich,' 'copious,' 'exuberant,' 'figurative,' 'outlandish' and 'coarse' – were regarded as the enemies of scientific discourse. Sprat usually expresses himself with moderation, but he admits to 'just anger' when he contemplates the writing of some authors past and present – full of 'vicious abundance of phrase,' 'trick of metaphors,' 'volubility of tongue.'[7] The philosopher John Locke agrees. His *Essay Concerning Human Understanding* has a chapter entitled 'Abuse of words.' 'If we would speak of things as they are,' he says, 'we must allow that all the art of rhetoric ... [is] for nothing else but to insinuate wrong ideas ... and mislead the judgment.'[8] He goes on to describe rhetoric as a 'powerful instrument of error and deceit.' Puns were particularly disdained. They involve double meanings, allowing multiple levels of interpretation. For writers concerned with scientific clarity, ambiguity and interpretative multiplicity were to be avoided – along with extravagance, fulsomeness, outlandishness, figurativeness and coarseness.

If English was to become a fit vehicle for scientific development, it clearly needed to be 'corrected,' or 'cleaned-up.' Linguistic 'clean-up operations' were already taking place in other parts of Europe. The earliest attempt was in Florence in the 1580s, where the Accademia della Crusca was set up. *Crusca* is the Italian for 'bran,' the husks remaining in the flour-making process, and the idea was that the new Academy would 'sift through' the language, 'separating the wheat from the chaff.' The Accademia published an Italian dictionary in 1612. In France, a French Academy was proposed in 1635. Its aim was 'to labor with all the care and diligence possible, to give exact rules to our language, to render it capable of treating the arts and sciences.'

Though the English eventually baulked at the idea of an English Academy, in some respects the Royal Society acted like one. In 1664 it set up a committee to look at ways of 'improving' the English language. It was headed by one of the Society's founders, John Wilkins, and had 22 members 'whose genius was very proper and inclined to improve the English tongue.'[9] Their number included John Dryden, Thomas Sprat, and the writer and diarist John Evelyn. The committee never presented a final report, but the direction in which it was moving was clear. Rhetoric and all the 'devices of fancy' would have to go. As Sprat put it, 'eloquence ought to be banished out of all civil societies'; 'we generally love to have reason set out in plain, undeceiving expressions.' He praised Royal Society members for 'bringing all things as near Mathematical plainness, as they can: and preferring the language of Artizans, Countrymen, and Merchants, before that, of Wits, or Scholars.'[10] The avoidance of 'coarseness' was also important, and much store was put on politeness.

It is not surprising that, in this new linguistic climate, there were aspects of Shakespeare's language that did not go down at all well. As Taylor (1989) elegantly puts it: 'anyone who disliked puns, metaphors, vulgar similitudes, fanciful schemes of speech, or excessive emotion could not care much for Shakespeare.'[11] So it was, by this declension, that talk of 'honey-tongued melliflousness' changed into mutterings about 'affected obscurity'?

1.3 Criticisms and, sometimes, reverence

1.3.1 Jonson and Dryden

But despite all this, many seventeenth-century commentators cared very much for Shakespeare. Even though they criticized his language, they remained respectful. Ben Jonson is like this. His view that Shakespeare would have done well to 'blot' [erase] many of his lines is well known, and it is supported by some detailed critical statements. For example, late in his life, Jonson wrote *The English Grammar*, published in 1640, three years after his death. In this, he expresses strong views regarding certain grammatical constructions, some of which were used by Shakespeare. Use of the word *his* in possessive constructions is one of his targets. This occurs in phrases like *the King his fool*, meaning *the King's fool*. The form probably came about for phonetic reasons. In Middle English (ME) the *–'s* genitive was often pronounced /ɪs/ or /ɪz/ and written *is* or *ys*; so *King's* could be written *Kingys*. This meant that *the King's fool* would look and sound rather like *the King his fool*. Since the two forms looked the same, there were doubtless those who used one for the other.[12] The form was common in the sixteenth century, and Shakespeare uses it at least three times:

- *Now where's the Bastard's braves* [threats] *and Charles his gleeks* [taunts]? (1H6 3.2.123);
- *Once in a seafight 'gainst the Count his galleys / I did some service* (TN 3.3.28);
- *Nor Mars his sword, nor war's quick fire shall burn* (Sonnet 55).

Jonson is intemperate in his condemnation. The form shows, he says, 'monstrous syntax.'[13] His criticism is not of course directed specifically at Shakespeare, but at a linguistic habit of his time. Indeed, in his youth, Jonson himself was guilty of the same 'monstrous syntax,' with two of his early plays entitled *Sejanus His Fall*, and *Cataline His Conspiracy*!

But Jonson's linguistic criticisms were accompanied by reverence. Later in life, remembering his comment about blotting lines, he adds: 'I lov'd the man, and doe honour his memory ... There was ever more in him to be praysed, than to be pardoned.'[14] It is that same note of reverence which we found in Jonson's First Folio commemorative verse.

John Dryden is the same. Like Jonson, his linguistic attacks are often aimed at the language itself, rather than specifically at Shakespeare. He wrote about the Elizabethan playwrights in three works. His 1668 *Essay on Dramatic Poesy* was followed in 1672 by the *Defence of the Epilogue*, a piece bearing the subtitle 'An essay on the dramatic poetry of the last age.' Then, in 1679 his adaptation of Shakespeare's *Troilus and Cressida* appeared. It had a Preface 'containing the grounds of criticism in tragedy.' In these three works – *The Essay*, *The Defence* and *The Preface* – he often claims the superiority of the English of his day over that of the past. The aim of his *Defence*, he says, is to clarify, 'that the Language, Wit and Conversation of our Age are improved and refin'd above the last [age].'[15] His claim about the speed of this improvement is somewhat intemperate: in *The Preface* he states that as far as some aspects of the language are concerned 'a greater progress has been made ... since his majesty's return, than, perhaps since the conquest to his time.'[16] From the Norman Conquest till the Restoration ('his majesty's return') is 594 years; from the Restoration to the time of writing (1697), just 19. Then, in the *Defence*, he concentrates on the 'writers of the last age (in which I comprehend Shakespear, Fletcher and Johnson).' His verdict: 'Let any man who understands English read diligently the Work of Shakespeare and Fletcher, and I dare undertake that he will find in every Page either some Solecism of Speech, or some notorious Flaw of Sense.' The reason is not the fault of the writers, but the fact that 'the Times were ignorant in which they liv'd.'[17] Shakespeare, the argument runs, was alive in linguistically barbarous times and inherited the vices of the age.

It is not surprising that many of Dryden's linguistic criticisms of Shakespeare should reflect the views of the Royal Society. There is bombast: in the *Essay* he talks of Shakespeare's 'serious swelling into bombast,' and in *The Preface* of his 'blown puffy style.' Figurative language comes in for attack: 'The fury of his fancy' he writes in *The Preface*, 'often transported him beyond the bounds of judgment.' He was also obscure – a cardinal sin in the seventeenth century where (as we have seen), clarity of expression was all important. 'Many of his words,' *The Preface* says, 'and more of his phrases are scarce intelligible' 'And of those which we understand,' Dryden continues, 'some are ungrammatical, others course [coarse].'

Shakespeare's language can also lack decorum or 'wit' – terms which refer to the suitability of style to subject manner and literary genre. Here is what Dryden says in the *Defence*:

> Shakespear, who many times has written better than any Poet, in any Language, is yet so far from writing Wit always, or expressing that Wit according to the Dignity of the Subject, that he writes in many Places, below the dullest Writers of ours, or any precedent age.[18]

All Dryden's detailed comments about language in *The Defence* are focused on Jonson, not Shakespeare. The briefest of looks at Jonson's play *Cataline His Conspiracy*, Dryden says, leads to the conclusion that he 'writ not correctly.' For example, Jonson uses *his* for the possessive pronoun *its*. This comes about because in Old English (OE), *his* was the genitive of *hit* ('it'). Dryden's example from Jonson's *Cataline* is *Though Heav'n should speak with all his wrath*. Here, Dryden complains, Jonson 'makes false construction.' Then there is the use of adjectival double comparatives. 'I think few of our present writers,' Dryden says, 'would have left behind them such a line as this: *Contain your spirit in more stricter bounds*.' But then, he concedes indignantly, 'that gross way of two comparatives was then ordinary.'[19] In the same spirit, Dryden rails against Jonson's use of *be* for *are* ('false English,' Dryden calls it) in: *When we, whose virtues conquered thee, / Thus by thy vices ruin'd be*. In earlier forms of the language, *be* and *are* were competing forms, with the *are* form not stabilized until the seventeenth century.[20] Yet another grammatical mistake Dryden notes is the placing of a preposition at the end of a sentence, as in Jonson's *The Waves, and Dens of beasts could not receive / The bodies that those Souls were frighten from*. This is a common fault in Jonson, though Dryden is honest enough to admit having 'observed [it] in my own writings.'

Though Dryden's examples are all from Jonson, they are the complaints of a seventeenth-century critic looking back to a linguistically barbaric age. Dryden could easily have chosen his examples from Shakespeare, who is equally guilty:

His for *its*

How far that little candle throws his beams.

(MV, 5.1.90)

Double comparative

This was the most unkindest cut of all.

(JC, 3.2.184)

Be for *are*

Be there bears i'th'town?
I think there are, sir. I heard them talked of.

(MW 1.1.268)

(The second line here suggests that the forms *be* and *are* could be interchangeable.)

Final preposition

The heartache and the thousand natural shocks
That flesh is heir to.

(Ham, 3.1.63)

Dryden, like many other seventeenth-century commentators, is not really correcting Shakespeare, but the language of his age. And Dryden, like Jonson, accompanies his critical statements with respect. In the *Essay* he attacks bombast, but he also says: 'I admire [Jonson] but I love Shakespeare ... he is always great.' And in *The Defence*: 'Let us therefore admire the beauties and the heights of *Shakespeare*,' without being deflected by his instances of carelessness.[21] It is no wonder that Dryden, for all his comments about 'puffiness' and the like, did much to bolster Shakespeare's reputation in the seventeenth century.

1.3.2 Rymer: critical, without reverence

Jonson and Dryden were reverential as well as critical, but Thomas Rymer was just critical. He was a historian whose major work (in his position as historiographer royal) was a sixteen-volume catalogue of all the agreements between England and foreign powers. It took him 20 years to write. In earlier days, he tried his hand at drama, writing a tragedy called *Edgar*. But this was a flop, and he subsequently turned part of his attention to criticizing the dramas of others. His 1693 *Short View of Tragedy* has a long chapter on *Othello*, and a shorter one on *Julius Caesar*. Rymer has been called 'the first professional English critic,' and his critical comments are often incisive and perceptive. They are also often scathing, so much so that he has been dubbed 'the bogeyman of Shakespeare idolatry.'[22] He even scared Dryden, who comments in a letter: '[I] thinke my selfe happy that he [Rymer] has not fallen upon me, as severely and as wittily as he has upon Shakespeare.'[23]

Many of the aspects of Shakespeare (and other dramatists) that Rymer attacks are not language-related. He was a defender of the classical rules of dramatic unity (which Shakespeare scarcely ever followed). He also believed that justice should prevail at the end of a tragedy, another thing that did not much happen in Shakespeare. His criticisms were often detailed and amusing. Here, for example, he is concerned with the lighting arrangements in *Julius Caesar*: 'Another Poet wou'd have allow'd the noble Brutus a Watch-Candle in his Chamber this important night, rather than have puzzel'd his Man Lucius to grope in the dark for a Flint and Tinder-box, to get the Taper lighted.'[24] And on Desdemona's handkerchief: 'This third Act begins in the morning, at noon she [Desdemona] drops the Handkerchief, after dinner she misses it, and then follows all outrage and horrible clutter about it.'[25]

But there were many language-based criticisms, and Shakespeare's verbosity was a main target. When Roderigo says he will bang on Desdemona's father's door to wake the household, Iago encourages him: *Do, with like timorous accent and dire yell, / As when, by night and negligence, the fire / Is spied in populous cities* (Oth 1.1.76). 'Would not a rap at the door better express Iago's meaning?,' Rymer dryly comments, 'he might be content at Bedlam to hear such a rapture [emotional state].'[26]

Inappropriacy of language is another of Rymer's targets. When Othello hears of Cassio's fight, the Moor curses all-too mildly, and describes his disquiet with impressive eloquence. But Rymer is not convinced:

> In the days of yore, soldiers did not swear in this fashion. What should a soldier say farther, when he swears, unless he blaspheme? Action should speak the rest ... by the style one might judge that Shakespeare's soldiers were never bred in a camp, but rather had belonged to some affidavit office.[27]

And when Cassio describes the arrival of the Iago's ship there are references to *tempests, high seas, howling winds*, and *traitors enscarped to clog the guiltless keel*. Rymer finds the description overblown. There is situational inappropriacy too: when Othello (in murderous mood) enters Desdemona's bedchamber to kill her, his words are: *Put out the light, and then put out the light* (5.2.7). 'Hear with what soft language, he does approach her ... Who would call him Barbarian, Monster, Savage?'[28]

Perhaps the closest Rymer came to reverence was an acknowledgement that Shakespeare's verse could be pleasing. But, the critic adds, it failed in two important aspects – it was devoid of meaning, and poorly expressed. 'In the Neighing of an Horse,' Rymer says, 'or in the growling of a Mastiff, there is a meaning, there is as lively expression, and, may I say, more humanity, than many times in the Tragical flights of Shakespear.'[29]

1.4 Shakespeare adaptations

Charles II enjoyed drama, and once London theatres were re-established, he went almost daily while the court was in London. His patronage helped drama to flourish. But there was a shortage of plays, and it was the constant need for material that partly led to the procedure of adapting Elizabethan plays. William D'Avenant (who eventually became poet laureate) played an important role. He 'humbly presented ... a proposition of reformeinge some of the most ancient playes that were played at Blackfriers and of making them fitt.' From 1660 to 1700, 486 performances in London were old plays, 473 new.[30] From the theatres' point of view, one of the attractions of restoring the old was that royalties did not have to be paid; the authors were dead.

The tastes of the age made Jonson, Beaumont, and Fletcher particularly popular as providers of plays for restoration. But Shakespeare was in demand too. As we saw in 1.1, Charles gave patents to put on plays to two theatrical impresarios. One of them was D'Avenant, and he had special Shakespearean connections. His father had run the Crown Tavern in Oxford, where Shakespeare may have stayed on his journeys backwards and forwards between Stratford and London. According to some stories, Shakespeare was D'Avenant's godfather, or even indeed his biological father – a rumour attributed to D'Avenant himself. Whatever the truth of these connections, D'Avenant was a keen Shakespearean, and he adapted several of Shakespeare's plays.

Adaptations were often more popular than the original plays. They had the advantage of retaining the good qualities of the originals, while dispensing with their undesirable characteristics, some of which were linguistic. The theatre-going habits of the diarist Samuel Pepys (1633–1703) testify to this popularity. He saw 12 different Shakespearean dramas on 41 occasions 'between 1660 and 1669 – *Macbeth* nine times and *The Tempest* eight. Both were in adapted form on most, if not all, occasions.'[31]

Table 1.1 shows some of the main Shakespeare adaptations produced in the period up to 1710. Seventeenth-century adaptations were certainly not attempts to restore original texts. If anything, the originals were being 'improved,'

12   *Till 1950*

Table 1.1 Some important seventeenth-century Shakespeare adaptations

D'Avenant (1606–1668)
(a) *The Law against Lovers*. Based on *Measure for Measure*, with elements of *Much Ado* added. 1673
(b) *Macbeth* 1674
(c) *Hamlet* 1676

Dryden (1631–1700)
(a) *The Tempest* (with *D'Avenant*). 1670. An opera version (with D'Avenant and Shadwell). 1674. Opera was a genre in some ways closer to today's musicals than what we now call operas. They were mixtures of spoken and sung text.
(b) *All for Love, or The World Well Lost (Antony and Cleopatra)*. 1677
(d) *Troilus and Cressida, or Truth Found Too Late*. 1679

Nahum Tate (1652–1715)
(a) *King Lear* 1681
(b) *Richard II* 1681
(c) *Coriolanus* 1682

Others
(a) Colley Cibber (1671–1757), *Richard III*. 1700
(b) George Granville (1666–1735), *Merchant of Venice*. 1701

it was believed, in the light of contemporary views on literature. Many of the changes made were non-linguistic. The emerging style of the day was for elaborate and picturesque productions. D'Avenant introduced movable scenery, utilizing machines where necessary, with added music. Dryden, Shadwell, and D'Avenant's *Tempest*, for example, had 'aërial wires …, a tricksome table that whisked up and down' through a trapdoor, a rising son, 'and various other excellencies, not to mention a chorus of devils, ballets of winds and Tritons, and a band of 24 violins assisted by harpsicals and theorbos [lutes].'[32]

Different adaptations involved differing degrees of variance from Shakespeare's originals. The changes could indeed be significant. D'Avenant had no compunction in creating his *The Law against Lovers* by adding elements of *Much Ado* to the basic framework of *Measure for Measure*. In the version of *The Tempest* which he produced along with Dryden, a 'man who had never seen a woman' is introduced, adding numerous dramatic possibilities as this new character meets with Miranda, the 'woman who had never seen a man.' Nahum Tate is particularly celebrated for his even more violent changes. He made the ending of *King Lear* a happy one: Lear lives to regain his throne, while Cordelia and Edgar marry. The word 'tatification' is sometimes used pejoratively to describe what Tate did to Shakespeare.

Many of the seventeenth-century adaptations related to language, and these could indeed be numerous. Hence D'Avenant made no fewer than 300 small word changes to his version of *Hamlet*.[33] To give a feel for the kind of changes that the adapters made, Table 1.2 shows a passage from *Macbeth* (1.5.38–52). The version on the left is one we are used to today (taken from Crystal and

Table 1.2 D'Avenant's adaptation of a Lady Macbeth speech

Shakespeare	D'Avenant
Come, you spirits	Come all you spirits
That tend on mortal thoughts, unsex me here	That wait on mortal thoughts: unsex me here:
And fill me from the crown to the toe top-full	Empty my Nature of humanity, And fill it up with cruelty: make thick
Of direst cruelty. Make thick my blood;	My bloud, and stop all passage to remorse;
Stop up the access and passage to remorse,	That no relapses into mercy may
That no compunctious visitings of nature	Shake my design, nor make it fall before
Shake my fell purpose, nor keep peace between	'Tis ripen'd to effect: you murthering spirits,
The effect and it. Come to my woman's breasts	(Where ere in sightless substances you wait
And take my milk for gall, you murdering ministers,	
Wherever, in your sightless substances,	On Nature's mischief) come, and fill my breasts
You wait on nature's mischief. Come, thick night,	With gall instead of milk: make haste dark night,
And pall thee in the dunnest smoke of hell,	And hide me in a smoak as black as hell;
That my keen knife see not the wound it makes,	That my keen steel see not the wound it makes:
Nor heaven peep through the blanket of the dark	Nor Heav'n peep through the Curtains of the dark,
To cry, 'Hold, hold!'	To cry hold! hold!

Crystal's *Shakespeare's Words* website). The one on the right is from D'Avenant's 1674 adaptation.

For anyone reading through these two versions, a legitimate first reaction would be that D'Avenant has sacrificed poetry for clarity. Figurative expressions have been removed: *Come, thick night* becomes *make haste dark night*, while *Fill me from the crown to the toe top-full* turns into *fill it* [my Nature] *up*. Rhetorical flourishes disappear: *the access and passage to remorse* becomes *all passage to remorse*. Potentially obscure expressions disappear: *compunctuous visitings of nature* become *relapses into mercy*, and *my fell purpose* is rendered *my design*. Note also that the words *dunnest, knife*, and *blanket* have been replaced. We shall have something to say about these later.

Shakespeare adaptations over time have been the subject of a number of scholarly studies. Fischlin and Fortier (2000), for example, look at adaptations up to the present day, including a version of *Othello* taking place in black New York. Two studies focus on Restoration adaptations. Spencer (1927) gives an overview of these, while Spencer (1965) contains the texts of five adaptations from the period.[34] The earlier book considers the work of the various adapters separately, and identifies categories of change used by each. The list in Table 1.3 is a composite of all Spencer's categories taken together, so it can be said to show the main areas of language-related changes made in seventeenth-century adaptations:

14   *Till 1950*

Table 1.3 Categories of changes to Shakespeare's texts, based on the analysis of Spencer (1927)

(a) condensing long speeches;
(b) changing prose passages into blank verse (regarded as the suitable vehicle for drama);
(c) making metrical 'improvements,' often 'regularizing' lines where there are irregularities (for example, in iambic pentameter lines);
(d) correcting perceived grammar mistakes;
(e) modernizing text;
(f) clarifications (including the removal of ambiguities);
(g) toning down fanciful, imaginative outbursts;
(h) literalizing figurative expressions;
(i) eliminating indecency (sexual, and foul language);
(j) avoiding offences against decorum (seemly style);
(k) capricious (at the whim of the adapter, following no apparent principles).

Here are illustrations of some of the more important of these categories:[35]

(a) Condensing long speeches

Many of Shakespeare's lengthy speeches are cut down, just as a scientific writer might cut down a text, making the main points succinctly, and eliminating unnecessary flourishes. In this example from *Troilus and Cressida* Ulysses is answering the question *What's his excuse?*:

> He doth rely on none,
> But carries on the stream of his dispose,
> Without observance or respect of any,
> In will peculiar and in self-admission.
>
> (2.3.161)

Dryden's version just has:

> Why he relies on none
> But his own will.

Brief and to the point. The desire for reduction took its toll on some of Shakespeare's celebrated lengthy speeches. Hence Tate's version of *Richard II* reduced Gaunt's celebrated 'happy breed of men' speech (2.1.31–68) from 38 lines to just 8.

(b) Correcting perceived grammar mistakes

A piece of grammar that attracts the attention of more than one adapter is *that* used as a relative. In Present-Day English (PDE) *that* is usually confined to restrictive (or 'identifying') clauses. *Who/which* can be used in both restrictive and non-restrictive ('non-identifying') clauses. So today we say *Where's the girl that sells the tickets?* but *This is Naomi, who sells the tickets*.[36] In

Shakespearean English, *that* was the most common relative form, and it was often used in non-restrictives, as well as restrictives. But the rule confining *that* to restrictives was established by 1700, and the seventeenth-century adapters followed it. So D'Avenant changes Shakespeare's *All hail, Macbeth, that shalt be king hereafter!* (Mac 1.3.49) to *All hail, Macbeth, who shall be King hereafter.*

Tate does not like adjectives to be used as adverbs, and in his *Lear* he changes *late* into *lately*: *It pleased the King his master very late* (2.2.114) becomes *It pleas'd the King his Master lately.*

In English, from OE to PDE, there are some irregular verbs which have the same past tense and past participle forms (PDE *bought* for example). In others, these forms are different (e.g. *rode* and *ridden*). Sometimes Shakespeare uses a past form instead of the different past participle. In *Henry VI, Part 3* (4.6.2) you find *have shaken*, but these lines are from *Troilus and Cressida* (3.3.222):

> Cupid
> *Shall from your neck unloose his amorous fold,*
> *And, like a dew-drop from the lion's mane,*
> *Be shook to air.*

Dryden 'corrects' this to:

> *And love shall from your neck unloose his folds;*
> *Or, like a dew-drop from a lion's mane,*
> *Be shaken into air.*

Notice here in passing how the personification *Cupid* is changed into the more literal *love* – a small example of how figurative expressions are made literal.

(c) Clarifications

Any expression deemed difficult or obscure was a candidate for omission or change. Tate, for example, changes Goneril's *Sir, I love you more than word can wield the matter* (KL 1.1.55) into *Sir, I do love you more than words can utter.*

D'Avenant was particularly concerned with clarity, and has a real 'zeal in elucidation.'[37] He goes out of his way to ensure that meanings are clear, with all ambiguities removed. Macbeth's *To be thus is nothing;/ But to be safely thus!* (3.1.47) becomes D'Avenant's *I am no King till I am safely so.* Nor is D'Avenant averse to going well beyond the text to add an explanation where necessary, as in this exchange from *Measure for Measure*. Shakespeare has:

> Claudio: *Perpetual durance?*
> Isabella: *Ay, just. Perpetual durance, a restraint,*
> *Though all the world's vastidity you had,*
> *To a determined scope.*
>
> (3.1.70)

16 *Till 1950*

D'Avenant's explanation runs like this:

> Claudio: Perpetual durance?
> Isabella: 'Tis worse than close restraint, and painful too
> Beyond all tortures which afflict the body;
> For 'tis a Rack invented for the mind.

(d) Literalizing figurative expressions

Here is *Measure for Measure* (1.3.2):

> No, holy father, throw away that thought;
> Believe not that the dribbling dart of love
> Can pierce a complete bosom.

Talk of the *dribbling dart of love* was not to seventeenth-century taste at all. Hence what D'Avenant gives us is:

> No, Holy Father, throw away that thought,
> Lov's too tender to dwell in my cold bosom.

Classical references could disappear in the interests of clarity. Here is another example from Dryden, who replaced *Cupid* with *love* in an earlier example. In *Troilus and Cressida* (1.3.38) Shakespeare has: *But let the ruffian Boreas once enrage / The gentle Thetis.* Dryden's version is: *But let the Tempest once inrage that Sea.* In the same vein, the opening lines of Richard in *Richard III* – *Now is the winter of our discontent / Made glorious summer by this son of York* – disappear entirely from Cibber's version, thus dispensing not just with the figurative *winter of our discontent*, but with the 'son/sun' pun too.

(e) Eliminating indecency

Though many seventeenth-century writers were far from being prudes, the King's patent allowing D'Avenant to produce plays specified that they 'should not contain any passages offensive to piety and good manners.' Sexual references were thus removed. D'Avenant replaces:

> Lucio: Lechery?
> Claudio: Call it so.

(MM 1.2.138)

with

> I believe 'tis that which the precise call incontinence.

Similarly

> *Dost thou think, Claudio,*
> *If I would yield him my virginity,*
> *Thou might'st be freed?*

(MM 3.1.101)

becomes in D'Avenant:

> *Speak, Claudio, could you think, you might on earth*
> *Be guiltless made by him, if I would Heaven,*
> *Which never injur'd us, foully offend?*

Other types of offensive language were also taken out. Horatio's line (Ham 5.1.254) *For, upon my life,/ This spirit, dumb to us, will speak to him* becomes D'Avenant's *perhaps/This spirit dumb to us will speak to him*. Similarly Shakespeare's *The devil take thy soul* is changed to *Perdition catch thee*.

(f) *Avoiding offences against decorum*

Ordinary 'household' words were not seen as proper for serious drama, and sometimes they had to go. A clutch of words in Lady Macbeth's 'Come, you spirits' speech (given earlier) offended in this way. Shakespeare's *blanket* was changed, as we saw, into D'Avenant's *curtains*. The same word, along with *clout* ('cloth'), also arouses Dryden's irritation in a passage in *Hamlet* (2.2.504), leading him to ask: 'Would not a man have thought that the Poet had ... followed a Ragman, for the clout and blanket.'[38] Lady Macbeth's *knife* (suggesting a household kitchen implement) is also changed by D'Avenant into *steel*, and in his adaptation of *Troilus and Cressida*, Dryden replaces *knife* with *sword*. The adjective *dun* also disappears from the Macbeth speech. In 2.4 we will see that such words continued to attract adverse attention in the eighteenth century.

Another 'unseemly' household word was *bucket*. Shakespeare's *Richard II* has:

> *Now is this golden crown like a deep well*
> *That owes two buckets, filling one another*

(2.4.83)

In Tate this becomes:

> *Now is this Crown a Well wherein two Vessels*
> *That in successive Motion rise and fall.*

(g) *Capricious*

Some of the changes made by adapters seem to be motivated by no more than personal whim. In *Richard II* (3.4.29) Shakespeare's Gardener says *Go, bind thou up young dangling apricocks* [apricots]. For some reason Tate (whose adaptations are often the loosest) changes *apricocks* ('apricots') to *peaches*.

Here, to conclude, is a longer example, showing more instances of the categories we have been discussing. It is from a speech of Thersites in *Troilus and Cressida*. One might expect this character to be a prime target for the seventeenth-century adapter – he is rhetorical, colourful, and crude – and it is indeed the case. Here is what he says about his master, Ajax:

> Why, he stalks up and down like a peacock, a stride and a stand; ruminates like an hostess that hath no arithmetic but her brain to set down her reckoning; bites his lip with a politic regard, as who should say there were wit in his head, an 'twould out – and so there is; but it lies as coldly in him as fire in a flint, which will not show without knocking. The man's undone for ever, for if Hector break not his neck i'th' combat, he'll break't himself in vainglory. He knows not me: I said 'Good morrow, Ajax' and he replies 'Thanks, Agamemnon.' – What think you of this man, that takes me for the general? He's grown a very land-fish, languageless, a monster. A plague of opinion! A man may wear it on both sides, like a leather jerkin.
>
> (TC3.3.251)

Dryden's version is very much more tame, and a good deal shorter:

> Why, he tosses up his head as he had built castles in the air; and he treads upward to them, stalks into the element; he surveys himself, as it were to look for Ajax: he would be cried, for he has lost himself; nay, he knows nobody; I said, 'Good-morrow, Ajax,' and he replied, 'Thanks, Agamemnon.'

1.5 From adaptation to restoration

Lewis Theobald was an eighteenth-century scholar who produced an edition of Shakespeare's plays. In 1726, before this edition appeared, he wrote a book with a lengthy subtitle which reveals how competitive eighteenth-century editing could be. The 'Mr Pope' he refers to here is the poet, Alexander Pope, who had also produced a Shakespeare edition. The subtitle is:

> a Specimen of the many Errors as well Committed as Unamended by Mr Pope in his late edition of this poet; designed not only to correct the said Edition, but to restore the true Reading of Shakespeare in all the Editions ever published.

The book's main title, *Shakespeare Restored*, is also revealing. It says something about the differences between seventeenth- and eighteenth-century Shakespeare studies. As in the seventeenth, there were plenty of adaptations of Shakespeare's plays in the eighteenth century. But the spirit of the new century was not so much to adapt as to restore – 'going back to Shakespeare' rather than 'bringing Shakespeare forward.' The next chapter looks at this move from Shakespeare adapted to Shakespeare restored.

Notes

1. The list is from Vickers (1974), p. 2.
2. Firth and Rait (1911), pp. 26–7.
3. Dryden (1679), p. 15.
4. Sprat (1667), p. 114.
5. *Ibid.*, p. 42.
6. Glanvill (1676), pp. 41–2. Cited by Taylor (1989), p. 37.
7. Sprat (1667), p. 112.
8. Locke, J. (1689), p. 146.
9. 'Minute of meeting on Dec 7, 1664.' Birch (1756), Vol. 1, p. 499.
10. Sprat (1667), pp. 11, 40, 112.
11. Taylor (1989), p. 37.
12. This explanation is suggested by Baugh and Cable (2013), p. 234.
13. Jonson (1640), p. 87.
14. Jonson (1640a), p. 584.
15. Dryden, J. 1672), p. 213.
16. Dryden (1679), p. 50.
17. Dryden (1672), p. 214.
18. *Ibid.*, p. 222.
19. *Ibid.*, p. 220.
20. Lass (1999b), p. 176.
21. Dryden (1672), p. 227.
22. Both titles, 'critic' and 'bogeyman,' are from Taylor (1989), pp. 33 and 135 respectively.
23. Bentley (1945), p. 6.
24. Rymer (1693), p. 154.
25. *Ibid.*, p. 126.
26. *Ibid.*, p. 5.
27. *Ibid.*, p. 113.
28. *Ibid.*, p. 134.
29. *Ibid.*, p. 95.
30. Quotation and figures from Vickers (1974), pp. 5, 6.
31. Spencer (1927), p. 3.
32. *Ibid.*, p. 204.
33. Taylor (1989), p. 47.
34. Spencer (1965).
35. Most, though not all, of the examples are taken from Taylor (1987).
36. Examples from Swan (1995).
37. Spencer (1927), p. 169.
38. Taylor (1989), p. 41.

2 'Retrieving original purity'
The eighteenth century

2.1 Mouldy bread

In the *Dramatis Personae* of Shakespeare's *Troilus and Cressida*, Thersites is sometimes described as 'a deformed and scurrilous Greek.' He and his master, the Greek prince Ajax, share a tempestuous relationship. They are very rude to each other. Here is part of their first exchange in the play. Ajax calls Thersites over, and is angry when he gets no response. Thersites' reaction (2.1.13): *The plague of Greece upon thee, thou mongrel beef-witted lord!* But Ajax can give as good as he gets: *Speak, then, thou vinewed'st leaven, speak,* he says.

Leaven is the fermenting mixture from which bread is made, and *vinewed* is glossed by Crystal and Crystal (2002) as 'mouldy, rotten, decaying.' The word came in for lengthy discussion in the eighteenth century. One who considers it is a clergyman turned scholar, John Upton. His 1746 book, *Critical Observations on Shakespeare* is full of detailed linguistic observations on Shakespeare's texts. On *vinewed'st leaven* he begins like this: 'Tis a common expression in the western counties to call an ill-natured, sour person, *vinnid*.' Upton mentions various forms of the word – *vinnid, vinewed, vinowed, vinny* and *vinew*. They all mean 'mouldy'; hence his version of the phrase – *vinnid leaven* – means 'mouldy sourdough.' Some versions, Upton notes, have *whinnid* for *vinnid*. This is because, according to him, the people of Kent regularly pronounce 'v' as 'wh.' In this case, he feels, "twas some Kentish person who occasioned the mistake.'[1] Incidentally, there is still today, in Dorsetshire, a cheese known as 'Blue Vinney'; like blue cheeses in general it has been intentionally left to develop some mould.

Upton has still more to say. Talk of bread sends him – a true lover of linguistic exploration – off in search of other Shakespeare 'bread references.' He finds another in *Troilus and Cressida* (5.1.4), where this time it is Achilles and not Ajax who is insulting Thersites, calling him a *crusty batch of nature* (a batch is anything baked).[2] Then Upton turns to the word *leaven*. It is, he notes, a scriptural expression, used for example in *1Corinthians 5. 6* which announces that 'a little leaven leaveneth the lump.' Upton finds another Shakespearean usage in *Measure for Measure* (1.1.51): *We have with a prepared and leavened choice/Proceded to you.* The word means, Upton says, 'hand prepared and rightly seasoned.' But he also notes that there can be an undertone of 'sour and corrupting nature.' This is particularly clear in a quotation from *Cymbeline* (3.4.63): *So thou, Posthumus,/Wilt lay the leaven to all proper men;/Goodly and gallant shall be false and perjur'd/From thy great fail*. Upton's paraphrase is: 'will infect and corrupt their good names, like sour dough that leaveneth the whole mass.'[3]

Nor does discussion stop there. In his edition of the plays, Samuel Johnson – one of the most celebrated of the many eighteenth-century editors – has no fewer than 24 lines of notes on the phrase. He observes that in a slightly earlier edition of Shakespeare, by the poet Alexander Pope, the phrase appears as *unsalted leaven*. But, Johnson argues, that version has 'no authority or countenance from any of the copies' that he has consulted. The 'old reading,' Johnson says, was '*whinid'st leaven*.' But what does this mean? Johnson finds the phrase 'corrupted and unintelligible.' The version of yet another editor, Lewis Theobald (mentioned at the end of Chapter 1), makes more sense to Johnson. It is *unwinnowed'st leaven*. Johnson then lists other forms that have appeared in various editions, including the Fourth Folio's *whinid'st leaven*, where the adjective means 'most windy' (it is 'leaven made by a great fermentation'). Then there is *vinew'd*, in the sense of 'mouldy.' When the time comes for a conclusion, Johnson stays with *unsalted*. Why? Because this is what appears in what he calls the 'old quarto' (Quarto 1, dated 1609). Johnson thinks that Shakespeare subsequently realized that 'want of salt was no fault in leven,' so he changed *unsalted* into *vinew'd*. But Johnson wants to stay as much as possible with originals, so *unsalted* it is.[4]

This lengthy example has been pursued to the bitter end to show how scholarship came into Shakespeare studies in the eighteenth century. It is true that some of scholarship may be rather speculative, with questionable conclusions: was it really a person from Kent who brought in that 'wh' instead of 'v,' as Upton suggests? But there is in general a clear search for evidence in support of assertions made. Examples are sought both inside and outside Shakespeare (as we saw, Upton cites the *Bible*). Texts are examined in detail, and what other editors have said is considered. Importance is also clearly given to 'going back to originals.' Johnson talks about 'authority ... from the copies,' about an 'old reading,' and about the 'old quarto.' He agonizes to find original version. He selects *unsalted* because it appears in Quarto 1, even though Shakespeare may have later amended it. These are the beginnings of Shakespearean scholarship. How did they come about?

2.2 Shakespeare's 'meridian blaze' …

Francis Gentleman was an Irish actor and a dramatist. In 1770 he produced a book of critical writings entitled *The Dramatic Censor*. He finds plenty to admire in Shakespeare, and at one stage talks of the poet's 'meridian blaze of … brightness.'[5]

Shakespeare's reputation did indeed reach glorious heights in the eighteenth century. His genius was extravagantly proclaimed time and time again. For William Richardson, a Scottish literary scholar, 'the genius of Shakespeare is unlimited';[6] for the actor David Garrick he was 'the greatest dramatic poet in the world';[7] Horace Walpole – a scholar as well as a politician – declared him to be 'superior to all mankind'; and the literary critic Samuel Badcock classed him 'among the most astonishing phaenomena of human genius.'[8] As some of these comments suggest, praise for Shakespeare occasionally reached the level of 'bardolatry,' defined by the *OED* as 'worship of the Bard of Avon.' There was plenty of bardolatry around in the eighteenth century. In fact, Shakespeare's status was such that he was often compared to the classical and Renaissance giants. In a single paragraph of his *A Fragment on Shakespeare*, the clergyman and critic, Martin Sherlock, talks of Shakespeare in the same breath as a clutch of celebrated figures – artists as well as writers: Homer, Dante, Michaelangelo, Corregio, Voltaire, Demosthenes, La Fontaine, Virgil.[9]

As Shakespeare's reputation grew, he was cited more and more. Collections showing off his 'meridian blaze' were very popular. In 1752, William Dodd, an Anglican priest (as well as a forger who was eventually hanged, but that is another story) produced one such collection called *The Beauties of Shakespeare*. Between its publication and 1893, no fewer than 39 editions were produced.[10]

The newly elevated status of Shakespeare had some important beneficial effects. One was that it led him to be taken seriously as a subject worthy of scholarship. The celebrated classical authors – Homer, Virgil, and the rest – were acknowledged fit subjects for scholarly treatment, and once Shakespeare was admitted to their company, he attracted the same scholastic attention. The beginnings of Shakespeare scholarship came about when he was deemed worthy of such scholarship.

A second important effect of Shakespeare's elevated status was a change of attitude, dampening the fashion for modern adaptations of the plays that were characteristic of the seventeenth century. Adaptations certainly did continue to appear: Pope produced a version of *King Lear*, David Garrick one of *Romeo and Juliet*, and the actor/playwright Theophilus Cibber wrote a version of *Henry VI*. Like many of the seventeenth-century adaptations, these often unashamedly strayed far from Shakespeare's texts. They may have been popular with audiences – there is always (including today) an appetite for modern versions. But the elevated image of Shakespeare as an author comparable to classical writers pulled in another direction – back towards original texts, towards what the writer actually wrote. Hence Johnson's concerns with Quarto 1 of *Troilus and Cressida*.

This attitude was an important factor in the beginnings of Shakespearean scholarship in general, but it was particularly important for language studies. There were still (as we are about to see) concerns with what Shakespeare 'should have written,' to conform to contemporary standards of linguistic acceptability; and Shakespeare was still sometimes 'corrected' to conform with the language of the day. But gradually interest moved towards what Shakespeare actually wrote – turning away from an entirely prescriptive linguistic approach, in the direction of a descriptive one.

2.3 … and his 'dark spots'

Francis Gentleman – he who spoke of the 'meridian blaze' – was by no means blind to Shakespeare's faults. Like many in the period, he was proud of his even-handed approach. Thus along with the blazes of brightness, he also talks of 'dark spots which [Shakespeare's] genius shares in common with the sun.'[11] Pope too was very aware of the dark spots. In the *Preface* to his edition, he says that 'of all the English poets, Shakespeare must be confessed … to afford the most numerous, as well as the most conspicuous instances, both of beauties and faults of all sorts.'[12] Then there is Theobald, who in the Introduction to *Shakespeare Restored*, talks about the 'vast crop of errors, which has almost choak'd up his beauties.' And Johnson: 'Shakespeare never has six lines together without a fault. Perhaps you may find seven, but this does not refute my general assertion.'[13]

Faults there were, then. How can a writer like Shakespeare, whose genius was now coming to be fully recognized, be so full of blemishes? In the *Preface* to his Shakespeare edition, Johnson wrote that 'the faults are more than could have happened without the concurrence of many causes.'[14] There was some 'blame,' Johnson suggests, attached to Shakespeare himself, and his style, which 'was in itself ungrammatical, perplexed and obscure.' Upton voices a particularly common criticism. Shakespeare, he said, was 'labouring with a multiplicity of sublime ideas … hence he crowds various figures together, and metaphor upon metaphor, and runs the hazard of far-fetched expressions; whilst, intent on nobler ideas, he condescends not to grammatical niceties.'[15] Notice that even in these critical comments, Upton presents Shakespeare's fault as a *felix culpa*: the sublime Shakespeare has his head so full of glorious ideas that he has no time for niceties.

Despite the admitted 'shortcomings' of Shakespeare, it fits in well with his new elevated status to attribute much blame elsewhere, and Johnson – along with many others – does this. It was partly the age. Johnson in the *Preface* again: 'The English nation, in the time of Shakespeare,' he says, 'was yet struggling to emerge from barbarity.'[16] And Gentleman: 'no other charge will be laid against Shakespeare than the barbarous and credulous taste of the times in which he wrote.'[17] But carrying most of the blame were those involved in the transmission process – the people who brought the texts to the public. As Johnson put it: 'his works were transcribed for the players by those who may be supposed to have seldom understood them; they were transmitted by copiers equally unskilled, who still multiplied errors; they were perhaps sometimes mutilated by the actors.'[18] Another type of person also came in for criticism: the editors. As Theobald said in the very first paragraph of *Shakespeare Restored*, much blame attached to the 'indolence and … ignorance of his [Shakespeare's] editors.' In order to obliterate such errors, we need an editor who

> would befriend the memory of this immortal poet, and contribute to the pleasure of the present and future times, in retrieving, as far as possible, the

original purity of his text, and rooting out the vast crop of errors, which has almost choak'd up his beauties.[19]

So we return to the idea of 'going back to originals,' as a way of eliminating transmission faults.

2.4 What the dark spots were

As in the seventeenth century, many of the faults found in Shakespeare were not to do with language. His failure to observe the unities comes up again, and indeed his general lack of conformity to the strictures of French drama (derived, of course, from classical Greek ideas). But there is an interesting shift in attitude. It is not so much that Shakespeare fails to conform to these rules. Given his elevated status, in the eyes of some it was the strictures themselves that were at fault. The vicar John Brown talks of the 'noble irregularities of Shakespeare.'[20] He may not be a 'correct and regular writer,' but he 'opens a mine which contains gold and diamonds in unexhaustible plenty,' even though these may be, as Johnson observes, 'clouded by incrustations, debased by impurities, and mingled with a mass of meaner minerals.'[21]

What, then, were the language faults? They were not dissimilar to those noted by seventeenth-century critics like Dryden. As we saw in Chapter 1, puns ('clenches' or 'quibbles'), and word play, were one of his prime targets. Here is an eighteenth-century view in verse, from the poet David Mallet. He is talking about the character of Hamlet:

> *Now eagle-wing'd, his heavenward flight he takes;*
> *The big stage thunders, and the soul awakes:*
> *Now, low on earth, a kindred reptile creeps;*
> *Sad HAMLET quibbles, and the hearer sleeps.*[22]

Lord Kames was trained as a lawyer, but he wrote some highly popular critical works, including *Elements of Criticism*. He is another who is highly critical of Shakespeare's word play – often nothing more than 'hocus-pocus tricks,' according to him. He is particularly disapproving when word play is introduced into serious contexts, where it creates an unfortunate 'discordance between the thought and expression.'[23] One of his examples comes from *Julius Caesar* (3.2.23), when Brutus is talking to the Plebeians after Caesar's death. The seriousness of the topic does not stop Brutus from playing with words around the ideas of living and dying: *Had you rather Caesar were living, and die all slaves, than that Caesar were dead, to live all free men?*

The use of ornamental language in situations of high emotion exercises some eighteenth-century critics, because it sounds unnatural. For example, in the *The Elements of Dramatic Criticism*, William Cooke focuses on the moment in *Richard III* when Queen Elizabeth finds out that her two sons have been murdered (4.4.9):

Ah, my poor princes! Ah, my tender babes!
My unblown flowers, new-appearing sweets!
If yet your gentle souls fly in the air
And be not fixed in doom perpetual,
Hover about me with your airy wings
And hear your mother's lamentation!

Such 'imagery and figurative expression,' Cooke says, 'are discordant in the highest degree with the agony of a mother who is deprived of two hopeful sons by a brutal murder.'[24] Much more to the taste of the age was Macduff's cry on the death of his children: *What, both my children! Both, both my children gone*. Richard Steele admired this (though he is in fact quoting from D'Avenant's adaptation; the First Folio version is a little less plain and simple, with mention of the murderer as a *hell-kite*).[25]

In fact, bombast and excess of conceit – in any context – are frequently criticized by eighteenth-century commentators. Johnson speaks of Shakespeare's 'disproportionate pomp of diction,' and 'wearisome train of circumlocution.'[26] Here are two examples from Johnson's edition. In *Love's Labour's Lost* (1.1.77), Berowne has the line: *Light, seeking light, doth light of light beguile*. Johnson's comment: 'The whole sense of this gingling [jingling, full of repetitions] declamation is only this, that *a man by too close study may read himself blind*, which might have been told with less obscurity in fewer words.' Then, in *The Winter's Tale* (1.2.260), Camillo says: *Whereof the execution did cry out/Against the non-performance*. 'This is one of the expressions,' Johnson complains, 'by which Shakespeare too frequently clouds his meaning. This sounding phrase means, I think, no more than *a thing necessary to be done.*'[27]

Dislike of figures of speech led Steevens to change Hamlet's *to take arms against a sea of troubles* to 'assay of troubles' (3.1.59), while Macbeth's *Glamis hath murder'd sleep* becomes 'murder'd a sleeper' (2.2.42). A figure of speech particularly unpopular with the critics was the 'ploce,' pronounced in British English /pləʊsiː/, and defined in the *OED* as 'the repetition of a word in an altered or more expressive sense, or for the sake of emphasis.' There is an example in Macbeth's line *Cleanse the stuffed bosom of that perilous stuff* (5.3.44). One editor, Steevens, changes *stuffed* to *foul*. Another, Malone, keeps *stuffed*, but comments that the repetition 'is very unpleasing to the ear.' He notes that 'our author was extremely fond of such repetitions.' Among Malone's other examples are *Now for the love of love* (AC), *The greatest grace lending grace* (AW), and *Our means will make us means* (AW).

Shakespeare's language, then, could be criticized for being inappropriately florid. But inappropriacy could also occur for the very opposite reason, through the use of ordinary, everyday words not suitable for high drama or poetic diction. It is extraordinary how the words *blanket* and *knife*, in Lady Macbeth's *Come, you spirits* speech (1.5.51), have attracted so much critical disdain. As we saw in Chapter 1, D'Avenant dispenses with both words in his adaptation. We also saw there that Dryden too objected to these words. Johnson picks the same targets. Lady Macbeth's speech is, he says, particularly 'debased by two unfortunate words.' He continues: 'I can scarce check my risibility when the expression forces itself upon my mind; for who, without some relaxation of his gravity, can hear of the avengers of guilt *peeping through a blanket?*'[28] Here is Gentleman's view of that same blanket:

> her invocation to spirits of evil influence is worthy of a powerful imagination, and Macbeth's interruptive entrance extremely well timed; but we must offer some doubt whether the word *blanket* of the dark does not convey a low and improper idea.[29]

As we shall see in Chapter 3, these same words, extraordinarily, continue to attract attention in the nineteenth century.

Moving from the everyday to the profane: the Scottish classicist, William Richardson talks of Shakespeare's 'vulgarity, and even indecency of language,'[30] while Johnson dismisses the whole of *The Merry Wives of Windsor* because of 'the frequency of expressions so profane, that no necessity of preserving character can justify them.'[31]

There were grammatical infelicities too. Edmond Malone – often considered the century's best Shakespearean editor – talks of Shakespeare's 'offences against grammar' (while, incidentally, still proclaiming Shakespeare 'the great refiner and polisher of our language').[32] When Hamlet sees the ghost of his father, he wonders why it is appearing *making night hideous? and we fools of nature* (1.4.54). Theobald picks up this use of *we*. It should be *us*, he says – *making us fools of nature*. Existing editions, Theobald argues, keep *we*; but 'that authority must not give a sanction to nonsense, and false grammar.' There are a number of times in Shakespeare where Theobald has 'observ'd that nominative of pronouns is used, tho' grammar requires the accusative.'[33] He enumerates: there is another *we* instead of *us* in *Coriolanus*; a *they* for *them* in *Measure for Measure*, and a *she* for *her* in *Anthony and Cleopatra*. He also finds a relative pronoun *who* for *whom*, in *Macbeth*. Another particularly common complaint was the use of singular verbs occurring with plural nouns. The author and antiquarian Joseph Ritson gives an example from *The Merchant of Venice* (4.1.50). He says that the lines in 'all the old editions' is: *Masters of passion sways it to the mood / Of what it likes or loaths*. His comment: 'If *sways* be objected to, it may be easyly altered to *sway*. But there are above fifty instances in Shakspeare, where a verb of the singular number is made to agree with a noun of the plural.'[34] Eighteenth-century critics assumed that these singular/plural mismatches were due to carelessness on Shakespeare's part, or some error in transmission. But it is worth remembering that –*es* was a present plural verb form in Northern dialects of ME, and though this was dying out in Shakespeare's time, 'such forms occur too frequently,' Mason says, 'for them to be dismissed as printers' or copyists' errors.'[35] We will return to these singular/plural mismatches in Chapter 3 (3.4).

Another comment about a singular/plural mismatch is made by John Monck Mason in relation to another Shakespearean target – his rhyme. Mason was an Irish scholar who had ambitions to produce his own Shakespeare edition. This did not happen, and instead he produced two booksworth of Shakespeare criticism, one entitled *Comments on the several editions of Shakespeare's plays extended to those of Malone and Steevens*. Mason says that Shakespeare 'knowingly, sacrificed grammar to rhyme … when he found it convenient.'[36] The example he provides relates to this verse of a song from *Cymbeline* (2.3.19):

Hark, hark, the lark at heaven's gate sings,
And Phoebus gins arise,
His steeds to water at those springs
On chaliced [with cup-shaped blossom] *flowers that lies*

What Mason calls 'false concord' (between *springs* and *lies*) is tolerated to make the rhyme between *arise* and *lies*.

Gentleman is once again on the scene when it comes to rhyme. Of the lines in *Measure for Measure* (3.2.26) – *He who the sword of heaven will bear/ Should be as holy as severe* – he says: 'The sentiments … are just and instructive; but the namby-pamby versification is abominable.'[37]

2.5 Editing Shakespeare

Eighteenth-century Shakespeare editors saw it as part of their duty to correct errors, to eliminate the dark spots. Indeed, editions like the ones we have mentioned were a major vehicle through which the eighteenth century developed its scholarship. There were plenty of them. Table 2.1 lists nine of the most important:

Table 2.1 Some eighteenth-century Shakespeare editions

Date	Editor	Comments
1709	Nicholas Rowe	First major edition. Added stage directions and *dramatis personae*. Also included a biography.
1725	Alexander Pope	Consulted quarto texts. Intrusive editing (put about 1560 lines into footnotes, regarding them as so bad that Shakespeare could not have written them).
1733	Lewis Theobald	More scholarly than Pope. Concerned with play sources as well as 'original' versions.
1744	Thomas Hanmer	Much based on Theobald and Pope. Poorly regarded.
1747	William Warburton	Based on Theobald. Often unscholarly and fanciful.
1765	Samuel Johnson with George Steevens	Major edition, with a celebrated *Preface*. Had elements of variorum.
1768	Edward Capell	Scholarly work, taking 30 years to produce, and based on a collection of quartos.

(continued)

Table 2.1 (Cont.)

Date	Editor	Comments
1773	George Steevens	Based on (and supported by) Johnson, and appearing in various editions.
1790	Edmond Malone	Very highly regarded. Included history of the stage, and a Shakespeare biography. Also interested in chronology and questions of attribution (did not believe *Henry VI* to be by Shakespeare).

Editing Shakespeare in the eighteenth century could be a vitriolic and aggressive business. Each new edition had to justify its existence in an increasingly full marketplace, and one way of doing this was by drawing attention to the shortcomings of earlier editions. Thus Johnson preceded his edition with a document entitled *Proposals for printing the dramatick works of William Shakespeare* – the eighteenth-century equivalent perhaps of the kind of publishing proposal that aspiring authors today are expected to produce. To prove the need for a new edition, Johnson attacks the opposition. Pope, he says, was ignorant of ancient literature, Warburton was 'detained by more important studies' (an elegant put-down!), while Theobald was just interested in the money. We have already seen the full title of Theobald's *Shakespeare Restored*, with its claim to 'correct' Pope's edition, and 'restore the true reading of Shakespeare in all the editions ever yet published.' In this age of polemic, it was to be expected that Pope should strike back. He did so by finding a place for Theobald in his poem, *The Dunciad*. The work celebrated the goddess Dulness and her agents. Pope made Theobald one of the agents, and indeed today this is for many how the name Theobald is known. He, and others like him, Pope writes, *Old puns restore, lost blunders nicely seek/And crucify poor Shakespear once a week*.[38]

Theobald deserves a better fate in posterity than being the butt of Pope's satire. Indeed, he is generally regarded as a better Shakespeare editor than Pope. The quality of the scholarship involved in eighteenth-century Shakespeare editions was certainly variable. Posterity has judged Theobald, Johnson, Capell, and Malone particularly well. Hanmer and Warburton have been less highly regarded. But despite the shortcomings – and idiosyncracies – of particular editors, the eighteenth-century editions were a great advance in Shakespearean scholarship. The editors were keen to show their adherence to the 'going back to originals' principle. So Steevens tells us that his own text 'has been constantly compared with the most authentic copies.'[39] Johnson makes a further claim: 'The edition now proposed will at least have this advantage over others. It will exhibit all the observable varieties of all the copies that can be found.'[40] This is the beginning of the variorum principle, which brings together the commentaries of a number of available editions.

Johnson's comments on the *vinewed'st leaven* phrase, discussed at the beginning of this chapter, show this principle at work: as well as looking at what the 'old quarto' has, he also tells us what other eighteenth-century editors – Pope and Theobald – have to say.

A consequence of the 'back to originals' principle was for contemporary editors to exercise restraint in the number of changes proposed to texts. Otherwise transmission faults might be multiplied, rather than eliminated. Eighteenth-century editors often state this as a conscious policy. Johnson puts it like this: 'As I practised conjecture more, I learned to trust it less; and after I had printed a few plays, resolved to insert none of my own readings in the text.'[41] A 'make fewer changes' principle.

Although the editions were the most substantial Shakespeare-related productions in the eighteenth century, they were not the only ones. We need also to look at various other types of publication. Some were produced as adjuncts to specific editions, others not. We start with a dictionary.

2.6 Word lists

2.6.1 Johnson's Dictionary

A clear sign that Shakespeare had 'arrived' was the role he was given in Johnson's 1755 *Dictionary of the English Language*. As we saw in the last chapter, the Royal Society, like the Academies in other European countries, felt the need for authoritative dictionaries of their language, as part of the process of helping the language become accepted. Johnson's 1755 *Dictionary* contributes in a major way to this process. It was as innovatory as it was comprehensive. One of the innovations was to include quotations exemplifying word uses. Because it was, as Johnson saw it, the duty of a lexicographer to produce a repository of good writing, only the best authors were quoted. Lexicographers also had a duty, he believed, to look after the moral welfare of their readers, and for this reason cited writers had to be ethically as well as aesthetically acceptable. An example of a writer who failed the 'ethics test' was the philosopher Thomas Hobbes (1588–1679). His views were, for Johnson, too deterministic, and Hobbes' idea that life was 'solitary, poor, nasty, brutish and short' was not morally uplifting at all.

According to Woudhuysen (1989), the *Dictionary* contained about 116,000 quotations, illustrating some 40,000 words. No fewer than a third of these came from Shakespeare, and the high number bears witness to the high regard in which Shakespeare was held.[42] Woudhuysen gives some statistics for the Shakespeare quotations in the *Dictionary*, based on a study of two letters, 'G' and 'T.' *Macbeth* and *King Lear* are the most commonly cited plays, with *Henry VIII* and *The Merchant of Venice* also scoring highly. Johnson also has his favourite passages. In one, from *Macbeth*, there are two and a half lines used to illustrate no fewer than eight separate words. The passage is the First Murderer's description of dusk (3.3.6):

> *The west yet glimmers with some streaks of day.*
> *Now spurs the lated traveller apace*
> *To gain the timely inn*

The words are *west, glimmer, streak, day, lated, gain, timely, inn*.[43]

There are occasions when Johnson's moral impulses get the better of him in his use of quotations. For example, one sense of the verb *to learn* that he discusses is 'to teach' (a usage that is now obsolete). Johnson exemplifies with a quotation from *The Tempest*. His version reads:

> *You taught me language, and my profit on't*
> *Is, I know not how to curse. The red plague rid you*
> *For learning me your language!*
>
> (1.2.363)

But the First Folio text says quite the opposite: *I know how to curse*.[44] It has been suggested that Caliban, as a colonial, would have been taught not to curse, robbing him of his ability to protest, and perhaps Johnson believed this.[45]

Sometimes too, the quotations seem like a decoration, added for aesthetic rather than lexicographical reasons. Under *investment*, for example, there is a nine-line passage from *Henry IV, Part 2* (4.1.42). The passage is an impressive one (perhaps Johnson's main reason for including it), but such a lengthy quotation can hardly be justified, and in fact it does not provide a particularly revealing clarification for the one word *investment*.

Johnson is not frightened to lay bare what he sees as inappropriate or incorrect uses of words, even when this involved highly admired writers like Shakespeare. Prescriptivism is still at work. Take his treatment of the noun *prejudice* for example. As well as the meaning of 'judgement made beforehand,' Johnson also includes the sense of 'mischief, detriment, hurt, injury.' Employing the 'back to originals' principle, Johnson says that this meaning 'is not derived from the original or etymology of the word: it were therefore better to use it less; perhaps *prejudice* ought never to be applied to any mischief, which does not imply some partiality or prepossession.' Among his examples is this, from Shakespeare's *Henry VIII*. Buckingham is talking about Wolsey (1.1.182):

> *England and France might through their amity*
> *Breed him some prejudice, for from this league*
> *Peeped harms that menaced him.*

Despite shortfalls and personal idiosyncracies, Johnson's use of Shakespeare in his *Dictionary* is a substantial contribution to Shakespeare studies. Indeed, 'in the process of compiling the *Dictionary*,' Woudhuysen claims, 'Johnson had also in effect produced the first, primitive, concordance to Shakespeare's works.'[46] A concordance, in this sense is, according to the *OED*: 'an alphabetical arrangement of the principal words contained in a book, with citations of the passages in which they occur.'

2.6.2 Glossaries

The eighteenth century developed an awareness of the need for glossaries for old books. It was part of the 'going back to originals' principle – the desire to describe and understand historical texts, rather than modernize them. In 1715, John Hughes produced a glossary of old words occurring in Spenser's *Faerie Queene*. At the other end of the century, Joseph Ritson wrote a 'Glossary of obsolete or difficult words' to supplement his three-volume *English Anthology* (1793), a collection of poetry from the sixteenth century onwards. Shakespearean glossaries were sometimes associated with new editions. George Sewell for example produced a list of 174 'old words' for a supplementary volume to Pope's edition. Hanmer also added a 550-word glossary to his edition. Edward Capell's edition was supplemented by a mixture of comments, notes and a glossary of 3,000 obsolete words.

Another Shakespeare glossary was produced by the botanist and scholar, Richard Warner. He wanted to write a Shakespeare edition of his own, and with this in mind, he sent a long letter to the influential actor, David Garrick. It was subsequently published in 1786 under the title: *Concerning a Glossary to the Plays of Shakespeare*. Warner expresses the view that Shakespeare's

> very frequent use … of words obscure, now disused and obsolete, of technical terms not universally known, and of words, though common, yet made use of by him in a sense uncommon, and sometimes peculiar to himself, seem to give an opening for a Glossary.[47]

The glossary was never written, but Warner's letter contains copious examples of the types of words he wanted to include, and gives a good sense of the scholarly way in which he would have gone about it. The letter also contains an extended sample of the proposed Glossary, for the letter 'A.'

The scope of Warner's proposed glossary is ambitious, and it is based on a (albeit rather rudimentary) classification of words to be covered. One of his categories is where Shakespeare uses a word in its original sense, perhaps no longer in common use by the time Warner was writing. The word *bombast*, for example, originally meant 'wadding,' or 'cotton' – indeed there is a genus of plants called 'Bombax' (the silk/cotton family). Warner's Shakespeare example is from *Henry IV, Part 1* (2.4.320) where Falstaff is described as a *sweet creature of bombast* (meaning 'well-padded'). The word was still found in this sense in the eighteenth century, but by then today's meaning of 'inflated, turgid language' (*OED*) was also in use. Another word in the same category is *buxom*, which meant 'obedient,' 'obsequious' ('bow-some' – pliant like a bow). Hence in *Henry V* (3.6.25), Bardolph is described as a soldier of *buxom valour*. Today – and in Warner's time – it means 'plump and comely.' Incidentally, the path by which *buxom* changed from 'obedient' to its modern meaning seems to have been: obedient → amiable → full of health → plump and comely. Warner's etymological explorations show scholarship. They are often wide-ranging too. In the case of *buxom* he cites both Milton, and the book known as the *Polychronicon* ('comprehensive, universal history') written in the fourteenth century by the chronicler Ranulf Higden.

Warner has another category of words which he calls 'technical.' One such is the verb *to ear*, from (as erudite Warner states) the Latin *arare*, meaning 'to plough' – it is associated with the word 'arable' which we still use today in the sense of 'capable of being ploughed,' and hence 'suitable for growing crops.' His Shakespearean example is from *Richard II* (3.2.212), where King Richard talks of going *to ear the land*. A third word category is 'local' (dialect) words, and one of Warner's examples is the Midlands word *quat*, meaning a 'pimple.' One of the *OED*'s citations for this word is from the *English Dialect Dictionary*,[48] dated 1903: *what's that there quot on yer nose?* It is used (less colloquially) in *Othello* (5.1.11). when Iago says of Roderigo:. *I've rubbed this young quat almost to the sense* [quick]/*And he grows angry*.

In section 2.7.3 we will make mention of yet another Shakespearean glossary, by Richard Roderick.

2.7 Attempts to systematize

Other eighteenth-century authors attempted classifications, making efforts to be systematic about Shakespeare's language – stating the linguistic rules he follows, making generalizations about his language use. Several are worth a look.

2.7.1 Shakespeare's 'language rules': Upton

Upton's commentaries on Shakespeare were not associated with any specific edition. We have already met him in relation to the *vinnid leaven* discussion at the beginning of this chapter. His *Critical Observations on Shakespeare* is full of similarly detailed reflections on specific language points. He is one of those writers on language who, while not entirely avoiding prescriptiveness, is concerned less with judging 'what Shakespeare ought to have written' and more with trying 'to discover and retrieve what he did write.'[49] To achieve this, Upton says, we need to understand the linguistic rules Shakespeare follows. The way to do this is by looking at his texts, rather than at exemplars of 'refined' eighteenth-century usage. The last part of Upton's book lists 14 of Shakespeare's 'language rules.' These are given in Table 2.2:[50]

Table 2.2 Upton's 14 Shakespearean 'language rules'

	Rule	Example(s)
1	Shakespeare anglicizes proper names.	'Shylock' for the original 'Scialac' in MV; 'Montagues' for 'Montecchi' in RJ.
2	He anglicizes Latin words, keeping their Latin senses.	*subscription* from Latin *subscriptio*, literally 'writing underneath.' The word came to mean 'allegiance,' which is how Shakespeare uses it in KL (3.2.18): *You owe me no subscription.*

Table 2.2 (Cont.)

	Rule	Example(s)
3	He sometimes uses a word in a secondary, but not its primary sense.	Upton: 'because the popish and heathenish mysteries are vain … [Shakespeare] therefore uses *mysteries* for "vanities".' For example, H8 (1.3.1): *Is't possible the spells of France should juggle/Men into such strange mysteries.*
4	He changes parts of speech: adjectives to verbs.	'to safe.' AC (1.3.55): *And that which most with you should safe my going/Is Fulvia's death.*
	verbs to nouns	2H6 (3.1.160): *accuse* for 'accusation'; LLL (1.1.149) *affect* for 'affection.'
	adjectives to nouns	*little*. Cor (1.9.51): *As if I loved my little should be dieted/In praises.*
	nouns to verbs	'to scale' = weigh, measure. Cor (1.1.89): *I will venture to scale it a little more.*
	nouns to adjectives (in apposition)	JC: *Tiber banks, Philippi fields.*
	He expresses one idea by two nouns (one acting adjectivally). Called hendiadys: defined in *OED* as 'a single complex idea … expressed by two words connected by a conjunction.'[67] We discuss hendiadys further in 11.5.1.	AC (4.2.44) *Where rather I'll expect victorious life/Than death and honour.* (= 'honourable death').
	adjectives to adverbs	Ham (3.1.122): *I am myself indifferent honest.*
5	He uses active participles passively.	*feeling* = causing themselves to be felt. KL (4.6.222): *Who by the art of known, and feeling sorrows/Am pregnant to good pity.*
	He uses passive participles actively.	TN (1.5.261): *the reverberate hill* = 'causing to be stricken [sounded] back again.'
6	He has verbs expressing intention, desire.[68]	*would* expressing desire. MM (3.1.8): *If I do love thee, I do love a thing/That none but fools would keep.*
7	He has double comparatives/superlatives.	KL (2.2.100): *more corrupter*; H8 (1.1.147): *more stronger.*
8	He can omit the verb *be*, and some prepositions.	Mac (1.4.1): *Is execution done on Cawdor yet?/Or not those in commission yet returned?*
9	He uses *but* for *other than*, or for *before*.	Tem (1.2.118): *I should sin,/To think but nobly of my grand-mother. But* = 'otherwise than nobly.'
10	He uses abstract nouns for concrete notions.	MND (1.1.219): *companies* for 'companions'; AC (2.2.51): *reports* for 'reporters.'

(continued)

Table 2.2 (Cont.)

	Rule	Example(s)
11	He omits a word or phrase already used.	Tem (4.1.26): *The strongest suggestion/Our worser genius can* (= can suggest).
12	He uses the nominative absolutely (*anacoluthon* – defined in OED as an instance of anacoluthia = 'a want of grammatical sequence; the passing from one construction to another before the former is completed').	Ham (3.2.251): *Your majesty and we, that have free souls, it touches us not.* Upton: 'he begins with the nominative case ... but cutting short his speech makes a solecism. Many kinds of these embarrassed sentences there are in Shakespeare.'
13	He has plural nouns with singular verbs.	AC (2.1.10): *My powers are crescent, and my auguring hope/Says it will come to th' full.* Upton says *it* refers to *my powers*.
14	He shortens words by omission of the first or last syllable. He lengthens words by adding a Latin suffix.	TA (1.2.236): *serving* for 'observing'; Per (1.2.25): *ostent* for 'ostentation.' Ham (3.4.47): *contraction* for 'contract.'

Several of Upton's 'rules' exercised others in the eighteenth century. His point (no. 5) about participles, for example, is discussed by Johnson, in relation not just to participles but to adjectives in general. Thus Johnson takes exception to this passage from *Henry V* (Chorus, 17): *And let us, ciphers to this great account,/ On your imaginary forces work. Imaginary* here means 'imaginative'; the word used is passive – 'being imagined' – but the sense is active: 'imagining.' Johnson comments: 'active and passive words are by this author frequently confounded.'[51]

Not just by 'this author' either. Often Upton's rules are characteristic of Early Modern English more generally. Here are some examples related to Upton's point 4. The *OED*'s first citation of *imaginary* meaning 'imaginative' is dated 1500. The *-ary* suffix is from the Latin *-arius*, and this could have the general sense of 'pertaining to,' a meaning which could be said to apply as much to *imaginative* as to *imaginary*. In fact, Onions (1986) glosses *imaginary* as 'of or belonging to the imagination.' Shakespeare, along with other writers of the period, often use *-ive* in a passive sense. *Troilus and Cressida* has *uncomprehensive deeps*, and *As You Like It*, *unexpressive she*. Milton too does this. In his *Hymn of the Nativity* he speaks of a choir's *unexpressive notes*. Today we would say *inexpressible*. Others too were using *indifferent* as an adverb in the sixteenth century. Often Upton's examples contain words that precede Shakespeare: the *OED*'s first citation for *accuse* meaning 'accusation,' for example, is 1439, while *affect* was recorded as a noun in 1398.

The accuracy of some of Upton's points is open to doubt. His gloss of *mysteries* as 'vanities,' for example (point 3 in Table 2.2), is apparently based on the belief that 'popish' mysteries are 'vain.' Johnson's explanation in his edition might be regarded as equally fanciful. *Mysteries*, he says. were mummers' plays, and Shakespeare here means that 'the travelled Englishmen were metamorphosed, by foreign fashions, into such an uncouth appearance, that they looked like mummers in a mystery.'[52] This is certainly an ingenious interpretation. A more plausible recent one is based on a now-obsolete meaning of *mystery*: 'ministry' or 'occupation,' extended here to signify 'way of behaving.' According to the *OED* the 'ministry' meaning may have come about by confusion of the Latin word *ministerium* ('ministry') with *mysterium*.

Despite such doubts, Upton's work impresses as a serious early attempt at Shakespearean linguistic description. Since his work was done, more than 250 years ago, our knowledge has increased considerably, and present-day accounts of Shakespeare's 'language rules' are naturally much richer and more evidence-based. But Upton provides an impressive starting point. What he says, for example, about Shakespeare's word formation processes now seems to us bare and incomplete. But he captures to some basic processes.

2.7.2 Word formation: Hurd

Shakespeare's methods of word formation also interested Richard Hurd. He was a preacher who produced commentaries on Horace, and in his notes we find discussion of Shakespeare's 'creative vocabulary.' Table 2.3 lists the 11 processes he identified:[53]

Table 2.3 Hurd's classification of Shakespeare's word formation strategies

1	compound epithets	*high-sighted* (tyranny)(JC) = 'arrogant'; *arm-gaunt* (steed)(AC); in good condition(?) *lazy-pacing* (clouds) (RJ).
2	adding an affix	*discandy* (AC) = 'to dissolve,' by reversing the caramelizing process; *dislimn* (AC) *limn* = to paint, *dislimn* means 'to obliterate.'
3	changing nouns into verbs	*feature* (Cym); *medicine* (Cym); *virgin* (Cor).
	changing verbs into nouns	*retire* = 'a retreat' (Cym); *stirs* = 'agitation' (Cym).
4	'using active verbs neutrally' (intransitively)	*inform* (Mac); *destroy* (AC).
	using 'neutral' verbs actively (making intransitive verbs transitive)	*dance* (Cor); *glow* (AC).

(continued)

Till 1950

Table 2.3 (Cont.)

5	changing adjectives to nouns	*outward* as a noun = 'exterior' (Cym).
6	changing participles to nouns	*thankings* (Cym); *strewings* e.g. of flowers on a grave (Cym).
7	changing participles to adverbs	*tremblingly* (AC); *smilingly* (KL).
8	using unusual figurative terms	*When snow the pasture sheets* (AC).
9	using words in their literal senses	*disasters veil the sun*. Disaster = an unfavourable planet (Ham).
10	'by transposition of words, unauthoriz'd use of terms, and ungrammatical construction'	No examples given; 'instances in all his plays, *passim*.'
11	use of foreign idioms	*Quenched of hope* (Cym 5.5.195).[69]

Hurd, like Upton, is not talking of processes used by Shakespeare alone. Many are characteristics of the Early Modern English period in general. Thus affixation (Hurd's point 2) is regarded as 'by far the most usual method of word-formation' in the Early Modern period.[54] Similarly, the first *OED* citation of *to medicine* (Hurd's example under point 3) is 1425, and the nouns *retire* and *stir* are both found elsewhere in the sixteenth century.

2.7.3 Identifying characteristics of individual plays: Richard Roderick

Richard Roderick was a scholar who contributed to a book produced by Thomas Edwards entitled *The Canons of Criticism, and a Glossary, being a Supplement to Mr. Warburton's edition of Shakspear*. In this volume, Edwards attacked – in that eighteenth-century polemic way – Warburton's Shakespeare work. Roderick (1758) provides what have been described as 'pioneering analyses' – the first attempt to define the styles of single plays.[55] Not all the points Roderick makes are linguistic, but many are. For example, in his treatment of *Henry VIII*, he identifies three metrical characteristics which distinguish the drama. One is that there are more verses ending with 'redundant' syllables, twice as many as in other plays in fact. In the following lines the syllables in question are the final ones on *admirer* and *ague*:

> *Healthful and ever since a fresh admirer.*
> *Of what I saw there. An untimely ague.*
>
> (H8, 1.1.3)

'A good reader,' Roderick notes, 'will, by a gentle lowering of the voice and quickening of the pronunciation, so contract that pairs of syllables ... as to make them have only the force of one syllable each ...'[56] He also observes that in the play, the caesuras often fall on the seventh syllable, rather than on the more usual fifth or sixth syllable. The third characteristic is that there is an unusual number of clashes between where the sense expects emphasis, and where it naturally falls in the metre.

In only slightly later times, stylistic analyses of this sort, involving linguistic evidence, will play an important role in attribution issues, deciding on the authorship of specific works. *Henry VIII* is in fact one of the plays where there are attribution questions – we now regard it as a joint effort between Shakespeare and Fletcher. But Roderick's own conclusions regarding the play's metrical characteristics have nothing to do with attribution. Indeed, he is himself not sure what they are to do with. He says: 'What Shakespeare intended by all this I fairly own myself ignorant, but that all these peculiarities were done by him advertently and not by chance is, I think, … plain …'[57] He then argues that since such characteristics are intentional, they should not be altered lightly. He is adhering to the 'make fewer changes' principle.

2.7.4 Verse: Daniel Webb and Edward Capell

Rhyme was, as we saw in 2.4, regarded by some as something of a Shakespearean 'dark spot.' As for verse in general, Daniel Webb, an Irish writer on aesthetics, provided what has been described as the 'first detailed appreciation of Shakespeare's verse,'[58] discussed particularly in his *Remarks on the Beauties of Poetry*. He shows how Shakespeare avoids monotony by changing pause positions and by 'varying the movement' of the verse. 'Nothing,' Webb says, 'could be more opposite to the genius and character of this poet than a constant equality of versification.'[59] His comments reflect a line of argument already mentioned – that irregularity, rather than being a negative quality (as the French critics would have it), is in fact a good thing. The varying movements of the verse, Webb says, are certainly not the result of carelessness. They often signal transitions of mood. In this example from *King Lear*, Webb sees 'a most affecting transition in the sound, corresponding with a sudden and pathetic change in the idea' occurring in the last line and a half:[60]

> *I tax not you, you elements, with unkindness;*
> *I never gave you kingdom, called you children.*
> *You owe me no subscription; then let fall*
> *Your horrible pleasure. Here I stand, your slave,*
> *A poor, infirm, weak, and despised old man.*

(3.2.16)

Capell was another interested in verse. His 1774 *Notes and various readings to Shakespeare*, includes *A brief essay on verse, as of Shakespeare's modelling; its principles, and its construction*. In fact the essay is not so brief: it is 44 pages long, and provides a detailed and scholarly look at metre in Shakespeare and Milton. The essay includes a substantial appendix full of examples illustrating the points

Capell makes. Like Webb, he is concerned to show that the variations within Shakespeare's verse were not careless irregularities to be abhorred, but deliberate measures to ensure variety. Indeed, out of such variety comes, he feels, 'some of the most striking beauties' of Shakespeare and Milton's work.[61] Capell is particularly concerned with caesuras, and with 'redundant syllables,' both of which occurred in various positions in Shakespeare's lines. We have seen two examples from Roderick of a line-final 'redundant' syllable. Here are two from Capell showing redundancy in middle and initial positions (the relevant syllables are underlined):

> *Will love you| but stir| not you| 'till you| have well* (MM 5.1.256)
> *Sir, will you| with those| infir|mities| she owes* (KL 1.1.202)[62]

Capell castigates former editions where Shakespeare's lines are cut short, or drawn out – forced to fit in 'to the measure of their sorry bed, which is one of five feet, and that precisely, without want or exceeding.'[63]

Shakespeare's versification also played a role in what was becoming a topic of scholastic interest – the chronology of the plays. For Malone, the more rhyme, the earlier the work: 'whenever, of two early pieces it is doubtful which preceded the other, I am disposed to believe … that play in which the greater number of rhymes is found, to have been first composed.' In later works, he conjectured, Shakespeare 'grew weary of the bondage of rhyme.'[64] The nature of the verse was relevant too. Steevens argues that the early works have more irregular verse: polish came later, with age. Capell sees it the other way round; the earlier verse is regular. Irregularity – and with it more expressiveness – comes in later works.[65]

Metre and verse will be discussed again in Chapter 3 (3.2), as well as in Chapter 10, where we shall see that they have been the subject of much scholastic attention since the middle of the twentieth century. In that chapter we will return to notions like 'redundant syllables' and 'pause position.' Roderick, Webb and Capell are precursors to these more recent treatments.

2.8 Seventeenth-century plays and eighteenth-century books

In his account of the 'reinvention' of Shakespeare over the centuries, Taylor (1989) points out that the seventeenth century regarded Shakespeare's dramas as plays: 'they happened; they enacted a story temporally.' 'In the eighteenth century,' he continues, 'they became things; they became, primarily, books. Books are spatial, not temporal and as the eighteenth century progresses Shakespeare editions surround the text with an expanding border of annotation, and undertext of commentary that repeatedly interrupts a reading of the uppertext.'[66]

The 'expanding border of annotation' could indeed be substantial. As an example, which also aptly finishes the chapter with a reminder of how Shakespeare scholarship grew during the eighteenth century, we will take a look at the first few lines of *King Lear*.

Kent: I thought the King had more affected the Duke of Albany than Cornwall.
Gloucester: It did always seem so to us. But now in the division of the kingdom it appears not which of the Dukes he values most, for qualities are so weighed that curiosity in neither can make choice of either's moiety.

Nahum Tate's seventeenth-century adaptation of the version does not have the passage at all. He had no desire to be faithful to the original, and this part of the scene, one might argue, does not contribute sufficiently to the 'temporal enactment of the story.' So it is not there.

In Johnson's edition, it could not be more different. The 'expanding border of annotation' is there with a vengeance. In fact these few lines of text are accompanied by no fewer than 62 lines of notes. The first page has just Kent's short speech, with the rest of the page taken up with 31 lines of footnotes. Page 2 has the remaining five lines of text (plus a few more), followed by another 31 lines of notes. It is true that these dramatic figures are distorted by the fact that the lines are the opening ones of the play, which means that some of Johnson's discussion is about the origins and sources of the play in general. But thereafter you find:

- a comment on *division of the kingdom*. Does this make sense, Johnson asks, given that the rest of the scene suggests the division has not yet been made?
- *equalities*, Johnson notes, is from the quartos. The First Folio has *qualities*. He observes that Steevens finds similar use of *equalities* in the *Flower of Friendship*, a popular 'conduct book' on marriage, produced by Edmund Tilney in 1568.
- *that curiosity in neither*. Johnson provides a paraphrase from Warburton's edition. Johnson glosses *curiosity* as 'scrupulousness,' and notes (from Steevens) a use of *curious* in the sense of 'scrupulous' in *The Taming of the Shrew*.
- *make choice of either's moiety*. Strictly, Johnson points out, *moiety* should mean 'half,' but Shakespeare's sense is simply a 'part' or 'portion.' Johnson mentions an example Steevens cites from *Henry IV, Part 1*, where *moiety* refers to a third part. Malone, Johnson also says, finds a similar use in Heywood's book, *History of Women* (1624).

Malone's edition, appearing at the end of the century, makes the same points, cites Johnson, and adds a few more instances of the use of the word *curious*. His edition is a century – and a world – away from Tate's adapted 'temporal enactment.'

Notes

1 Upton (1746), p. 210.
2 *Botch* (meaning 'ulcer') is found in some editions today, which would make *crusty* mean 'scabby.' This reading certainly makes the insult clearer; indeed for us today, baking that is 'crusty' is sought after!

3 *Ibid., p.* 212.
4 Johnson and Steevens (1765), p. 236.
5 Gentleman (1770), p. 2.
6 Richardson (1774), p. 38.
7 Garrick (1769). In Vickers (1979), p. 344.
8 Both citations from Vickers (1981), p. 1.
9 Sherlock is extracted in Vickers (1981), pp. 435–9.
10 Taylor (1989), p. 91.
11 Gentleman (1770), p. 2.
12 Pope and Warburton (1747), p. xxiii.
13 Cited in Raleigh (1908), p. xxii.
14 Johnson (1765), p. 42.
15 Upton (1746), p. 137.
16 Johnson (1765), p. 31.
17 Gentleman (1770), 'Comments on *Macbeth*.' Extracted in Vickers (1979), pp. 373–409.
18 Johnson (1765), p. 42.
19 Theobald (1726), p. i.
20 Brown (1751), p. 34. Cited in Vickers (1975), p. 2.
21 Johnson (1765), p. 34.
22 Mallet (1733), p. 21.
23 Kames, Lord (1762), p. 481.
24 Cooke (1775), p. 149.
25 Approved of by Richard Steele in *The Tatler*, No. 167, May 1710.
26 Johnson (1765), p. 22.
27 Johnson *Notes on The Winter's Tale*. In Johnson (1765), p. 89.
28 Johnson (1751), p. 217.
29 Gentleman (1770), p. 386.
30 Richardson (1774), p. 238.
31 Johnson *Notes on the Merry Wives of Windsor*. In Johnson (1765), p. 95.
32 Malone (1790), p. 529.
33 Taylor (1989), pp. 39, 40.
34 Ritson (1781), p. 54.
35 Barber (1997), p. 170.
36 Mason (1785). Cited in Vickers (1981), p. 37.
37 Gentleman (1773), p. 92.
38 The website http://smallnotes.library.virginia.edu/2016/06/28/shakespearean-insults/ contains a lengthy list of eighteenth-century editor insults.
39 Steevens (1773), p. 69. Cited in Vickers (1981), p. 336.
40 Johnson (1756), p. 5.
41 Raleigh (1908), p. xxiv.
42 Woudhuysen (1989). Others have a smaller number – for example, Brewer (2010).
43 The *Macbeth* example is given in Lim (1986).
44 Information from Woudhuysen (1989). The error was corrected in later editions.
45 Sorensen (2000), p. 98.
46 Woudhuysen (1989), p. 11.
47 Warner (1786), p. 4.
48 Wright (1905).
49 Upton (1746), p. 284.

50 Most of the examples are Upton's own, and on several occasions, the texts used today differ from the one Upton uses. Sometimes he does not give examples of a point, in which case these have been added.
51 Johnson (1756) *Notes on Henry V.* In Raleigh (1908), p. 126.
52 Offor (1819). *King Henry VIII*, Act 1, line 550.
53 Hurd (1748), p. 77.
54 Barber (1997), p. 232.
55 The description is Vickers' (1976), p. 34.
56 Roderick (1758), p. 226.
57 *Ibid.*, p. 228.
58 Vickers (1974), p. 35.
59 Webb (1762), p. 49.
60 *Ibid.*, p. 45.
61 Capell (1774), p. 191.
62 Both lines have different forms in modern editions.
63 Capell (1774), p. 194.
64 Malone (1816), p. 247.
65 Vickers (1981), p. 37.
66 Taylor (1989), p. 108.
67 Discussion of hendiadys here may seem a little out of place at this point in Upton's system, but his order has been followed.
68 Upton's exact words are: 'He [Shakespeare] uses the thing done, for the intention and desire to do it.' He gives an example from Milton's *Paradise Lost* (Book IV): *The undergrowth / Of shrubs, and tangling bushes, had perplex'd / All path of man, or beast, that pass'd that way.* Here, Upton says, *pass'd that way* means 'should now or hereafter endeavour to pass that way.'
69 This phrase is listed in the *Encyclopaedia Britannica, Volume 16* Edinburgh: Constable, (1823), p. 770, under Greek and Latin idioms 'common in English poetry,' but not found in prose.

3 Measuring and classifying
The nineteenth century

3.1 A problematic relationship with the truth

In the pictures that we have of him, John Payne Collier (1789–1883) looks like an amiable, even jolly, man. He was indeed said to have been a kind and generous person, devoted to his family. The problem was his relationship with the truth. He began life as a journalist. Trouble started in 1819, when he was called before the House of Commons for incorrectly reporting a politician's speech. After a spell as a lawyer, he turned his attention to Shakespeare studies, and in 1852 produced a book claiming to have uncovered – as its title states – *New Facts, New Particulars and Further Particulars respecting Shakespeare*. Before long, scholars were casting doubt on the veracity of his 'new' Shakespeare facts and particulars, suspecting him of forgery. Collier then turned his forger's gaze in the direction of Shakespeare's actual texts. In 1852, he announced that he had bought a dusty copy of the Second Folio for 30 shillings. He found within it – behold! – copious marginal notes and emendations which threw new light on Shakespeare's texts. It showed new punctuation and stage directions, and even revealed some new lines. The book had 'Tho. Perkins, his booke' inscribed on the outer cover, and hence became known as the 'Perkins Folio.' The truth about Collier's forgery was fully exposed over time. Another lawyer turned scholar, Clement Ingleby, demolished Collier's claims in his *A Complete View of the Shakspere Controversy*. The amiable, jolly forger was silenced, but he remained unrepentant. Indeed, in his later life there were the beginnings of an attempt to do to Milton what he had done to Shakespeare, through the 'discovery' of another forged document. Despite his unwillingness to come clean, Collier did, at the very end of his life – when he was 93 and nearly blind – admit: 'I am bitterly sad and most sincerely grieved that in every way I am such a despicable offender I am ashamed of almost every act of my life … My repentance is bitter and sincere.'[1]

What has this story to do with Shakespeare's language? One answer relates to how Ingleby exposed Collier's claims. His main sources of evidence are handwriting and palaeography, but he also uses more recognizably linguistic means. He employs, for example, 'philological tests': 'The obvious method of testing the genuineness of the corrections,' he says, was to select a word or phrase which had the appearance of being modern in sense, or idiom, … [and to show] … that such a word or phrase was not in use at all, or in a particular sense, till a period later than when the document was produced.[2]

One such test-word was *cheer*, used as a countable noun. Coriolanus (4.7.51) has the lines: And power, unto itself most commendable,/ Hath not a tomb so evident as a chair/ T' extol what it hath done. The forgery replaces *chair* with *cheer*. But, Ingleby argues (at some length), this sense of the word 'was not in use till the present century, and that consequently it is a test-word which proves the manuscript notes … to be of recent origin.'[3] Ingleby's book has many such examples of language analysis being used to detect forgery.

3.2 Two societies, for Shakespeare and Shakspeare

Another reason why the story has to do with Shakespeare's language is that Collier was associated with a group of scholars who made efforts to push Shakespeare studies forward. 'It is remarkable,' Collier says,

> that all that has hitherto been done for the illustration of Shakespeare has been accomplished by individuals, and that no literary association has yet been formed for the purpose of collecting materials, or of circulating information, by which he may be thoroughly understood and fully appreciated.[4]

To make up for this lack, Collier and his colleagues formed the Shakespeare Society (SS) in 1840. The Society met regularly, with members presenting and discussing papers. They also supported various Shakespeare-related publications. Collier himself, who became director, contributed no fewer than 21 papers. Suspicions of Collier's forgery cannot have helped the Society's reputation, though it seems to have been mainly financial problems that caused its demise in 1853.

But in 1873 a New Shakspeare Society (NSS) was founded. This spelling of Shakespeare's name was, it was argued, the original and correct one. The NSS was the brain-child of Frederick James Furnivall, a scholar who (as we shall see in 3.5) was also an important figure in the development of the *Oxford English Dictionary*. The NSS had similar aims to the earlier SS: to meet and discuss matters Shakespearian, and to foster Shakespeare publications. It was particularly concerned with a common nineteenth-century occupation, to establish chronological sequence. The way of tackling this was also very nineteenth century, by using scientific means to reveal progression in Shakespeare's development as an artist. In Furnivall's words, the Society aimed

> by very close study of the metrical and phraseological peculiarities of Shakspere, to get his plays as nearly as possible into the order in which he wrote them … and then to use that revised order for the purpose of studying the progress and meaning of Shakspere's mind.[5]

One prominent member of the NSS was Frederick Gard Fleay, a minister of the Church of England until late in life. He in particular was determined to develop a scientific approach towards Shakespeare studies. His creed: 'if you cannot weigh, measure, number your results ... you must not hope to convince others, or claim the position of an investigator; you are merely a guesser, a propounder of hypotheses.'[6]

Fleay was an energetic scholar, so much so that he earned himself the nickname of 'the industrious flea.' A paper which shows how he weighed, measured, numbered, was delivered to the NSS under the title of 'On metrical tests as applied to dramatic poetry.' The paper is particularly concerned with establishing the chronology of Shakespeare's plays. To illustrate his approach, Fleay begins by comparing two plays, *Love's Labour's Lost* (considered an early play), and *The Winter's Tale* (regarded as late). He believed that 'in general terms ... we may expect to find, that in Shakspere's development he gradually dropped the rhymed dialogue, adopted double endings, Alexandrines, and broken lines.'[7] 'Double endings' were lines with an extra unstressed syllable after the iambic pentameter sequence; 'broken lines' had fewer syllables than iambic pentameters, and Alexandrines had more (six iambic feet). Table 3.1 shows the results of his counting.

Fleay divides the plays that he regards as having been written just by Shakespeare into four groups:

Table 3.1 Metrical features of *Love's Labour's Lost* and *The Winter's Tale*

	LLL	WT
Rhyming lines	over 1000	0
Double endings	7	639
Incomplete lines	few	many
Alexandrines	1	16

Table 3.2 Fleay's chronology of Shakespeare's plays

1. **Rhyming period.**
   LLL has more than 1000 rhymes, MND has 850, CE 380, RJ 650, R2 530.
   No other play has as many as 200 rhymes. Fleay argues: 'Shakspeare joined the advocates of rhyme at first, and gradually learned to feel the superiority of blank verse.'[8]

2. **Comedy and history period.**
   TGV, MV, TN, AYLI, MWW, MAAN, R3, KJ, H4, H5.
   These plays have fewer rhymes (100–200 per play). There is an increase in the number of short lines; also in feminine endings and Alexandrines.

3. **Tragedy period.**
   Mac, Cym, Ham, Oth, KL, TC, MM, AWEW.
   The metres here are more free, intermingling of prose and verse. There are abundant short lines, and many double endings.

Table 3.2 (Cont.)

---

4. **Roman and final period.**
   JC, Cor, AC, Tem, WT.
   The metres here are more regular.

It is not surprising that, with the benefit of later scholarship, we should arrive at an order different from Fleay's, and from others of the nineteenth century. He puts *Twelfth Night*, *Macbeth*, and *Cymbeline* earlier than we place them today, while he has *Richard* III and *Julius Caesar* later. But the chronology is largely accurate. At least (following Malone) he places *The Tempest* at the end of Shakespeare's career rather than the beginning, which is where earlier chronological attempts had placed it.

Fleay's chronology does not include *The Taming of the Shrew*, *Henry VI*, *Timon of Athens*, *Pericles*, *Henry VIII*, or *Two Noble Kinsmen*. These are plays which he regarded as having been written either entirely or completely by other authors. As well as chronology, Fleay – like many nineteenth-century scholars – was interested in questions of attribution, using his scientific methods of measuring and counting to determine 'the genuineness of the works traditionally assigned to a writer.'[9] Another of Fleay's papers for the NSS shows how he used his measurement techniques in relation to an attribution issue. It was entitled 'On the authorship of *The Taming of the Shrew*,' and was read at the third NSS meeting. The paper begins: 'There is something in the first aspect of this play so different from the generality of Shakspeare's work that I have long since excited suspicion as to its authorship.'[10] Fleay puts forward a number of non-linguistic arguments in support of the idea that the play was largely written by someone other than Shakespeare. The play is, for example, the only instance in Shakespeare where an Induction (with Sly) is used. But his main case is made through linguistic means. He uses his metrical counting methods, showing, for example, that TS has over 20 lines where the first foot has just one syllable. He claims that the figure for the rest of Shakespeare's entire output is just 12. He also uses lexical information. He observes, for example, that 'the frequent contraction of the word *gentlemen* into *gent'men* in TS is also noticeable.'[11] More significantly, he comes up with a list of words found in the play that do not occur in what he calls Shakespeare's 'undoubted plays' – where authorship is not contested. There are no fewer than 130 items. Among those only occurring in TS are: *plash* (a pool), *devote*, *dough*, *incredible*, and *pithy* (powerful).

Methods of linguistic analysis like these were highly controversial, so much so that the heat they generated ended in the disbanding of the NSS in 1894. Furnivall and Fleay were on the 'scientific' side. A major opponent was the poet Algernon Swinburne. His 1880 book *A Study of Shakespeare* contains an Appendix entitled 'Report on the proceedings on the first anniversary session of the Newest Shakespeare Society.' It is an amusing satire on the NSS's ways of working. It is presented as a paper submitted to the NSS about the authorship of *A Midsummer Night's Dream*, which, it is satirically suggested, was written by Shakespeare's contemporary, the dramatist George Chapman. Soon the discussion widens to these lines from Shakespeare's Sonnet 37: *So I, made lame by fortune's dearest spite, / Take all my comfort of thy worth and truth.* The supposed author suggests that these lines show that Shakespeare was lame. The question then becomes: lame in which leg? Evidence on this issue is taken from some discussion about shoes in *Two Gentlemen of Verona*, and the final suggestion is that Shakespeare was made lame in the left leg, following an accident in his early life. This delightful spoof ridicules the use of textual analysis in Shakespearean scholarship.

The bad feeling between the two camps descended, alas, into personal abuse. Furnivall referred in print to Swinburne as 'Pigsbrook,' derived from the Anglo-Saxon *swin*, meaning 'pig' and *burn* meaning 'brook.' Swinburne countered by calling Furnivall 'Brothels-dyke,' combining the Latin *fornix* ('brothel') and *vallum* ('dyke').[12] Less publically, Swinburne also called Furnivall 'Fartiwell,' and the term 'Shitspeare Society' was also bandied about. The society ceased to exist in 1894.

3.3 Editions, long, short, and sometimes expurgated

Forgery is, one might say, a sincere form of flattery, and Collier's attempts to forge Shakespeare are evidence of the dramatist's standing, which was now very high. For Coleridge, Milton, and Shakespeare were 'the two glory-smitten summits of the poetic mountain,' while Carlyle saw Shakespeare as the 'priest of mankind' – 'the greatest intellect who, in our recorded world, has left record of himself in the way of literature.'[13] Shakespeare was now part of the cultural fabric of England. As Jane Austen put it in *Mansfield Park* (written early in the nineteenth century): 'His celebrated passages are quoted by every body; they are in half the books we open, and we all talk Shakespeare, use his similes, and describe with his descriptions.'[14] It is said that Hazlitt quotes Shakespeare no fewer than 2,400 times, a fifth of these being from *Hamlet*.[15] Dickens, who revered Shakespeare, says in a letter that he is aware of his habit of falling into iambic pentameters in his prose, doubtless partly due to the influence of, and exposure to, Shakespeare.[16] He was also now playing a role in education, with speeches given as practice texts for budding orators. And (as we shall see in 3.4), school pupils were being made to study Shakespeare's language.[17]

One result of this increasing reverence was a proliferation in editions of the works. In the seventeenth century there were four, in the eighteenth, 80, and in the nineteenth some 800.[18] Variorum editions were particularly popular. One, sometimes called the 'first variorum,' was produced by Isaac Reed in 1803. A variorum contains a scholarly collections of comments, rather than personal statements of interpretation. While in the eighteenth century, well-known characters (like Pope and Johnson) produced the editions, in the nineteenth the editors were often expert scholars, and not necessarily known names.[19]

But not all editions were heavy tomes, weighed down by decades, even centuries, of scholastic comment. A particularly successful edition was *The Globe*, produced by a group of Cambridge academics. Its popularity was huge, with 95,000 copies sold by 1870, and 244,000 by 1911. It had the advantage of being reasonably portable and, since it divided plays into acts, scenes, and gave line numbers, it was useful as a reference text for scholars. There was also a proliferation of 'pocket' editions, textbook editions, editions appearing in serialized form. Shakespeare was being made accessible to everyone. For young readers, there was Mary and Charles Lamb's 1807 *Tales from Shakespeare*. In the same year, another adapted and 'sanitized' version appeared, with a slightly different audience in mind. *The Family Shakespeare* was an edition 'which the parent, the guardian, and the instructor of youth, may place without fear in the hands of the pupil,'[20] and which could be read by, for example, well-bred young ladies. The words are those of the most famous of the expurgators, Thomas Bowdler (who gives us the word 'bowdlerize'). He and his sister Henrietta Maria Bowdler were responsible for *The Family Shakespeare*. A number of other editions in one way or another expurgated, appeared during the rest of the century.

Here are some examples of Bowdler's expurgation, some of them linguistic:

- In *Hamlet*, Ophelia is said to have drowned in an accident, rather than killing herself.
- The whore Doll Tearsheet disappears completely from *Henry IV, Part 2*;
- Shakespeare's 20 lines given to the foul-mouthed Porter in *Macbeth* becomes six rather tame lines in Bowdler.
- Lady Macbeth's *Out, damned spot* becomes *Out, crimson spot*.
- Many references to 'God' and Jesus' were cut out. So Gobbo's *I will run as far as God has any ground* becomes *as far as there is any ground* (MV 2.2.102). And while the Traveller in *Henry IV, Part I* says *Jesus bless us* (2.2.81.), in Bowdler he says nothing.
- *Romeo and Juliet*'s line (1.1.214): *Nor ope her lap to saint-seducing gold* is simply omitted; the word 'lap' could refer to the female pudendum.

Three facsimiles of Folios also appeared during the century, in 1866, 1876, and 1895, and there were quarto facsimiles too. These 'original versions' enabled editors to eradicate some of the 'faults' that eighteenth-century interpreters had introduced. An editor who is particularly concerned with historical fault-eradication is the publisher, and member of the NSS, Charles Knight. Here he describes the process he followed in the production of his edition, *The Pictorial Shakespere*:

> I diligently applied myself to a critical examination of the text to be adopted. I procured a copy of the First Folio, which was read aloud to me whilst I marked upon a copy of the common trade edition, all the variations that presented themselves. I found that no book could be more incorrectly printed than this booksellers' stereotyped volume. I subsequently expressed

my belief that the text of Shakspere had not been compared with the originals carefully and systematically for half a century.'[21]

A particular concern of Knight's was with punctuation which, in modern editions, was, he said, 'in the most confused state.' Consequently he makes a good number of punctuation changes. His procedure is invariably the same. He notes points where 17th to 19th century editions differ from what is in the First Folio; he argues against these changes, and comes down in favour of the First Folio version. Here is an example, which will need some context to clarify. In *Much Ado About Nothing*, Claudio and Hero are to marry, but the Machiavellian Don John has contrived to make Hero appear to have been unfaithful, so when it comes to the marriage ceremony, Claudio makes it clear he does not want to marry the girl. As a result, when the Friar, undertaking the ceremony, asks *You come hither, my lord, to marry this lady,* Claudio replies *No.* Leonato assumes there has been some linguistic misunderstanding, which he tries to clear up by saying, *To be married to her: friar, you come to marry her.* Claudio is to be 'married to her,' Leonato is saying, and the Friar is doing the marrying (undertaking the ceremony, that is). The lines and its punctuation, as above, are what is in the First Folio, and they are what Knight uses. There are some editions today (like Wells and Taylor, 2005) which have *To be married to her. Friar, you come to marry her* – slightly different punctuation but conveying the same sense. But the editions of Pope, Theobald, and Malone all have *To be married to her, friar; you come to marry her.* Knight comments: 'We follow the punctuation of the original. The meaning is destroyed by the modern mode of pointing the passage.'[22] 'Destroyed' is perhaps too strong a word, but one can see what Knight means.

There was, then, a proliferation of Shakespeare editions during the century. One linguistic consequence was, as we have seen, to 'clean-up' the language to make it suitable for new audiences. But there was also, at the same time, an increase in scholarship, with editors not so much providing 'interpretations' as assembling collections of comments, as well as making a real effort to look back to what the Folios and quartos reveal.

3.4 Abbott and an educational grammar

Writing grammars, like producing forgeries, might be regarded as a sincere form of flattery. It was one which Edwin Abbott (1838–1926) showed to Shakespeare. He was a theologian, writer, and perhaps above all an educationalist. He became headmaster of the City of London School at the early age of 26. There he made considerable innovations both in terms of teaching methods and of curriculum, introducing, *inter alia*, the study of Shakespeare's language as a subject. Poor health made him retire at 50 and he then devoted himself to writing. Some of his works were educational: one book was entitled 'How to write clearly,' another 'Via Latina: First Latin Book.' He also wrote a novella called *Flatland*, a social satire with elements of science fiction; it was made into a feature film as recently as 2007. Abbott also produced *A Shakespearian Grammar,* a work which turned out to be so popular that it ran into second and third editions within a year of its initial publication in 1870.

The *Grammar*'s subtitle is 'An attempt to illustrate some of the differences between Elizabethan and modern English.' This correctly suggests that though the prime focus is on Shakespeare, the Elizabethan period as a whole is covered, with other writers like Jonson being mentioned. The title also suggests that the book has a comparative perspective, focusing on differences between Elizabethan and Victorian English. Nevertheless, at almost 500 pages long, the book presents an extremely thorough analysis of Elizabethan English grammar.

The book is divided into two main parts: 'Grammar' and 'Prosody,' and these are subdivided into sections – 529 in all; the coverage is indeed extremely thorough. There are 14 pages dealing with the articles, 24 dealing with auxiliary (and modal) verbs, and no fewer than 46 pages covering prepositions. Consider too how Abbott treats the mismatches of singular verbs and plural nouns. As we saw in 2.4, the eighteenth century took note of these mismatches, and the belief was often that they were the result of carelessness, either by Shakespeare or through errors in transmission. But Abbott relates them to the existence of an alternative plural form. He has a long section on the topic, speaking of Shakespeare's 'general predilection for the inflection in –s which may well have arisen from the northern E.E [Early English] third person plural in –s.'[23] The section contains over 20 examples. He notes that modern editors generally 'correct' the mismatch by altering the verb or the noun. This sometimes, he shows, leads to the wrong sense being conveyed. For example, *Hamlet* in the First Folio has: *The great man down, you mark his favourites flies* (3.2.214), with the noun plural, and the verb apparently singular. The Globe edition (and indeed, it must be said, most editions today) solve the mismatch by making the noun singular (*favourite*). But for Abbott this completely misses 'the intention to describe the crowd of favourites scattering in flight.'[24] He concedes that sometimes there are nouns which, though plural, might be regarded as carrying a singular sense, for example in *Romeo and Juliet*'s *What manners is in this?* (5.3.214). But as a rule this does not apply, as in *The Tempest*'s *My old bones aches* (3.3.2). In this case, The Globe edition changes the verb to plural (rather than the noun to singular): *My old bones ache*.

The Introduction to Abbott's *Grammar* perceptively covers the main areas of difference between Elizabethan and Victorian English. Particularly noteworthy are the sections dealing with semantic change. One covers 'Words then [in Elizabethan times] used literally [which] are now used metaphorically.' Included in his examples is the word *extravagant*. The literal meaning from Latin is 'wandering out of bounds,' which is how Horatio uses it when he describes the Ghost in *Hamlet* as an *extravagant and erring spirit* (1.1.55). In Victorian English, Abbott says, the word has become restricted in sense, meaning 'wandering beyond the bounds of economy' – the major sense of the word today. Another of Abbott's examples is *aggravate*, which in Shakespeare could mean 'add to the weight of.' This is how the word is used in *The Merry Wives of Windsor*, when Falstaff says he will *aggravate* Ford's *style* ('form of address') – by calling him a knave (2.2.271). In Victorian English its meaning had narrowed to 'add to a mental burden.' These examples, as Abbott notes, show a narrowing of meaning, which occurs when new words enter the language and come into conflict with already-existing words; 'specialisation of meaning' occurs. But sometime, Abbott continues, the new words can take on wider, rather than narrower, senses. One of his examples is *influence*. In Shakespeare it refers to the effect of stars: Horatio talks of *the moist star* [the Moon]/ *Upon whose influence Neptune's empire stands* (Ham 1.1.119). In Victorian English (as today) the word refers to more general sorts of effect. Another category Abbott discusses is where the semantic specialization of words results in pejorative meanings. Hence Elizabethan *impertinent* meant 'not to the point': Prospero in *The Tempest* (1.2.138) talks about a story being *impertinent* ('irrelevant') to him. Today the word has a pejorative sense ('disrespectful' or 'rude'). Another example: when Leontes calls Antigonus *tenderly officious* (WT 2.3.158) he means 'obliging.' Today *officious* carries a pejorative sense. Such categories of semantic narrowing, widening, and pejorative change are recognized in more recent discussions of semantics, like Ullman (1964).

When comparing Elizabethan and Victorian English, Abbott notes that 'in the former any irregularities whatever, whether in the formation of words or in the combination of words into sentences, are allowable.'[25] He suggests reasons for this. One is 'the natural results of a spirit which preferred clearness and vigour of expression to logical symmetry.'[26] This explanation is used to account for the occurrence of double negatives, as when, in *As You Like It*, Celia announces *I cannot go no further* (2.4.8). Abbott, who notes that the structure is 'quite common in Early English' accounts for it in terms of a 'desire for emphasis.'[27] Another difference between Elizabethan and Victorian, Abbott says, is that Elizabethan English tended to 'overburden' words, giving them multiple meanings. Victorian English shows more 'division of labour.' One of his examples is the Elizabethan *by* which could mean, among other things, 'near,' 'in accordance with,' 'by reason of,' and 'owing to.' Victorian English would use prepositional phrases like these to distinguish the various meanings. Ellipsis is another characteristic Abbott notes, claiming that Elizabethan authors freely used ellipsis 'provided the deficiency could be easily supplied from the context.'[28] Thus in these lines from *The Rape of Lucrece* (930): *O hear me then, injurious shifting time; / Be guilty of my death, since of my crime*, it is clear from the context that the second line means 'since thou art guilty of my crime.'[29]

It was part of the spirit of the age that Abbott's *Grammar* should show a characteristically Darwinian evolutionary perspective, seeking to reveal 'progression' in the development of the language. This belief in progression leads in the direction of a central message which says 'Victorian English good, Elizabethan English bad.' But to Abbott's credit this is not quite his conclusion. He is aware of this danger, saying that 'the enumeration of the points of difference between Shakespearian and modern English may seem to have been a mere list of irregularities and proofs of the inferiority of the former to the latter.' He also concedes that 'we may perhaps claim some superiority in completeness and perspicuity for modern English.' But at the same time he is prepared to admit that 'for freedom, for brevity and for vigour, Elizabethan is superior to modern English.'[30] In addition, Shakespeare's English gives 'a liveliness and wakefulness ... which are wanting in the grammatical monotony of the present day.'[31] This is a far cry from seventeenth- and eighteenth-century complaints about the 'barbarousness' of Elizabethan English (as we discussed in 2.3).

Grammars of the time often had educational aims. William Cobbett's 1819 volume, for example, was subtitled: *Intended for the use of schools and young persons in general, but more especially for the use of soldiers, sailors, apprentices and plough boys*. Abbott, ever the pedagogue, also proclaims on his *Grammar*'s title page that it is 'for the use of schools.' To this end, there is a 'Notes and Questions' section near the end of the book, intended for use with students. All the questions are based around Act 3 of *Macbeth*. Here is an example for the line *So weary with disasters, tugged with fortune* (3.1.113). Abbott asks: 'parse and explain *tugged*. How does the meaning differ from the modern meaning? Compare.' Often the questions require students to refer back to sections of the *Grammar*. Thus there is a question which deals with the line: *You have displaced the mirth, broke the good meeting* (Mac 3.4.108). The question is: 'What is here contrary to common usage?' He refers students to the *Grammar*'s section 343, which deals with the Elizabethan tendency to drop the inflection *–en* in past participles, and use past forms for the participle. This was 'common in Early English,' Abbott says.[32] He does not give *broke* as an example, but lists similar forms, like *drove* for *driven*, *took* for *taken*; in 1.4 we saw Dryden objecting to Shakespeare's use of *shook* for *shaken*. Abbot's questions are worthy of modern-day linguistics students, and certainly the section indicates the extent to which the study of Shakespeare's language was making inroads into the nation's educational system.

There were some grammars of Elizabethan English that Abbott was able to draw on, Jonson's *The English Grammar* for example. He acknowledges a few specific sources in his Prefaces to the various editions, particularly (in relation to the third edition) the three-volume, 1700-page *Englische Grammatik* written by Eduard Mätzner and published in Berlin in 1860. But a lot of Abbott's work seems to have been original scholarship. His *Grammar* has to be regarded as a major development in Shakespearean language studies.

3.5 Two concordances, one lexicon, and a very large dictionary

Abbott's *Grammar*, with its 529 sections, shows just how passionate nineteenth-century scholars were about listing and classifying. The various Shakespearean 'word-lists' that the century produced show the same.

A concordance is 'an alphabetical arrangement of the principal words contained in a book, with citations of the passages in which they occur' (*OED*). An early nineteenth-century Shakespeare concordance was produced by an English lady, Mary Cowden Clarke. She worked together with her husband on a Shakespeare edition, and in 1864 she produced *The Complete Concordance to Shakspere; being a verbal index to all the passages in the dramatic works of the poet*. It took 12 years to complete, and was published in 18 monthly parts. Its coverage was comprehensive, though there are, she admits in her *Preface*, some omissions. Titles like *master, mistress, lord, lady, king* are not there, and for reasons of space she leaves out some common words or usages. The auxiliary use of *let*, for example, is not covered; 'the space gained [by omitting this use] is,' she says, 'the enormous difference between 17 and 2184 [instances], or six printed pages of three columns each.'[33] Note though, that in order to be able to calculate this saving, Clarke has clearly had to do the work of collecting all the auxiliary instances – before deciding to omit them. Clarke's volume is indeed a *Concordance*. Words are not defined; the quotations given are brief, with play, act, and scene references given; line numbers did not come into popular scholastic use until the publication of The Globe edition in 1864.

It had long been recognized that glossaries would be a helpful accessory to understanding Shakespeare fully. Some editions accordingly provided these. Alexander Dyce's 1857 edition, for example, had an associated glossary, 500 pages long in fact! The *OED* defines a glossary as 'a list with explanations of abstruse, antiquated, dialectal, or technical terms; a partial dictionary.' They were lists of difficult words, and did not cover the entire word-stock. A German scholar, Alexander Schmidt, who worked in Königsberg, felt the need for something more comprehensive, and in 1874 produced his *Shakespeare-lexicon: A Complete Dictionary of All the English Words, Phrases and Constructions in the works of the poet*. Earlier Shakespeare glossaries focused on 'obsolete and unintelligible' words, but Schmidt's *Lexicon* aimed 'to contain [Shakespeare's] whole vocabulary, and subject the sense and use of every word of it to careful examination.'[34] As befits a lexicon, there are word definitions. But there are quotations too – more than 50,000 in fact – citing play, act, scene, and The Globe line numbers. These are organized round definitions which have sub-classifications. Thus – to select an example at random – for the word *abandon*, Schmidt has three meanings: 'to leave,' 'to desert,' and 'to give up,' each with associated quotations.

In addition to all this, Schmidt adds an Appendix divided into four sections. There are 'Grammatical observations,' some of which are lengthy. For example, several pages are dedicated to adjectives forming the first element of compound nouns. The next section on 'Provincialisms' is much shorter, and focuses mainly on Edgar's use of dialect in *King Lear*, employing such forms as *ch'ill* for 'I will' – *Ch'ill not let go, zir* he says (4.6.235). The third section covers 'Words and sentences taken from foreign languages.' These are, naturally (given Schmidt's thoroughness), classified according to language. For Latin you have, for example, the use by Holofernes in *Love's Labour's Lost* of *canis* (*canus*) for 'dog,' when he describes Cerebus as a *three-headed canus*. One of Schmidt's examples from Italian (again used by Holofernes, but also twice in *The Taming of the Shrew*) is *ben venuto*, meaning 'welcome.' There is just one entry for Dutch: *lustique* in *All's Well that Ends Well*. It means 'lively' (*Lustique, as the Dutchman says* is Lafew's line – 2.3.40). Schmidt's fourth section is a 'List of words forming the latter part in compositions [compounds],' and his examples include *apparent* in 'heir-apparent,' and *babe* in 'cradle-babe.' Sometimes his compounds have no more than an added prefix, like *-cave* in 'concave.' The very thorough Professor Schmidt is almost apologetic about the fact that his work ignores etymologies, which a 'general dictionary' might include.

The American John Bartlett, a descendent from one of the *Mayflower* pilgrims, was a publisher and author. Like Clarke and Schmidt, his Shakespeare volume was a massive one, with an appropriately lengthy title: *A new and complete concordance or verbal index to words, phrases, and passages in the dramatic works of Shakespeare with a supplementary concordance to the poems.* It was published in 1894. It took him, he says, some 16,000 hours to produce. But this was amidst an energetically active life: 'the work has been prepared,' he casually announces, 'chiefly in the leisure taken from active duties.'[35] His *Concordance* claims to be more comprehensive than previous ones. It includes 'normal' words, like verb *be*, *have*, *may*, though he admits that items like *the*, *a* and some interjections, are not there. As a concordance rather than a lexicon, the work consists of quotations only which, he says, are given 'independent of context.'

A comparison of how Clarke, Schmidt and Bartlett handle the word we randomly selected earlier – *abandon* – shows only slight differences. Clarke and Bartlett have separate entries for *abandon* and *abandoned*, while Schmidt deals with the two together (identifying, as we have seen, three meaning sub-classifications). But all three have the same total number of quotations (12: 4 for *abandon* and 8 for *abandoned*). Clarke's quotations are slightly longer than Schmidt's (providing, that is, a little more context), but Bartlett's are significantly longer (nearly twice as long in fact). To illustrate these differences in quotation length: here are those for the word *abandoned* in *As You Like It* (5.4.192):

>   *Schmidt*   ... at your abandoned cave
>   *Clarke*   I'll stay to know at your abandoned cave
>   *Bartlett*   What you would have
>   I'll stay to know at your abandoned cave.

Bartlett's longer quotations partly explain why his is by far the longest volume. Another reason is that he considers items that the other choose to omit. Bartlett's entry for the verb *have*, for example, fills an entire column, while there is no entry in Clarke.

It is more telling, perhaps, to compare the three works with a modern 'word-list' like Crystal and Crystal (2008). This too has 12 quotations for *abandon/abandoned*, suggesting that (at least for this one selected example) the nineteenth-century authors have located all instances of the word.[36] A look at some other words suggests the same; to choose two more random examples: for *calamity* and *generally*, the number of quotations in all four sources is almost identical. But the more interesting comparison is in terms of the mode of production. Today a concordance is based on a corpus of the texts, electronically organized into entries. This involves a good deal of work, to be sure. But doing the same thing manually – laboriously going through the texts collecting quotations – is a task in an altogether different league. The nineteenth-century authors deserve credit not just for what they did, but also for how they had to do it.

The nineteenth century also heralded an important birth, of the *OED*. Frederick Furnivall, already mentioned in relation to the NSS, was there in attendance. He was one of a small group of scholars who formed the Philological Society. In 1857 they expressed the need for a comprehensive dictionary of English, and put forward a proposal for its development. Furnivall himself was an early editor, where he continued his predisposition to form new societies by creating the Early English Text Society (in 1864), and the Chaucer Society (in 1868), both partly with the intention of finding out about old words, and both hence valuable sources of information for the new dictionary. Furnivall was not entirely successful as a dictionary editor, and he recruited James Murray to replace him. In 1879 Oxford University Press officially invited Murray to edit what was to be called the *New English Dictionary*. The name was changed to *Oxford English Dictionary* in 1933.

The proposed scope of the *OED* was huge. It was to deal not just with modern words and their meanings, but to go back well into history. Definitions would be supported by copious quotations through the ages. For each word, the first quotation would be the first instance found, giving a sense of when a word came into the language. The initial plan was for a four-volume, 6,400 page work, to be finished in ten years. After five years, the team had only reached the word 'ant.' The task was clearly going to be very much more onerous and time-consuming than originally planned.[37] The ten-volume work appeared in 1928, some 13 years after Murray's death. When the second edition came out in 1989, it was 21,728 pages long, and filled 20 volumes.

The *OED* was important for Shakespeare language studies because he was used extensively as a source for example quotations. We will have much more to say about the dictionary, particularly in following two chapters.

Notes

1 Collier, (1882). Cited in Schoenbaum (1991), p. 266.
2 Ingleby (1861), p. 141.
3 *Ibid.*, p. 151.
4 Collier (1842), p. 2.
5 Furnivall (1861), p. vi.
6 Fleay (1874), p. 1.
7 *Ibid.*, p. 7.
8 *Ibid.*, p. 11.
9 *Ibid.*, p. 6.
10 *Ibid.*, p. 85.
11 *Ibid.*, p. 88.
12 Hollingsworth (2012).
13 Carlyle (1841), p. 100.
14 Austen (1814), p. 391.
15 Bate (1984), p. 26. Cited by Taylor (1989), p. 107.

16 Discussed in Hardy (2008), p. 22.
17 Taylor (1989), p. 197.
18 Decker (2014), p. 16.
19 The point is made by Taylor (1989), p. 189.
20 Bowdler (1843), p. viii.
21 Knight (1873), p. 285.
22 Knight (1851), p. 429.
23 Abbott (1870), sect. 333.
24 *Ibid.*, p. 235.
25 *Ibid.*, p. 5.
26 *Ibid.*, p. 5.
27 *Ibid.*, p. 295.
28 *Ibid.*, p. 279.
29 *Ibid.*, p. 283.
30 *Ibid.*, p. 16.
31 *Ibid.*, p. 16.
32 *Ibid.*, p. 244.
33 Cowden Clarke (1864), p. vi.
34 Schmidt (1874), p. v.
35 Bartlett (1894) Introductory Note.
36 In fact Crystal and Crystal (2008) have one more entry for *abandon*, because they treat *Edward III* as a Shakespeare play, while Clarke does not.
37 This information about the *OED* and its history is taken from https://public.oed.com/history-of-the-oed/.

4 Making Shakespeare difficult
The early twentieth century

4.1 Ambiguity and the plain man

Robert Graves is best known today as a poet and novelist. But he was a critic also, and in 1926 wrote, together with Laura Riding, 'A study of original punctuation and spelling.' Their paper is mainly about the poet e e cummings, but it also deals with Shakespeare, and looks in detail at the punctuation and spelling changes that editors have made to Shakespeare's Sonnet 129 (*Th'expense of spirit in a waste of shame*). Their conclusion is that 'Shakespeare's editors, in trying to clarify him for the plain man, weakened and diluted his poetry ... Making poetry easy for the reader should mean showing clearly how difficult it really is.'[1]

Earlier, 3.3 showed how much effort the nineteenth century put into making Shakespeare easy: accessible to all, including to the 'plain man,' and this sometimes entailed making the works clean and wholesome as well. The early twentieth century could not have been more different. It was part of the spirit of the age that all forms of artistic expression had to be regarded as difficult, esoteric, accessible only to the intellectual elite. If the Victorian Shakespeareans made the dramatist comprehensible to the *hoi polloi*, it was (the early twentieth-century argument ran) by focusing on the superficialities of his work. But the true Shakespeare lay hidden under layers of superficiality. There were hidden depths – there had to be, because, the belief was, all art was deep – and these could only be found by 'excavating'; serious digging below the surface.

The sonnet which Graves and Riding discuss is about lust and its effects: before the lustful act, during it, and afterwards. Lust, Shakespeare says, is like a bait:

> On purpose layd to make the taker mad.
> Made In pursut, and in possession so,
> Had, hauing, and in quest, to haue extreame

These lines are from the 1609 version; Graves and Riding show how later editors render them:

> On purpose laid to make the taker mad:
> Mad in pursuit, and in possession so;
> Had, having, and in quest to have, extreme

There are two significant changes here. The *made* in the second line of the early version becomes *mad*, and the punctuation *in quest, to haue extreame* changes to *in quest to have, extreme*. In the early version, Graves and Riding argue, several 'interwoven meanings' are possible. Among these are:

(a) the man ('taker') is made to have extremes (i.e. to show extreme behaviour);
(b) all stages of lust – before, during and after – are extreme.

But 'with the emended punctuation,' Graves and Riding claim, 'the line has only one narrow sense' – *to have* is put together with *in quest*, and the third stage of lust is 'in quest to have.' The editors have removed ambiguities to simplify the meaning.[2]

Simplifying meaning was often just what editors in previous centuries did. The point is made by William Empson, whose 1930 book – *Seven Types of Ambiguity* – contains copious examples from Shakespeare. The traditional attitude towards ambiguity, Empson says, is that 'it allows a structure of associated meanings to be shown in a [foot]note, but not to be admitted.' Behind this attitude is the assumption 'that Shakespeare can only have meant one thing, but that the reader must hold in mind a variety of things he may have meant'[3]: ambiguities reveal alternative interpretations, only one of which can be the intended one. But for Empson, Graves and others in the twentieth century, ambiguities represent different layers of meaning intended by the author. They allow the artist to be interpretable on different levels … and hence to appeal to different kinds of listeners and readers at the same time – from the *hoi polloi* to the elite.

For Empson, ambiguity is 'any verbal nuance, however slight, which gives room for alternative reactions to the same piece of language.'[4] His book is certainly not written for the 'plain man' – more for the 'intellectual elite' – and it is often not at all easy to follow what he is saying. He is associated with the 'New Criticism' movement, a characteristic of which was the close reading of texts, with detailed attention given to verbal nuances. *Seven Types* is a clear example. Consider for example the detailed way in which Empson treats this celebrated line from Shakespeare's Sonnet 73 (*That time of year thou mayst in me behold*), where the poet is talking about the leafless tree boughs in winter:

Bare ruined choirs, where late the sweet birds sang.

The comparison between boughs and chancels holds, Empson says, for many reasons, which he details at length:[5]

> because ruined monastery choirs are places in which to sing, because they involve sitting in a row, because they are made of wood, are carved into knots …, because they used to be surrounded by a sheltering building crystallized out of the likeness of a forest, and coloured with stained glass and painting like flowers and leaves, because they are now abandoned by all but the grey

walls coloured like the skies of winter, because the cold and Narcissistic charm suggested by choir-boys suits well with Shakespeare's feeling for the object of the Sonnets, and for various sociological and historical reasons (the protestant destruction of monasteries; fear of Puritanism) …

Shakespeare's line is used by Empson as an example of his first type of ambiguity. All the seven types are given in Table 4.1, which includes some of Empson's Shakespearean examples. The seven types are not always easy to distinguish, and the criteria Empson uses to distinguish them seem mixed and even a little vague. But his close textual, language-focused, analysis was impressive, and the influential critic F. R. Leavis, described *Seven Types* as 'one of the most important critical books in the language' … ever.[6]

Ambiguity provides an author with a way for saying more than one thing at any given time, and we shall return to it in 4.3.1 when we look at Shakespeare's bawdy puns. One reason why early twentieth-century scholars and critics were interested in ambiguities was because they revealed 'other than-obvious meanings' which they believed to be characteristic of artistic works. In the next section we look at another way of exploring the 'other–than-obvious.'

4.2 Excavating images

4.2.1 *Spurgeon*

Caroline Frances Eleanor Spurgeon (1869–1942) was another who 'excavated' for hidden depths, looking not at ambiguities but at images. She became the first woman head of department at the University of London. In 1935, when she was in semi-retirement, she published her pioneering book, *Shakespeare's Imagery and What it Tells Us*. In its early pages she cites *Hamlet*'s Polonius whose son, Laertes, is living in Paris. Polonius wants his servant, who is going to Paris, to find out what kind of life Laertes is leading. The best way to discover this, Polonius says (2.1.64), is by using *assays of bias/By indirections* [to] *find directions out* (*assays* = attempts; *bias* = indirectness). 'Assays of bias,' Spurgeon says, would have made a suitable title for her book. It captures how she herself goes about her 'excavations.'[7]

Spurgeon believes that writers reveal their personality and temperament through images; they 'give themselves away.' 'In the case of Shakespeare,' she says, 'I believe one can scarcely overrate the possibility of what may be discovered through a systematic examination of [images].'[8] Sometimes what is 'given away' is personal, and she has a section entitled 'How images reveal the man.' One fascinating 'assay of bias' is recounted in a section dealing with river images in Shakespeare. She notes that on one occasion (in *The Rape of Lucrece*, 1667–73) Shakespeare describes a river eddy which swirls back on itself, returning the way it came. A Stratford local she consults observes that the current in the Avon river at Stratford, visible from the river bridge, has just this movement. Shakespeare, she claims, would have seen this eddy, and it makes its way into his

Table 4.1 Empson's seven types of ambiguity, with Shakespearean examples

The definitions given are Empson's (1977), from the contents page unless stated otherwise.

Type 1   *'when a detail is effective in several ways at once'*
This is metaphor, when 'one thing is said to be like another, and they have several different properties in virtue of which they are alike' (p. 2). The Shakespearean example given is from Sonnet 73, and is discussed in the text.

Type 2   *'two or more alternative meanings are resolved into one'* ['resolved' here means 'conflated']
This example is from Sonnet 32:

If thou survive my well-contented day,
When that churl Death my bones with dust shall cover,
And shalt by fortune once more re-survey
These poor rude lines of thy deceased lover,
Compare them with the bett'ring of the time

The ambiguity is that line 4 can go with previous line (with *re-survey* used as transitive verb), or with following line, in apposition to *them*.

Type 3   *'two apparently unconnected meanings are given simultaneously'*
This often occurs 'when there is reference to more than one universe of discourse'

In *Henry V* (1.2.187) a vision of human civil order is compared to the society of bees:

Obedience; for so work the honey-bees,
Creatures that by a rule in nature teach
The act of order to a peopled kingdom.
They have a king, and officers of sorts,
Where some, like magistrates, correct at home;
Others, like merchants, venture trade abroad;
Others, like soldiers, armed in their stings,
Make boot upon the summer's velvet buds;
Which pillage they with merry march bring home
To the tent-royal of their emperor;
Who, busied in his majesty, surveys
The singing masons building roofs of gold,
The civil citizens kneading up the honey

Empson looks particularly at the penultimate line, where (mason) bees 'sing' (buzz) as they work.

Type 4   *'alternative meanings combine to make clear a complicated state of mind in the author'*
Shakespeare's Sonnet 83 is analysed in detail. The first four lines are:

I never saw that you did painting need
And therefore to your fair no painting set;
I found, or thought I found, you did exceed
The barren tender of a poet's debt

Line 2 can go with first line. Empson's paraphrase for this interpretation is: 'I did not praise you in verse because I could not see that your reputation could be set any higher by my praise.'

But line 2 could also go with line 3, in which case a comma is needed after *therefore*. The paraphrase then becomes: 'And so, when no painting has been set to your fairness … I found that you exceeded [in beauty] …' (p. 134).

(continued)

Table 4.1 (Cont.)

Type 5 *'a fortunate confusion, as when the author is discovering his idea in the act of writing ... or not holding it in mind at once'*

When the author discovers his idea in the act of writing. Empson describes a simile that lies halfway between two statements made by the author.

For example, in *Measure for Measure* (1.2.128), lust is compared to rat's poison (*bane*):

Our natures do pursue,
Like rats that ravin [gobble] *down their proper bane,*
A thirsty evil, and when we drink we die.

According to Empson, Shakespeare starts with the idea of lust being the poison, with *proper* meaning 'suitable for rats.' But the poison makes the rat thirsty and drinking is a sign of imminent death. 'By reflection, then,' Empson says (p. 155), '*proper bane* becomes ambiguous, since it is now water as well as poison.' Notice that as well as meaning 'suitable,' *proper* can mean 'right and natural' – which is what the act of drinking is.

Type 6 *'what is said is contradictory or irrelevant and the reader is forced to invent interpretations'*
This occurs 'when a statement says nothing and the readers are forced to invent a statement of their own, most likely in conflict with one another' (p. 176).

This song from *Measure for Measure* (4.1.1) is given as an example:

Take, O take those lips away
That so sweetly were forsworn;
And those eyes, the break of day,
Lights that do mislead the morn:
But my kisses bring again, bring again;
Seals of love, but sealed in vain, sealed in vain.

There seems a contradiction between 'take ... away' which assumes the lovers are together, and 'bring' which suggests that they are not. Empson considers in detail what contradictory interpretations this can lead to.

Type 7 *'full contradiction, marking a division in the author's mind'*
Empson gives an example from *Macbeth* (1.3.146). At this point he is aware of the witches' predictions, and has already been made Thane of Cawdor. He has to decide what to do, but does not want to decide yet:

> *Come what come may,*
> *Time and the hour runs through the roughest day.*

If Macbeth wants to pursue his fate in the direction of murder, then this means the 'opportunity for crime ... will arrive whatever happens.' If he does not want to pursue this path, then it means: 'this condition of horror has only lasted a few minutes ... there is nothing for me to worry about yet' (p. 201).

---

writing. The frontispiece of her book shows the bridge and traces the direction of the current's movement.

Spurgeon does not classify Shakespeare's images by any linguistic criterion. She does it by subject matter, producing a chart which shows the subject matters and the relative frequency of images associated with each. The largest number, her study shows, are to do with simple everyday things, particularly associated with nature. There are many gardening images, though farming is relatively ignored. Weather images are also frequent, particularly related to sounds and movements of light. The sea is also referred to, though, Spurgeon says, Shakespeare sees it through the eyes of a landlubber. Animal images abound, particularly of birds and their movements. She identifies movement as an important theme. Shakespeare 'continually … endows inanimate and motionless objects with a sense of life,'[9] using 'action verbs' in relation to objects and ideas. Among her examples are these lines from *Henry IV, Part 1* (3.2.50):[10]

> And then I *stole* all courtesy from heaven,
> And *dressed* myself in such humility
> That I did *pluck* allegiance from men's hearts

Spurgeon also notes that Shakespeare is fond of verbs expressing 'swift, delicate and darting action.'[11] The verb *peep* is an example, as in these lines from *Macbeth* (1.5.51) that we have seen a number of times already:

> *Nor heaven peep through the blanket of the dark*
> *To cry, 'Hold, hold!'*

Spurgeon also notes some interesting omissions. There is little from town life – taverns and shops, for example.

In Part 2 of *Shakespeare's Imagery* Spurgeon looks at the comedies, histories, tragedies, and romances in turn, seeking in each play imagery 'somewhat analogous to the action of a recurrent theme or "motif" in a musical fugue or sonata, or in one of Wagner's operas.'[12] In *Romeo and Juliet*, for example, she finds frequent images of light; in *Richard II* it is garden images; war images in *Love's Labour's Lost* and *Much Ado About Nothing*. She gives lengthy consideration to image clusters in *Macbeth*. A predominant one – not immediately apparent to the theatre-goer or reader (and hence involving some 'excavation' to discover) – is to do with Macbeth and 'ill-fitting clothes.' She sees the hero as 'a small, ignoble man encumbered and degraded by garments unsuited to him.'[13] Among the many 'clothes' images she finds in the play is this one from Angus, expressing his view of how Macbeth seems since gaining power (5.2.21):

> *Now does he feel his title*
> *Hang loose about him like a giant's robe*
> *Upon a dwarfish thief.*

A second image area Spurgeon identifies in *Macbeth* is 'reverberation of sound echoing over vast regions.' Here she cites these lines (1.7.21):

> *And Pity, like a naked new-born babe*
> *Striding the blast, or heaven's cherubin, horsed*
> *Upon the sightless curriers of the air,*

> *Shall blow the horrid deed in every eye,*
> *That tears shall drown the wind.*

The lines have received their fair share of critical attention over the centuries; indeed, one nineteenth-century critic described them as 'pure rant, and intended to be so.'[14] After Spurgeon, the American critic, Cleanth Brooks, was to identify the passage as containing 'a central symbol of the play' – the naked babe: 'essential humanity, humanity stripped down to the naked thing itself.'[15]

There are several other images in the play: one is 'the symbolism that light stands for life, virtue, goodness; and darkness for evil and death.' Another – common in Shakespeare – is that sin is disease.

Spurgeon also has a chapter entitled 'Association of ideas' in which she shows how some images become linked to others. One set of associations she excavated is between 'a dog or spaniel, fawning and licking,' and 'candy, sugar or sweets, thawing or melting.'[16] Among the various examples she gives are these lines from *Antony and Cleopatra* (4.12.21):

> *The hearts*
> *That spanieled me at heels, to whom I gave*
> *Their wishes, do discandy, melt their sweets*
> *On blossoming Caesar*

In 1946 Edward Armstrong explored image clusters like this in further depth. The first chapter of his *Shakespeare's Imagination* is entitled 'Kites and Coverlets,' and it looks at how in Shakespeare kites are associated with images of bed sheets. This is because the kite, a bird of ill omen, is prone to snatching items, including pieces of laundry, to adorn its nest. These lines from *The Winter's Tale* (4.3.23) show the association:

> *My traffic is sheets; when the kite builds, look to lesser linen.*

Armstrong also uses the association of images to identify passages written by Shakespeare. In the case of *Macbeth*'s Porter's speech (which, it is sometimes claimed, was not written by Shakespeare), the images used lead him to argue that the Shakespeare attribution is correct, while in *The Two Noble Kinsmen* he finds little evidence of Shakespearean imagery.

4.2.2 Clemen

While most admit that Spurgeon's work was pioneering, not all were convinced by it. Hence the celebrated critic, John Dover Wilson, announced that he was not 'persuaded by her attempt to deduce Shakespeare's personal propensities' from the images she considers.[17] Much more convincing, for Dover Wilson, was the work of Wolfgang Clemen (1909–1990), whose *The Development of Shakespeare's Imagery* appeared in 1951. Clemen acknowledges a debt to Spurgeon. But while she focuses on the content of Shakespeare's images, Clemen's concerns are with their development over Shakespeare's writing career, and with their functions. He is unable, he says, to cover all the plays, but focuses selectively from different periods in Shakespeare's working life. While Clemen's need for selectivity is understandable, it is perhaps odd that one of the plays he does not discuss was *Macbeth*, a play so full of memorable imagery.[18]

Clemen shows that in the early plays Shakespeare's images are often not organic; it is 'imagery for imagery's sake.'[19] It sometimes seems as if they have been 'inserted' into the text. Indeed, occasionally they are so complex and peripheral that they have to be explained. An example is this passage from *Love's Labour's Lost*. The male characters, disguised as Muscovites, have wooed the ladies and then disappeared. Will they return, the Princess wants to know. Yes, replies Boyet (5.2.292):

> Boyet: *Therefore change favours, and, when they repair* [come],
> *Blow* [blossom] *like sweet roses in this summer air.*

The Princess asks for an explanation of these obscure lines:

> Princess: *How 'blow'? How 'blow'? Speak to be understood.*
> Boyet: *Fair ladies masked are roses in their bud;*
> *Dismasked, their damask sweet commixture shown,*
> *Are angels vailing clouds, or roses blown.*

The Princess' response is understandable: *Avaunt, perplexity*, she says.

In the early history plays like *Henry VI*, Clemen says, we find certain types of images associated with specific situations. Argumentative, protesting speeches, for example, attract proverb images. Thus when Suffolk attacks Gloucester for being a trouble-maker, his speech (2H6 3.1.50) contains two proverbs in three lines: *Smooth runs the water where the brook is deep* and *The fox barks not when he would steal the lamb*.

In *Romeo and Juliet* we find the beginnings of Shakespeare 'blending outer nature with the inner spirit of his characters.'[20] Following Spurgeon's discussion of light/dark images in the play, Clemen shows how images of night are used to reflect Juliet's dark moods.

In the tragedies, we find some images that 'implant anticipatory ideas.' He gives as example these lines from *Julius Caesar*, spoken long after Caesar has been killed (5.3.60):

> Titinius: *O setting sun,*
> *As in thy red rays thou dost sink to night,*
> *So in his red blood Cassius' day is set.*
> *The sun of Rome is set. Our day is gone;*
> *Clouds, dews, and dangers come; our deeds are done.*

The lines refer to three events: the actual setting of the sun in the evening; the death of Cassius (just about to die); and the end of the old era, with a new one about to begin. Having such multiple functions is characteristic of the late Shakespeare; it is common for his images to fulfil some symbolic function, but at the same time to help create an atmosphere.

A major function of images in the tragedies, Clemen says, is to lend 'a unifying colour and "key",' helping to create 'an organic unity.'[21] In *Hamlet*, for example, images referring to disease, poisoning, ulcers are common. Hamlet's father's ghost sets the scene early on as he describes how he was murdered (1.5.63):

> And in the porches of my ears did pour
> The leperous distilment; whose effect
> Holds such an enmity with blood of man
> That swift as quicksilver it courses through
> The natural gates and alleys of the body,
> And with a sudden vigour it doth posset
> And curd, like eager droppings into milk,
> The thin and wholesome blood. So did it mine.
> And a most instant tetter barked about,
> Most lazar-like, with vile and loathsome crust
> All my smooth body.

It is natural that different ages should show interest in different aspects of artistic creations, and so it certainly is with Shakespeare. Some ages have been particularly interested in his characters, others in his sense of drama, yet others in his poetry. In the early twentieth century, imagery became a main focus of attention. Their desire to excavate for deep, true, hidden meanings looked in that direction. For many, this kind of excavation is associated in the early twentieth century with Sigmund Freud. In his case, the hidden meanings sought were often sexual. Nor did Shakespeare escape his share of sexual searching.

4.3 Lexical excavations

4.3.1 Partridge and bawdy Shakespeare

We have seen that there were some Victorians who put effort into ridding Shakespeare of sexual references – to make him 'clean and wholesome.' The early twentieth-century's attitude to matters sexual was much more liberal, and some Shakespeare excavations dug down into the more bawdy seams in his writing. Eric Partridge's 1947 book, *Shakespeare's Bawdy*, led the way. It is subtitled 'A Literary and Psychological Essay and a Comprehensive Glossary.' The essay (Part 1 of the book) contains some generalizations about which bawdy topics did and did not interest Shakespeare. Thus we find little about clasping, but a lot on caressing, while female buttocks are featured more than male ones. The essay

The early twentieth century 65

also includes examples, one from *Much Ado* and another from *Henry V*, showing how Shakespeare contains extended passages of *double entendre*. A similar point is made in later times by Don Paterson (2010) who, when commentating on Sonnet 129 (the one about lust which we considered earlier), says: 'the poem is such a torrent of innuendo, with some kind of Elizabethan double-meaning in every second word, you can safely assume that if you think you've spotted something rude, you have.'[22]

Partridge's glossary indeed reveals the number of (relatively) innocent-looking words that can have double meanings. Hence *lap* can refer to female pudenda: Partridge provides five examples, including Hamlet's request to Ophelia: *Lady, shall I lie in your lap* (3.2.121). Other not-so-innocent words are: *lean* = 'worn thin by sexual excess'; *forks* = 'buttock and upper thighs, along with the gap between them'; and 'to speed' = 'to be sexually potent.' Sometimes Shakespeare's bawdy puns need considerable unravelling. Here for example is what Partridge has to say about the phrase *change the cod's head for the salmon's tail* (Othello 2.1.151: *She that in wisdom never was so frail / To change the cod's head for the salmon's tail*):

> a difficult phrase, even when we remember that *cod's head* probably refers to *codpiece* and that probably it therefore = penis (the head of the *cod* or scrotum), and that *salmon's tail* probably = pudend (cf. **fish**, q.v., and see **tail**, 1). A woman does not change, i.e. exchange, the former for the latter; she exchanges the latter for the former: the pun demands that *change ... for* = 'put ... in the place of,' hence 'put ... in.[23]

There is not much etymology in Partridge's book, nor much consideration of contemporary Elizabethan usage, but part of the glossary's value is the amount of erudite detail, cross-referencing, and fragments of critical discussion. Consider this entry for the word *bung*:[24]

> When Doll Tearsheet cries, 'Away, you cut-purse rascal! you filthy bung away!' (2*King Henry IV*, II iv 126–127), she is, I think, using *bung* in the sense of 'bung-nipper' or 'cut-purse.' Yet it is just possible that she is using it in the slang sense 'bung-hole' or anus, as Mr Eric P. Newman of St Louis, Missouri, maintains. For *bung* (and *bung-nipper*) in cant, see either the O. E. D. or my *Underworld*.

4.3.2 Unbawdy Onions

The library in Oxford's Magdalen College could be cold in winter, and a familiar sight in the 1920s was a figure wrapped in a blanket sitting in a bay surrounded with papers. He was Charles Talbot Onions (1873–1965). After a poor academic career, Onions started work with the *OED* team in 1895, and eventually became its fourth editor. He was a waspish man, known for his astringent wit. But he was also extremely productive – as well as working on the dictionary, he also wrote a book on English syntax, and *A Shakespeare Glossary*. This latter, in Onions' own words, aims 'to supply definitions and illustrations of words or senses of words which are now obsolete or which survive only in archaic or provincial use.'[25]

The *OED* used Shakespeare a great deal as a source, and it is thus no surprise that Onions should claim that his work on the *OED* helped him to clarify language points in Shakespeare's works. For example, *The Winter's Tale* has (4.4.258) *I love a ballad in print a-life*. Some editors, Onions notes, interpret *a-life* to mean 'on my life,' and sometimes put a comma after *print*, to suggest this interpretation. But Onions recognizes the word to mean 'dearly,' from 'lief' (meaning 'beloved,' 'dear'); thus the sentence means 'I dearly love a ballad in print.' A second example is in *The Two Gentlemen of Verona* which has the line (2.1.19): *to relish a love-song like a robin-redbreast*. Editors tend to leave the word *relish* unexplained, assuming it has the same meaning as today. But Onions identifies its meaning of 'to warble' – a sense listed in the *OED*, but no longer in use.[26]

Today we would describe *relish* used to mean 'warble' as a 'false friend': the word is in use today, so we assume we understand it, but it could have a different meaning in the past. False friends can be troublesome for readers today. Onions recognizes this, so as well as dealing with obsolete and archaic words, he deals with false friends too. An example is the word *conclusion*. Here are some examples of its use in Shakespeare, cited by Onions:

> *Hamlet* (3.4.194) has the phrase *to try conclusions*;
>
> *Cymbeline* (1.6.17): *is't not meet/ That I did amplify my judgement in/ Other conclusions?*
>
> *Anthony and Cleopatra* (5.2.353): *She hath pursued conclusions infinite/ Of easy ways to die.*
>
> *Othello* (1.3.325): *the blood and baseness of our natures would conduct us to most preposterous conclusions.*

In these examples (with the possible exception of the last one), *conclusion* means 'experiment.' One reviewer of Onions' *Glossary* suggests the same meaning for *foregone conclusion* in Othello (3.3.425), though this is doubtful since Onions also recognizes the meaning of 'end' – in Shakespeare as today, and this seems to be the sense here.[27]

Onions' *Glossary* was enlarged (though some of the entries are in fact shorter) and revised in 1986 by Robert Eagleson, and it is this version that is most in use today.

4.4 Shakespeare language studies and modern linguistics

Linguistics goes back a long way. The first linguist is sometimes said to have been Paṇini who lived in the Indian subcontinent between the 6th and 4th centuries BC, and who wrote a Sanskrit grammar known as the *Ashtadhyayi*.

As for the birth of 'modern linguistics,' certainly one important moment was the publication in 1915 of *Cours de linguistique générale*, based on notes of lectures given by the Swiss linguist, Ferdinand de Saussure. Another later milestone is Leonard Bloomfield's 1933 book *Language*. The exact birth date is not important. What is important is that in the second half of the twentieth century, and into the twenty-first, linguistics has grown hugely, and now flourishes, with very many universities having departments of linguistics offering a variety of courses in the area. Linguistics has become a 'subject.' Shakespeare language studies have grown along with it, taking on many of its aims and procedures. Lyons (1968) defines linguistics as 'the scientific study of language … investigation by means of controlled and empirically verifiable observations.'[28] There are now very many Shakespearean studies which are linguistic in this sense.

Indeed, the number of studies since 1950 is so large that the chronological approach we have so far been using no longer seems the best way of covering the ground. For this reason, the chapters in Part II of this book – covering the period from about 1950 until the present – each deal with discrete linguistic topics, like lexis, grammar, pragmatics, and so on. This quite dramatic change of organizational principle in mid-book does sometimes cause some chronological problems, and occasionally pieces of work done before 1950 will be mentioned in a Part II chapter. The advantage is that this new structure brings together within the same chapter work in the same area.

Notes

1 Graves and Riding (1926), p. 92.
2 *Ibid.*, p. 89.
3 Empson (1977), p. 81.
4 *Ibid.*, p. 1.
5 *Ibid.*, p. 2.
6 Leavis (1931), p. 180.
7 Spurgeon (1961), p. 3.
8 *Ibid.*, p. 5.
9 *Ibid.*, p. 51.
10 The italics are Spurgeon's.
11 *Ibid.*, p. 52.
12 *Ibid.*, p. 309.
13 *Ibid.*, p. 326.
14 Story (1891), p. 256.
15 Brooks (1947), p. 49.
16 Spurgeon (1961), p. 195.
17 Dover Wilson (1951), p. v.
18 Vickers (1968) also points out that Clemen does not deal with Shakespeare's prose.
19 Clemen (1951), p. 220.
20 *Ibid.*, p. 71.
21 *Ibid.*, p. 224.

22 Paterson (2010), p. 391.
23 Partridge (1947), p. 77.
24 Partridge (1947), p. 73.
25 Onions (1986), p. v.
26 These examples are taken from Macaulay (1912).
27 Macaulay (1912).
28 Lyons (1971), p. 1.

Part II
1950 on

5 From oxcart to computer
Lexical studies

5.1 Expressions of *zeitgeist*

Earlier chapters of this book have suggested how pervading ideas – expressions of *zeitgeist* – have influenced perceptions of Shakespeare's language in a particular age. During the late twentieth and early twenty-first centuries part of the *zeitgeist* was not an idea, but a piece of machinery, and it played a particular role in the development of Shakespearean lexical studies. That piece of machinery was the computer.

In 4.3.2, where there were no computers, we caught a glimpse of Charles Onions, the fourth editor of the *OED*, in the library of Magdalen College, Oxford. He was wrapped in a blanket against the cold, sitting in a bay poring over piles of papers full of words. Before about 1960, collecting and analysing large quantities of words was indeed a mammoth task. The German lexicogapher Friedrich Käding used 80 collaborators to analyse the eleven-million-word corpus collected for the production of his German frequency dictionary.[1] So too Michael West, who in the 1950s produced an English frequency dictionary – the *General Service List* – with the assistance of a phalanx of helpers. Such early efforts were truly, in the phrase of Elliott and Valenza (2011), 'road-bound and oxcart-borne.'[2] Computers were behind the big change, which occurred towards the end of the twentieth century. Texts, put into digital form, became machine-readable. This did not mean that the collection and analysis of large quantities of text suddenly became effortless. But it did become far more feasible, though still involving painstaking work.

One of the first to utilize computers for research in the humanities was an American Shakespearean scholar, Marvin Spevack. Between 1968 and 1980 he produced a *Concordance to Shakespeare* – the complete version in nine volumes, the Harvard edition in one-volume.[3] The following decades brought various equally ambitious initiatives involving digitalized texts. One was the *Early English Books Online* (EEBO) project. Behind this was a private company called ProQuestLLC, which started life in 1938 as a microfilm publisher in Michigan. In 1999 they started collaborating with the University of Michigan and Oxford University to form the 'Early English Books Online Text Creation Partnership.' The project is now well under way, and when completed will contain at least 134,000 works, adding up to more than 17 million pages.[4] Collections like this have truly revolutionized how we study lexis through history. Oxcarts have now disappeared. Or have they? Chapter 12, which is about future trends, discusses an approach to data analysis in which something akin to the oxcart plays a crucial role.

There is another piece of *zeitgeist* – not a piece of machinery this time – that is particularly relevant to Shakespeare lexical studies. As we have also seen in past chapters, bardolatry has often flourished. Shakespeare has been regarded as fault-free, in every way exceptional as an author, and even as a human being. To use a word invented by Taylor, he was 'Shakesperfect.'[5] We will see examples of claims about 'Shakesperfection' in the next few pages. But they will largely be refuted by those who follow a new *zeitgeist* and who, like Taylor, believe that 'by overestimating Shakespeare's importance and uniqueness, Shakespearean critics insult the truth,' and that 'he was no less and no more singular than anyone else.'[6] This iconoclastic 'debardolatrification' of Shakespeare is a theme we will come across particularly in this chapter. It is part of the spirit of our age. As the very last sentence of Taylor's book puts it: 'sycophancy is no more admirable in literature than in politics.'[7]

5.2 Counting Shakespeare's words

5.2.1 Total vocabulary size

Computers are particularly good at measuring quantities, and there are two quantity issues associated with Shakespeare's vocabulary: how large was it, and how many new words was he responsible for? His reputation as an author is huge, and it is a natural impulse to want everything else about him to be huge – to see him as a hugely prolific linguistic inventor, possessing a huge vocabulary. Theobald expressed this impulse in the eighteenth century: 'my partiality for Shakespeare makes me wish, that everything which is good, or pleasing, in our tongue, has been owing to his pen.'[8] Early in the twentieth century, Jespersen adds: 'Shakespeare's vocabulary is often stated to be the richest ever employed by any single man.'[9]

Exactly how large you consider Shakespeare's vocabulary to be depends on how you do your counting. Spevack's *Concordance* was used by a number of scholars to estimate Shakespeare's vocabulary size. The *Concordance* contains 884, 647 words, so it could be said that this is the size of his vocabulary. But of course this list includes different forms of the same word; so along with the verb *bear*, you also find *bears, bearest, beareth, bearing, boar'st, bore,* and *born*.[10] If you decide to include only 'headwords' (like *to bear*, under which all the other forms are subsumed), the number will drop dramatically. There are other issues about what to count. Most would consider spelling variants as single words, making *burthen* and *burden* one item, *crocodile* and *corocodile* another.[11] Then there are homonyms: *bear* (the animal) as a noun should presumably count as a separate lexical item from *bear* as a verb. Or take the word *carbuncle*, which Shakespeare uses to refer to a 'boil' or to a 'precious stone' (both meanings in fact in use today, though the latter is rare). One word or two? And what about the same word used in different parts of speech: Shakespeare uses the noun *lip* as a verb – in *Othello* (4.1.71) Iago says *To lip a wanton in a secure couch*. Compounds too will also raise counting issues: Shakespeare uses the both *waspish* and *headed* as separate words; and in *The Tempest* (4.1.99), Cupid is described as *waspish-headed*: a separate word or not? Then there is the question of foreign words, and proper nouns. Do we count these?

Clarke's *Concordance*, mentioned in 3.5, estimates Shakespeare's vocabulary at 21,000 'without counting inflected forms as distinct words.'[12] There are various claims above and below this figure, ranging roughly from 15,000 to 30,000.[13] But estimates in the region of 20,000 seem to be generally accepted. Word estimates, though, only really become meaningful when compared to other word estimates. One type of comparison is with 'ordinary people.' In early days, Shakespeare's vocabulary was made to look big by grossly underestimating normal vocabulary size. The nineteenth-century philologist Max Müller calculates that farm labourers have an active vocabulary of around 300 words, and the American Francis Wood (writing in 1896) thinks that 'the average man uses about five hundred words.'[14] Both are gross underestimations. More reliable tests mentioned by Crystal and Jespersen have 'run-of-the-mill college-educated moderns' with vocabularies of 50–80,000 words. But this is larger than Shakespeare's. How can that be? The answer is because the language has grown enormously since Shakespeare's day. Crystal calculates that the size of the lexicon at the end of the sixteenth century was 150,000, while the unabridged *OED* today has 600,000 words. Another type of comparison is with other authors. Jespersen calculates Milton's vocabulary size as 8,000 – considerably less than Shakespeare's 20,000. But others after Jespersen suggest that the figure for Milton is an underestimate because only his poetry, and not his prose, was included.

Two papers – Craig (2011) and Elliott and Valenza (2011) – show that interest in Shakespeare's vocabulary size has continued. They also show how, with the appearance of digitalized texts, methods of word counting have become not just easier but also more sophisticated. Craig's statistics still have Shakespeare with a larger vocabulary than his peers; his 20,000 compares with the dramatist George Peele's 6,000 and Jonson's 18,500. But, Craig argues: 'the obvious explanation for Shakespeare's relatively large vocabulary is that he had more opportunity to use different words';[15] 'Shakespeare has a larger vocabulary because he has a larger canon.'[16] Craig's statistics suggest that 'Marlowe, Middleton, Jonson … would have reached or exceeded Shakespeare's total dramatic vocabulary if they had written as much dialogue as he did.'[17] Hope (2012) illuminates the point well with a parallel related to goal-scoring statistics in football. He argues that if you consider the total number of goals scored by three players (let us say A, B and C) you might come up with a figure that A has scored the greatest number in his lifetime, B the second most, with C third. But if you then look at the number of games each player has participated in, and work out a total of 'goals per game,' the order might easily be quite different – perhaps even with C the most prolific, B the second, and A the least.

To counteract differences in the size of output of various authors, Craig compares segments of comparable size. When this is done, Shakespeare loses his lexical pre-eminence and is ranked seventh out of the 13 contemporary authors Craig looks at. Top of the list now are Webster, Dekker, Peele, and Marlowe. Elliott and Valenza also topple Shakespeare from his exalted position. Their vocabulary league table has Shakespeare in the middle of the pack, with Milton and Spenser higher: 'if anyone's vocabulary dwarfed others in size,' they conclude, 'it was Milton's, and maybe Spenser's, not Shakespeare's.'[18] 'Debardolatrification' is at work.

Though analyses like this push Shakespeare down the numerical scale, everyone who looks into Shakespeare's vocabulary admires his lexical skills. For Jespersen

> the greatness of Shakespeare's mind is ... not shown by the fact that he was acquainted with 20,000 words, but by the fact that he wrote about so great a variety of subjects and touched upon so many human facts and relations that he needed this number of words in his writings.[19]

Crystal (2004) reaches a similar conclusion. Bolton (1992) is another who argues that to appreciate the extent of Shakespeare's lexical achievement, we must do more than count words. He uses a type/token analysis of lexis in the history plays. His conclusion is that 'the real versatility of Shakespeare's vocabulary lies in the variety of his diction.'[20] In comparison with other authors, he uses a very large proportion of his words a few times only.

One reason for Craig's admiration relates to the nature of the words Shakespeare uses. He cites Slater who considers these four lines from Sonnet 13:[21]

> *Who lets so fair a house fall to decay,*
> *Which husbandry in honour might uphold*
> *Against the stormy gusts of winter's day*
> *And barren rage of death's eternal cold?*

The lines, Slater says, contain particularly flamboyant images. But the words are all common ones. Their effect comes from 'the context, the imagery, and particularly from the contrast between concrete and abstract, and a certain ambiguity of meaning.'[22] The words themselves are commonplace ones, not at all exotic or extravagant. This is one of a number of reasons which leads Craig to the conclusion that '[Shakespeare's] language is an extraordinary achievement with the regular resources of the English of his day rather than a linguistic aberration.'[23] Another clear case of 'debardolatrification.'

5.2.2 Neologisms

Before the Elizabethan period, the philologist Harold Bayley said, 'the English language was a slighted, poor, inexpressive and unseemly thing.'[24] But by Shakespeare's time moves were afoot to make it less poor, inexpressive, and unseemly. Particularly, the lexicon was greatly expanded – partly by borrowing, and partly by the creation of new words based on 'native' linguistic resources.

One reliable source has around 6,000 new words introduced during the time that Shakespeare was writing,[25] making it 'one of the most lexically inventive periods in the history of the language.'[26] There are occasional claims that Shakespeare was responsible for very few of these. According to Garner (1982), one anonymous author argues that Shakespeare's coinages 'do not amount to more than about a dozen.'[27] But most of the claims come at the other extreme. Crystal (2004) – a book which provides a readable and authoritative account of Shakespeare's vocabulary – reports such statements as 'Shakespeare invented a quarter of our language,'[28] while the American scholar Joseph Shipley claims that 'Shakespeare was the greatest word-maker of them all.'[29] As for actual numerical estimates, in 1906 Bayley had Shakespeare coining 9,450 words, a number which most today find exaggeratedly high. Crystal's estimate is around 1,700, and Elliott and Valenza arrive at a similar figure.

Why such different, and often inflated, claims? Counting neologisms involves all the difficulties we have seen in relation to calculating vocabulary size. One reason why Bayley's coinage count was so high was that he regarded each different meaning of a word as a separate item. He counted the word *go*, for example, no fewer than 22 times, because he calculated it had 22 different meanings. As with vocabulary size calculations, meaning shift is again an issue. When Othello asks that Desdemona should accompany him to Cyprus, he insists that she should have *such accommodation … as levels with her breeding* (*Oth* 1.3.236). She must, in other words, be given somewhere suitable to lodge. The word *accommodation* is used in the same sense today. But Shakespeare was possibly the first to employ it in this way. The word had come into the language earlier in the sixteenth century, but it meant 'the process of adaptation.' Then should malapropisms be counted as new words? The word *vagrom* for example, used by Dogberry in *Much Ado About Nothing* (3.3.18) for *vagrant*? And what about nonsense words? In the First Folio, *Twelfth Night* (2.3.25) has Feste saying: *I did impeticos thy gratillity*. *Impeticos* is a nonce word combining 'impocket' and 'petticoat' and means 'to pocket,' while *gratillity* is a humorous version of 'gratuity.'[30] Unsurprisingly, Crystal does not include either of these words in his neologism count. We must also remember that a proper count should consider not only words which have survived today, but also so-called 'stillborn neologisms' – words like *acture* ('action'), *adoptious* ('connected with adoption'), and *repasture* ('food,' 'repast') which were apparent Shakespeare coinages, but did not make it into PDE.[31] One calculation has it that more than half of Shakespeare's neologisms were stillborn.[32]

Bardolatry – making Shakespeare huge in every way – certainly fans the flames of lexical exaggeration. In a celebrated passage about Shakespeare's legacy to the English language, Bernard Levin (1983) listed a selection of words and phrases in use today that are found in Shakespeare. The passage begins:

> 'If you cannot understand my argument, and declare "It's Greek to me", you are quoting Shakespeare; if you claim to be more sinned against than sinning, you are quoting Shakespeare; if you recall your salad days, you are quoting Shakespeare.' On the long list of the words and phrases he cites are *tongue-tied*, *hoodwink* (as a verb), *eyesore*, and *bloody-minded*.

Though he does not say this in so many words, Levin seems to be claiming these words as Shakespeare neologisms. He is glorying in the influence and creativity of our greatest author. But where do these claims come from, and how accurate are they?

The *OED* is deeply implicated. As we saw in 3.5, a major feature of the dictionary is that it contains copious citations providing chronological records of words in use. It is perhaps natural for scholars to treat the *OED*'s 'first citation' of a word as if it were the first time it was ever used. In fact, those involved in producing the *OED* are cautious in their claims. The dictionary was, they point out, never 'meant to be the final word on the history of the English language,'[33] and the *OED* certainly does not claim 'that first citations are the actual first occurrence of a word.'[34] Nevertheless, the first citations are the result of the lexicographers' searches to find when a word was – as far as they could judge – first used, and many scholars do not resist the temptation to equate 'first citations' and 'first recorded use.' 'First citations' have become a major source of information about Shakespeare neologisms. Bayley's exaggerated claims, for example, involved use of the *OED*. But at the time he was working, the dictionary was not finished, so he decided to scrutinize available portions, choosing to focus on words beginning with the Latin prefix *ex-* and the Greek prefix *ge-*. He counted the Shakespeare first citations and assumed them to be Shakespeare neologisms. He then consulted the *OED* editor as to the likely eventual length of the completed dictionary, and was thus led to a predicted calculation of the total number of Shakespeare's inventions. Those doing more recent neologism counts have been able to work with a more 'complete' version of the dictionary (though as any lexicographer would admit, no dictionary is ever really complete). But the practice of using first citations to identify neologisms has often remained.

Writing early in the twentieth century, Jespersen notes that 'in turning over the pages of the *New English Dictionary* (the name initially given to the *OED*) ... one is struck by the frequency with which Shakespeare's name is found affixed to the earliest quotation for words or meanings.'[35] This over-representation of Shakespeare in the *OED* is partly responsible for the exaggeration of Shakespeare's inventiveness. How this came about has been the subject of much discussion, recently in Brewer (2007) and Goodland (2011). It is partly to do with the dictionary's original aims. The pamphlet which announced the completion of the *OED*'s first edition in 1928 heralds it as 'the supreme treasure-house of the riches of the English language'[36] – a phrase which gives Brewer the title of her detailed consideration of the *OED*. Indeed, the first volume of the *OED*, published in 1888, specifically states that 'all the great English writers of all ages' were first port of call for citations. Early contributors to the dictionary were asked to analyse 'the works of any of the principal writers.'[37] The citation statistics clearly show this. Milton, Chaucer, Dryden, and Dickens are all in the top ten of *OED* quotations sources. But at the very top is Shakespeare, providing no fewer than 33,000 quotations.[38] This top position reflects Shakespeare's eminence. But also, importantly, it reflects the scholarship which that eminence attracted. As we have seen in past chapters,

Shakespearean commentaries, concordances, and glossaries abound. The life of OED lexicographers searching for quotations was made more simple by the availability of these. Shakespeare was an easy – as well as (because of his celebrity) an appropriate – option when it came to looking for citation material.

A consequence of this focus on Shakespeare (and other 'principal writers') is that lesser known ones tended to be ignored, even though they may in fact have been prolific neologizers. Schäfer (1980) shows this by comparing how Shakespeare and Nashe are represented in the OED. Thomas Nashe – playwright, poet, and pamphleteer – was chosen partly because he was a close contemporary of Shakespeare. He was also known for his 'Rabelaisian gusto' in word coining.[39] To calculate neologisms, Schäfer uses sources like Schmidt's *Shakespeare-Lexicon*, mentioned in 3.5, and Stanley Wells' 'Glossarial notes and index' to his edition of Nashe's selected works.[40] Schäfer finds that 'the vocabulary of second-rank authors (like Nashe) is recorded less rigorously, to the point where items are simply omitted.'[41] In parallel first citations (where OED editors find occurrences by two authors for the same year), 'they preferred the Shakespeare passage.'[42] Schäfer is also interested in establishing the extent to which first citations actually represent first use. The reliability figure he arrives at is 60 per cent.

There are other biases in the dictionary's choice of citations. Literary, and particularly poetic, texts are favoured, and because spoken texts are difficult to collect, written texts are usually used as sources. Another major bias relates to time, and different periods are unevenly represented. Because of its abundant literature (including Shakespeare's works), the Elizabethan age is well-represented. 'The early Tudor period of Caxton and Skelton' far less so,[43] and Middle English texts are even more neglected. Figure 5.1 shows OED quotation numbers per decade. As well as the uneven coverage, you can also see the 'Shakespeare effect':

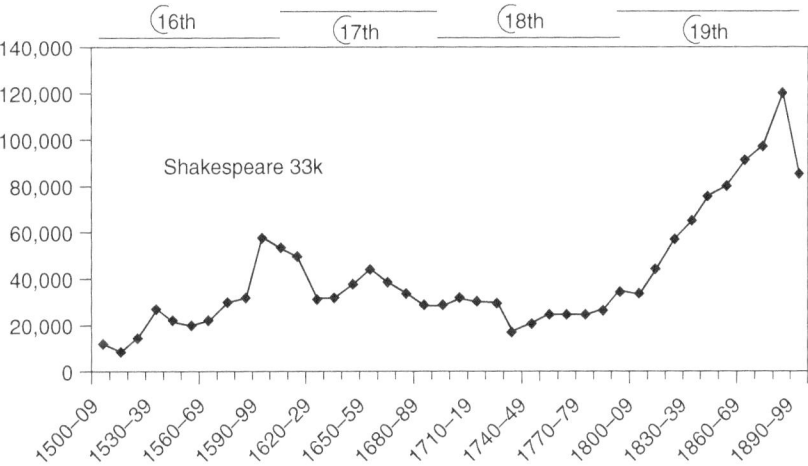

Figure 5.1 Quotation numbers per decade in OED data (gathered from the second edition). From Brewer (2007), p. 128

The problem of uneven chronological coverage can be largely put down to the lack of readily searchable texts. Now that digitalized texts are available this issue can be properly addressed. *Literature Online* (LION) is one of the resources that made available a good number of literary texts. Another digital collection, already mentioned in 5.1, is EEBO. Part of its importance is that it includes non-literary texts, and hence can help to counteract the 'treasure-house syndrome' – the over-representation of literature. There is also now a healthy number of corpora and concordances available, including the *The Helsinki Corpus of English Texts* which is 'multi-genred'; also the Toronto Lexicons of Early Modern English.[44] With this increase in searchable texts, Shakespeare's first citations have diminished. As Goodland (2011) put it: 'it is not that there was too much Shakespeare, it is that there was too *little* of other texts and writers.'[45] Goodland uses LION and EEBO to calculate the extent of the *OED*'s over-representation of Shakespeare and the underrepresentation of others. He focuses on entries in the *New English Dictionary* from P to Ra. and finds 122 coinages (7 per cent of Shakespeare's 1,700 total). He re-examines these in the light of the online sources like LION and EEBO and, employing various criteria, takes out 60 per cent of them. Here are four examples from Goodland, illustrating how the resources of EEBO have revealed so-called antedatings – first citations now pre-dated. None of these words has a Shakespeare first citation in the current *OED Online*, though all do in the earlier Second Edition's CD-ROM version; the Shakespeare first citation references in this version are given in brackets:

- *practisant* (n) found in a 1550 translation of Thucydides *History of the Peloponnesian War* (1H6);
- *precurse* (n) in Hatton *A Treatise concerning Statutes*, 1591 (Ham);
- *prodigiously* (adv) in a 1541 defence of the marriage of priests (KJ);
- *Prometheus* (n) in a 1549 translation of Erazmus' *Prasie of Folly* (Tit And).

If these revised first citation figures are projected onto Shakespeare's entire canon, the figure of 1,700 neologisms would be reduced to 680. In his conclusion, Goodland also makes the point that Shakespeare is not primarily in the business of coining new words for the sake of it. Hence 'the often-posed question, *how many words did Shakespeare coin?*, is largely false.'[46] Shakespeare was using language to create effects, and one of the processes involved would, in certain circumstances, entail the creation of new words.

At the time of writing, Giles Goodland is Senior Editorial Researcher for the *OED*, and his comments reveal that the *Dictionary* researchers are well aware (as indeed was the early editor James Murray) of the fact that antedatings are going to continue to occur in numbers. The *OED* has certainly taken on board the need for more even representation, and the result is that Shakespeare's word inventions are decreasing by the decade. To return to Levin's examples given earlier: all now have pre-Shakespeare first citations. The *OED Online* has a first quotation for *tongue-tied* in 1530, for *hoodwink* 1562, for *eyesore* in the 1300s, and for *bloody-minded* 1545. Sometimes the antedatings have been very recently added, and there are words which in the 1989 *OED* Second Edition were given Shakespeare first citations but which are now antedated. For example: in his performance 'Being Shakespeare,' the British actor Simon Callow gives the word *mewl* as a Shakespearean neologism (it occurs in Jaques' "Seven Ages' speech from *As You Like It* where the infant is described as *mewling and puking in the nurse's arms*: 2.7.145). Callow can be forgiven for this, since the line is indeed the first citation in the 1989 *OED*. But in the *OED Online* there is a first citation dated 1425. Callow also cites *puke* as a Shakespeare neologism. The *OED Online* has the *As You Like It* passage as its first citation in the general sense of 'vomit,' though a specialist use in falconry has an earlier date, referring to a hawk passing 'food from the crop to the stomach.' The noun *pukishness*, meaning 'queasiness' is dated 1581, 18 years before *As You Like It* was probably written, and the adjective *pukish* was even earlier. This example points to an important aspect of Shakespeare's neologisms, already touched on in relation to the word *accommodation*: that the creativity often involves not the introduction of a completely new word, but the adaptation of an existing word, frequently by extending its semantic range.

There is one study of Shakespeare's neologisms that focuses particularly on Latinate words. It is reprinted in a book which is a landmark collection of Shakespeare language studies – Salmon and Burness (1987). This collection of largely small-scale studies deals with linguistic particulars, and is one of the first in this genre. In one chapter, Garner (1982) focuses on Latinate neologisms, of which there were some 7,600 appearing in English during Shakespeare's professional lifetime. The words Garner considers all have a Latinate component, though this may just be an affix. Many are hybrid words, 'combining ... Anglo-Saxon roots with Latinate (or Gallic) prefixes or suffixes.'[47] One of Garner's examples is the word *blastment* ('blight'), used in *Hamlet* (1.3.42). The root 'blast' is Germanic, while the suffix *-ment* is Latinate. Nor are the rules of Latin word formation followed. Thus Shakespeare has *disquantity* (KL 1.4.245), using the Latinate prefix *dis-* together with a noun (*quantity*) to form a verb, a combination which did not occur in Latin. This breaking of the rules is not surprising: Shakespeare was not an academic classicist, and academic grammarians, of Latin or any other language, were not going to be consulted before new formations were introduced.

5.3 Shakespeare's word formations

Linguists have looked at the nature, as well as the quantity, of Shakespeare's neologisms. Given the large vocabulary expansion of the period, it is not surprising that there have been a number of accounts of EModE word formation strategies. A major one is Nevalainen's chapter in the authoritative *Cambridge History of the English Language, Volume 3*.[48] In a later publication, Nevalainen

(2001) focuses on Shakespeare, and describes three word formation strategies. One is compounding, a process natural to Germanic languages. Compounds often succinctly capture complex ideas that would otherwise be lengthy to express. So when the Chorus in *Romeo and Juliet* refers to the lovers as *star-crossed* (1, prologue, 6), they are economically expressing an idea about being thwarted by astrological incompatibility. Sometimes compounds can be so compact as to be ambiguous. Nevalainen's example is the expression *child-changed father* in *King Lear* (4.7.17). It can either mean, she notes, 'father changed into a child,' or 'father changed by his children.' One way of classifying compounds, Nevalainen notes, is in terms of the parts of speech involved. 'Noun + present or past participle' are particularly common ones: the thunderbolts in *King Lear* are *oak-cleaving* (3.2.5), and Juliet's body is described as *tempest-tossed* (RJ, 3.5.137). Salmon and Burness' collection includes a section entitled 'Lexical Innovation,' and in one chapter, Salmon (1970) discusses another means of compound classification – according to how they function. Two areas particularly attracting compounds are 'describing the natural world' (as in *Romeo and Juliet*'s *lazy-pacing clouds*, 2.2.31), and a function in which Shakespeare has exceptional skills: 'personal abuse.' The description of Lysander in *A Midsummer Night's Dream* as a *lack-love* and a *kill-courtesy* (2.2.83) are relatively tame examples.

Another of Nevalainen's strategies is affixation, and her chapter includes a valuable list of common Elizabethan prefixes and suffixes. Shakespeare, she notes, has his 'favourites' among these, and for some she proposes reasons for his preferences. For example, she considers the negative prefixes *un-*, *in-/im-* and *dis-*, noting that Shakespeare uses them all in neologisms – in *Antony and Cleopatra*, for example, you find *unseminared*, *immoment* and *discandy*. But Shakespeare has a preference of *un-*, perhaps because the other two have more restricted meanings; *un-* can be used most productively. She also shows the extent of linguistic choices which the Elizabethan spirit of innovation made available. For example, Shakespeare uses the apparently invented noun *insultment* (the *OED* definition is 'the action of insulting') in *Cymbeline* (3.5.142). But the language of the time offered various other options for him to choose from: *insult, insultation, insultance,* or just *insulting*. Such an embarrassment of choice suggests that English was no longer quite what Bayley had called it: a 'slighted, poor, inexpressive and unseemly thing.'

The third strategy Nevalainen discusses is functional shift, also called conversion. This is where a word is allowed to become a new part of speech. We have already seen an example in the word *lip*, used by Shakespeare as a verb as well as a noun. Here are some more examples, revealing that the most common results of functional shift are indeed new verbs:

Duke as a verb:

Lord Angelo dukes it well in his absence.

(MM 3.2.90)

Urn **as a verb:**

He will not suffer us to burn their bones, / To urn their ashes.

(TNK 1.1.43)

Furnace **as a verb:**

There is a Frenchman … that, it seems, much loves / A Gallian girl at home. He furnaces.

(Cym 1.7.64)

Safe **as a verb:**

I tell you true: best you safed the bringer / Out of the host.

(AC 4.6.26)

Window **as a verb:**

Wouldst thou be windowed in great Rome.

(AC 4.14.72)

Nevalainen points out that the strategy relies for its effect on economical usage. Her example is the use of *boy* as a verb, as in *I shall see / Some squeaking Cleopatra boy my greatness* (AC 5.2.218). This is effective partly because it stands out among the frequent uses (roughly 400) of the noun *boy* in Shakespeare.

There is an experiment, reported by Davis, which studies the effects of Shakespeare-like functional shifts on readers.[49] Part of its interest is its interdisciplinary nature, revealing how in recent decades literary studies have shown themselves open to influences from other academic areas, in this case neurolinguistics. Davis finds that 'the effect [of Shakespearean functional shifts] is often electric … like a lightning-flash in the mind.' With neuroscientific colleagues he set out to explore whether this 'electricity' can be actually detected in the brain when a functional shift was encountered. For his experiment he uses sets of four sentences (the key words are italicized):

(a) I was not supposed to go there alone: you said you would *accompany* me.
(b) I was not supposed to go there alone: you said you would *charcoal* me.
(c) I was not supposed to go there alone: you said you would *incubate* me.
(d) I was not supposed to go there alone: you said you would *companion* me.

Sentence (a) in each set is a normal English sentence. Sentence (b) is odd both syntactically and semantically (that is, in terms of both grammar and meaning): in the example above there is a noun where there should be a verb, and its meaning does not relate to the sentence. Sentence (c) each time is semantically unacceptable, but syntactically correct (*incubate* does not make sense here, but it is at least a verb, and is being used as one here). Sentence (d) is the most like Shakespearean functional shift; *companion* is semantically clear (we know immediately what it means), but syntactically odd because the word is a noun being used as a verb.

Subjects were asked to read each of the four sentences. The experimenters used various techniques, including placing electrodes on various parts of the subjects' brains to measure brain-events. Reactions to the different sentences types were assessed. It was found that type (d) sentences had 'distinct and unique' effects on the brain. One of these effects was to 'alert' the brain to further possible anomalies. Davis concludes that 'Shakespeare is stretching us; he is opening up the possibility of further peaks, new potential pathways or developments.' Interdisciplinary research of this sort is as welcome as it is new.

5.4 More 'interdisciplinariness': metaphor

In the past, the studies of literature and language were often treated together. But since the middle of the twentieth century, linguistics has very much become a separate discipline. So it happens that when literary scholars utilize linguistics, they are, like Davis and his neurolinguistics colleagues, indulging in a form of 'interdisciplinariness,' and they have not shrunk from this. One area where linguistics has touched on literature is in metaphor studies. There was a surge of interest in the study of metaphor at the beginning of the 1980s. Partly responsible was a book written by a linguist and a philosopher, Lakoff and Johnson's (1980) *Metaphors We Live By*. They regard metaphor not simply as a linguistic device used by writers for effect, but as an instrument of thought, profoundly affected by our culture, and profoundly affecting how we think. Their book talks in terms of systematic metaphorical concepts 'that structure our actions and thoughts ... they are metaphors we live by.'[50] This view became one of the central tenets of what is now called Cognitive Metaphor Theory (CMT).

Imagery, as we saw in 4.2, had already captured the attention of Shakespearean scholars, particularly Spurgeon and Clemen. Given Shakespeare's frequent and skilful use of metaphor, it is not surprising that he should become a major focus of attention when the 'surge of interest' occurred. Thompson and Thompson (1987) use a CMT perspective to look at Shakespearean metaphor. They concentrate on a number of Shakespearean metaphorical themes, some of which were discussed by Spurgeon and Clemen. Thompson and Thompson's themes include time metaphors in *Troilus and Cressida*, animal metaphors in *King Lear* and human body metaphors in *Hamlet*. They use a different view of metaphor to consider each of these, to see how well each is able to interpret Shakespeare, and hence the extent to which it can stand as a comprehensive theory of metaphor. For example, they use Lakoff and Johnson's perspective to interpret *Troilus and Cressida*'s time metaphors. Their work is presented as a 'series of meetings' between linguists and literary critics. They are explorations in interdisciplinariness.

Among those who have followed up these metaphorical explorations is Oncins-Martinez (2011). Recognising Thompson and Thompson's work as a 'turning-point' in the field, he focuses on Shakespeare's sexual language. One way of characterizing metaphors, common in recent studies, is to use an 'A IS B' formula. The one Oncins-Martinez focuses on in Shakespeare is SEX IS WAR. His section headings identify some of the metaphorical parameters:

- A fight is a sexual encounter;
- Military attributes are sexual attributes;
- Wooing is assailing;
- A woman is a walled city; to have a woman is to take a city;
- Trying to have a woman is besieging her;
- 'Breaches' and 'gates' are vaginas;
- A penis is a pistol or pointed weapon;
- Sex is archery;
- A vagina is a case (container).

Oncins-Martinez gives Shakespearean examples for all these. A particularly good example of the A WOMAN IS A WALLED CITY one comes towards the end of *Henry V*, where Henry discusses possible terms of agreement for his marriage to the King of France's daughter, Katherine. Burgundy teases Henry for being love-blind for Katherine. The dialogue continues (5.2.311):

> Henry: It is so; and you may, some of you, thank love for my blindness, who cannot see many a fair French city for one fair French maid that stands in my way.
> French King: Yes, my lord, you see them perspectively [symbolically], *the cities turned into a maid; for they are all girdled with maiden walls, that war hath never entered*.

Oncins-Martinez's chapter appears in the Ravassat and Culpeper (2011) collection. The book's subtitle is *Transdisciplinary Approaches*. It well demonstrates a fruitful 'series of meetings' (in Lakoff and Johnson's phrase) between linguistics and literature.

5.5 Dictionaries, concordances, glossaries

Specialized glossaries and dictionaries covering specific lexical areas in Shakespeare have also appeared since the mid-twentieth century. Williams (1997) – *A Glossary of Shakespeare's Sexual Language* – is an example. Another area that has attracted interest is Shakespeare's legal language. It has often been said that his writings 'supply ample evidence that their author ... had a very extensive and accurate knowledge of law.'[51] The Salmon and Burness collection has a chapter on legal language in *Coriolanus*,[52] and more recently a dictionary of Shakespeare's legal language has been produced by Sokol and Sokol (2000). The volume is welcome because so many dramatic conflicts in Shakespeare's plays involve some legal question, which modern readers cannot always be expected to understand. Sokol and Sokol's 'mammoth undertaking' is a 'groundbreaking enterprise.'[53] Entries have three parts. Part A explains the term, giving some history, Part B lists Shakespeare's uses, and Part C provides a relevant bibliography. A look at the entry for the word *appeal* will give a flavour of the book and the detail it goes into. It is all of four pages long. Shakespeare sometimes uses the term in its modern sense; Sokol and Sokol's well-contextualized example is

> Refusing to accept Cardinal Wolsey for her judge, Henry VIII's Queen Katherine wishes to *appeal unto the Pope/ To bring my whole cause 'fore his holiness/ And to be judged by him* (H8 2.4.119). She leaves the court, and Cardinal Campeius hopes she may be induced to *call back her appeal/ She intends unto his holiness.*
>
> (2.4.234)

But, Sokol and Sokol point out, the word had other meanings, one of which is 'accusation.' Their example is from *Measure for Measure* (5.1.299), where Isabella's charges against Angelo are called her 'manifest appeal.'

Both Williams' *Glossary* and Sokol and Sokol's legal dictionary are part of the Arden (previously Athlone) 'Shakespeare Dictionary Series.' Other titles deal with *Shakespeare's Medical Language*, *Shakespeare's Religious Language*, and *Women in Shakespeare*.[54] Some of these are dictionaries in the generally used sense of the word (the *OED* definition being 'a book which explains or translates, usually in alphabetical order, the words of a language or languages'). But the perfectly acceptable extended use of the word (*OED*: 'a book of information or reference on any subject in which the entries are arranged alphabetically; an alphabetical encyclopedia') is often more applicable to them – as it is also to Wells' *Oxford Dictionary of Shakespeare* (1998).

More general dictionaries and glossaries have also appeared since the middle of the twentieth century. Spevack's *Concordance* has already been mentioned. In the early volumes of the complete version, there is a chapter on each Shakespeare work. It begins with some statistics related to the work. Here, for example, is the information given about *The Tempest*. There are:

- 653 speeches of which 444 are verse, 206 prose, three verse and prose;
- 2,283 lines, of which 1835 verse, 448 prose, 236 split lines;
- 16,036 words in total, of which 12,812 are verse, 3,224 prose;
- 3,149 different words.

Then comes an alphabetical word list giving, for each word: the frequency, the relative frequency, the number of occurrences in verse and prose, line and scene references. So, to take the word *ashore* at random, the information for *The Tempest* is: frequency: 4; relative frequency: 0.024; Verse: 2; Prose: 2; occurrences: 1.2.158, 2.2.42, 2.2.121, and 2.2.125.[55] Later volumes of the complete version, plus the Harvard version, give examples of the words in short contexts, and figures for the entire words are also given (the total occurrence of *ashore* in Shakespeare is 13).

Sometimes statistical information like this sounds dry and valueless. But it can provide useful information. Among other things, the relative frequencies of verse and prose lines can distinguish plays – and characters too – as well as revealing interesting trends over the canon as a whole. Also, lists of all occurrences of particular words are invaluable for identifying their meanings. We will see this in a moment when we come to consider the word *ah*.

Many Shakespeare-dedicated websites, like *Shakespeare Online*,[56] contain glossaries, focusing on words which cause problems for modern readers. One impressive large-scale dictionary is Crystal and Crystal's *Shakespeare's Words* (2002a). It is subtitled 'A glossary and language companion.' The 'language companion' part includes boxes which bring together information on such topics as 'discourse markers,' 'address forms,' and 'politeness.' There are also appendices dealing with proper names, foreign words and phrases. The online version is accessed by subscription.[57] When you search for a word, all Shakespeare's uses appear on the screen. Clicking on any one shows it in full context. Both modern and First Folio texts are displayed, together with glosses of unfamiliar words. The site contains many other useful features. For example, if you click on a play's title, a list of dramatic personae appears (among other things); clicking then on a character's name shows all their lines, again in modern and First Folio texts. Another feature is a list of all Shakespeare's characters graded according to part size; Hamlet with 1506 lines is at the top. Iago is second; it is interesting that he speaks considerably more than Othello.

An exciting new dictionary project, at present in progress, is described in Culpeper (2011). He reviews dictionaries so far available and argues for 'a new kind of dictionary for Shakespeare's plays.' His 'new dictionary' will not deal just with 'hard' words, nor even just 'content' words, but all items. 'From a linguistic perspective,' he says, 'we know that all words change meaning: even the most frequent of items have incurred shifts of meaning which present-day readers must take on board.'[58] Culpeper looks at examples of words that tend to be omitted from previous Shakespeare dictionaries. One is the word *ah* – just the sort of word that is sometimes left out of a dictionary. It is a common word in Shakespeare, and has various different uses. Table 5.1 shows the ones Culpeper describes, and would want his dictionary to cover. Culpeper's dictionary will be corpus-based, describing meanings in terms of usage in context, and not just simply etymology. As he puts it, the question of 'what does X mean?' is pursued through another question: 'how is X used?'[59] It will also include the kind of information found in the 'reference book' sense of the word 'dictionary' discussed earlier (where Wells' *Oxford Dictionary of Shakespeare* was given as an example). Culpeper's ambitious project will also, *inter alia*:

- identify the patterns of language that constitute 'themes' in Shakespeare's work;
- look at similarities and differences between Shakespeare's linguistic usage and that of his contemporaries;

- explore the understandings that contemporary audiences had of Shakespeare's language.

Given the various types of information the work will provide, it would, Culpeper says, perhaps best be described as an 'Encyclopaedia of Shakespeare's language.' Its overall form, as conceived at present, will consist of three volumes.[60] Volume 1 would be the dictionary, focusing on the use and meanings of each of Shakespeare's words, both in the context of what he wrote and in the context in which he wrote. Volume 2 will be a compendium of semantic patterns, identifying patterns of words in Shakespeare's writings, and describing how they create the 'linguistic thumbprints' of characters, genders, themes, plays, and dramatic genres. Volume 3 will be a grammar, concentrating on grammatical words and patterns. At the time of writing, Culpeper's project is well under way, though not yet completed.[61]

Table 5.1 Uses of *ah* discussed in Culpeper (2011), pp. 68–70

Uses of *ah* from Culpeper

1. **Sorrow, emotional distress**
Othello (4.2.40):
Desdemona: *To whom, my lord? With whom? How am I false?*
Othello: *Ah Desdemon! away, away, away!*

2. **Pity**
King Lear (3.4.161):
Gloucester: *Canst thou blame him?…*
His daughters seek his death. Ah, that good Kent!

3. **Surprise, realization**
The Comedy of Errors (4.2.1):
[Enter Adriana and Luciana]
Adriana: *Ah, Luciana, did he tempt thee so?*

4. **Preface to the correction/rejection of the previous speaker's propositions, emotions or actions**
Antony and Cleopatra (2.7.70):
Menas: *These three world-sharers, these competitors,*
Are in thy vessel. Let me cut the cable;
And when we are put off, fall to their throats.
All there is thine.
Pompeius: *Ah, this thou shouldst have done*

5. **Reinforces elicitation**
Much Ado About Nothing (3.5.21):
Leonato: *All thy tediousness on me, ah?*
Dogberry: *Yea, an't 'twere a thousand pound more than 'tis, for I hear as good exclamation on your worship as of any man in the city; and though I be but a poor man, I am glad to hear it.*
Here, *ah* means something like 'is that what you mean?'

5.6 Attribution studies

Another area where the availability of digital texts has made a dramatic difference is in attribution studies. Craig and Kinney (2009) is representative of the stage these studies have now reached. Lexis is the main focus here, and computational stylistics, they say, 'has shown that … tests of common words, rare words, word pairing, especially when used in conjunction, can detect the similarities' which continue through all stages of a writer's work, however much this changes over time.[62] Craig and Kinney's methods of analysis are sophisticated, involving much more than simple word frequency counts, though even these are of interest: the fact, for example, that Shakespeare seems fond of the words *gentle* and *beseech*, and that his characters tend to use *hath* rather than *has*. This last example shows that attribution studies are now as interested in 'common,' functional words as they are in rarer, semantically fuller ones. Indeed, Craig and Kinney argue that particular importance should be given to function words since they make up the vast majority of texts. 'Pronouns, for instance,' they note, 'are among the strongest markers of genre (*me* is unusually common in Shakespeare comedies, as *we* and *they* are in Shakespeare's Roman plays).'[63] Among the conclusions reached by various contributors to their edited collection is the tentative one that Marlowe may have been responsible for some sections in the three parts of *Henry VI*, particularly in the Joan la Pucelle and Jack Cade scenes. Another conclusion is that some of the additions made to Kyd's *The Spanish Tragedy* after the author's death are 'Shakespearean in style' and may indeed have been written by him.[64]

5.7 Shakespeare's language in the pecking order

Thompson and Thompson note that in the past the detailed study of language has been 'rather low in the pecking order' of Shakespearean topics for study.[65] Kermode (2000) makes the same point, noting that 'every other aspect of Shakespeare is studied almost to death.'[66] These authors see their work as helping to counteract this. Kermode's book, full of insight, looks at a selection of the plays one by one and provides what amounts to a 'linguistic commentary' on each. Pecking-order position is also raised by the appearance of various collections of papers dealing with detailed aspects of Shakespeare's language, very much including lexis. Three have been represented in this chapter: the Salmon and Burness *Reader* (1987), Adamson et al.'s *Reading Shakespeare* (2001), and Ravassat and Culpeper's *Stylistics* (2011). A fourth, largely focused on lexical issues, appeared in 2015 – a collection edited by Yachnin. The book explores Shakespeare's 'world of words' through a series of chapters centred around selected words or phrases. One, for example, by Munro, gives an account of the words *antique* and *antic* ('ancient' and 'grotesque' respectively, among other meanings) in *Love's Labour's Lost*, and *Henry IV, Part 2*. She focuses particularly on the characters of Don Armado and Pistol, who manage simultaneously to be both 'antique' and 'antic' in their linguistic behaviour.[67] Then there is Shea's chapter on 'angling' in *The Winter's Tale*, which explores in detail the particular associations of the term with (among other things) various types of theft.[68] Jacobson's study looks at the verb 'to colour' in *Hamlet*. One connotation sees colouring as a 'masking' or 'disguising.' It is easy to see how the theme resonates through the play, among other things in Hamlet's 'antic disposition,' which might be seen as a form of 'colouring.'[69]

Often the appearance of edited collections like these proclaim that a subject has well and truly 'arrived.' So it is with Shakespeare language studies.

Notes

1. Heid (2008), p. 147.
2. Ward and Valenza (2011), p. 40.
3. Spevack (1973).
4. Figures from https://proquest.libguides.com/eebo.
5. Taylor (1989), p. 408.
6. *Ibid.*, pp. 407, 411.
7. *Ibid.*, p. 411.
8. Cited by Taylor (1989), p. 408.
9. Jespersen (1932), p. 199.
10. The example is from Crystal (2008), p. 4.
11. The examples are from Ward and Valenza (2011), p. 38.
12. Jespersen (1932), p. 199.
13. 15,000 is the estimate in Müller (1861), p. 254. Crystal (2004), p. 4 mentions the figure of 30,000.
14. Jespersen (1932), p. 200.
15. Craig (2011), p. 60.
16. *Ibid.*, p. 63.
17. *Ibid.*, p. 60.
18. Elliott and Valenza (2011), p. 45.
19. Jespersen (1932), p. 202.
20. Bolton (1992), p. 89.
21. Slater (1988). Cited in Elliott and Valenza (2011), p. 57.
22. Slater (1988), p. 78.
23. Elliott and Valenza (2011), p. 89.
24. Bayley (1906), p. 203.
25. Wermser (1976). Cited in Nevalainen (1999).
26. Crystal (2008), p. 9.
27. Garner (1982), p. 211.
28. Crystal (2004), p. 315.
29. Shipley (1977). Cited in Garner (1982), p. 211.
30. Elam (2008).
31. The examples are taken from Nevalainen (1999), p. 249, which contains a longer list.
32. Elliott and Valenza (2011), p. 49.
33. van Noppen (1983).
34. Goodland (2011), p. 12.
35. Jespersen (1932), p. 211.
36. Brewer (2007), p. 12.
37. *Ibid.*, p. 124.

38 *Ibid.*, p. 125.
39 Schäfer (1980), p. 7.
40 Wells (1964).
41 van Noppen (1983), p. 707.
42 Schäfer (1980), p. 17.
43 *Ibid.*, p. 4.
44 Details at www.helsinki.fi/varieng/CoRD/corpora/HelsinkiCorpus/ and http://leme.library.utoronto.ca/public/intro.cfm.
45 Goodland (2011), p. 13.
46 *Ibid.*, p. 31.
47 Garner (1982), p. 213.
48 Nevalainen (1999).
49 The article appeared in *The Reader*, but is no longer available online. It is described in 'The Shakespeared Brain,' *The Literary Review*, 356, July, 2006.
50 Lakoff and Johnson (1980), p. 55.
51 Greenwood (1908), p. 371.
52 Tanselle and Dunbar (1962).
53 Both phrases are used by Kreps (2003).
54 Iyengar (2014), Hassel (2015), and Findlay (2014).
55 Throughout this book, acts, scene and line references use those in Crystal and Crystal (2002a).
56 www.shakespeare-online.com/
57 www.shakespeareswords.com
58 Culpeper (2011), p. 65.
59 *Ibid.*, p. 58.
60 Some of this information on the project is taken from a presentation Culpeper made to the project's external panel, July, 2016.
61 The project's website is http://wp.lancs.ac.uk/shakespearelang.
62 Craig and Kinney (2009), p. 9.
63 *Ibid.*, p. 11.
64 *Ibid.*, Chapters 3 and 8, both by Craig.
65 Thompson and Thompson (1987), p. 3.
66 Kermode (2000), p. vii.
67 Munro (2015).
68 Shea (2015).
69 Jacobson (2015).

6 'A richness of variant forms'
Grammar

6.1 *Do* and NICE

Do is an important auxiliary in PDE. The acronym NICE describes its main roles:

N	Negatives	*I don't like chocolates.*
I	Inversion	*Do you like chocolates?*
C	Code (as a substitute verb)	*She likes chocolates, and so do I.*
E	Emphasis	*I really do like chocolates.*

Shakespeare uses *do* in all these ways:

N	*No, sir, it does not please me* (H8, 5.3.134)
I	*Now, fair one, does your business follow us?* (AW, 2.1.99)
C	*She for an Edward weeps, and so do I* (R3, 2.2.82)
E	*I do begin to perceive that I am made an ass* (MWW, 5.5.119).[1]

One of the themes of this chapter is the variability that EModE showed in grammar usage – much more than we find in English today. There was indeed 'a richness of variant forms and constructions.'[2] Thus it is with *do*, and alongside the 'N' and 'I' examples above, you commonly find in Shakespeare sentences where do is not used, like *Tut, I came not to hear this* (1H4, 4.3.89), and *Signor Gremio, came you from the church?* (TS, 3.2.148). Also, the use of *do* in positive affirmative sentences did not necessarily express emphasis. So *I do remember* might simply stand for PDE *I remember*.

Since the mid-twentieth century, when linguistics became a distinct discipline, the study of historical syntax has developed considerably, and we now have a number of complete EModE grammars, as well as very many studies of specific EModE grammatical structures. Among the complete grammars are Görlach (1991), Barber (1997), Nevalainen (2006), and a lengthy chapter on syntax by Rissanen in Lass (1999). The auxiliary *do* has always been of particular interest to historical linguists, because similar uses of such an auxiliary among the world's languages (to form negatives and interrogatives, for example) are rather rare. All the general grammars mentioned above discuss *do*, with

Rissanen's treatment being particularly detailed. There have also been a number of specific *do* studies in recent decades. These include Ellegård (1953), Miller and Leffel (1994), Nevalainen (1991), sections of Nevalainen and Raumolin-Brunberg (2003), Nurmi (1996) and (1999), Rissanen (1985) and (1991), Stein (1990). Several of these are full-length books on the topic.

So *do* has well and truly been 'done.' It is worth looking at the form in detail, to show just how well-developed EModE grammar studies now are. Certainly, a lot has happened since Abbott's 1869 *Grammar*. We will look at what Abbott says about *do*, describe what has been said since, and show how this has been represented in recent Shakespearean grammar studies. Because there is so much to say about *do* in all its forms and uses, we will concentrate mainly on *do* in positive affirmative sentences – just the 'E' of the NICE formula. We will call this 'PA *do*' for short.

Abbott devotes about four pages to *do*. He begins with a historical point, about the use of *do* in a causative sense in Early English. One of his examples is Gower's *They have done her understonde*, which means 'they have made her understand.' Abbott also mentions an EModE use of *do* with verbs which have similar-sounding tense forms. Tyndale for example has *did eat*, and Abbott supposes that this might be to clarify that the tense is past, since the present and past forms – *eat* and *ate* are phonetically quite similar. Concentrating then on Shakespeare, Abbott mentions the variability of PA *do* use. Sometimes it is there, sometimes not. In his words: 'slight causes determined [the] use or non-use' of *do*.[3] One of these 'slight causes' can be metre, and PA *do* is sometimes there for metrical reasons. When Horatio sees old Hamlet's Ghost (Ham, 1.2.216) he reports: *It lifted up it* [sic] *head and did address / Itself to motion*. Here, the use of *did* with *address* (and *lifted* up without) creates an iambic pentameter; *addressed* or *did lift* would lose this.

Abbott also notes that *do* can be used for various types of emphasis. His example creates what he describes as 'excited narrative,' when Calphurnia in *Julius Caesar* (2.2.23) reports:

> Horses did neigh, and dying men did groan,
> And ghosts did shriek and squeal about the streets.

But, Abbott says, unemphatic *do* is also found. So *I do remember* in *Twelfth Night*, can stand for our PDE 'I remember.' The rest of Abbott's treatment mostly deals with *do* in negatives and interrogatives.

Figure 6.1 shows that since Abbott the origins of *do* have been well-explored. Corpus-based studies show that the use of PA *do* peaked in the 1560–1600 period, with about 10 per cent of verb occurrences showing the form. The decline thereafter was rapid, as shown in Figure 6.2. The eighteenth century's dislike for 'using two words where one would do' doubtless contributed to the rapid decline. In the 'Grammar of the English Language' part of his *Dictionary*, Dr Johnson notes that '*do* is sometimes used superfluously, as *I do have* ... but this is considered as a vitious mode of speech.'[5]

92 1950 on

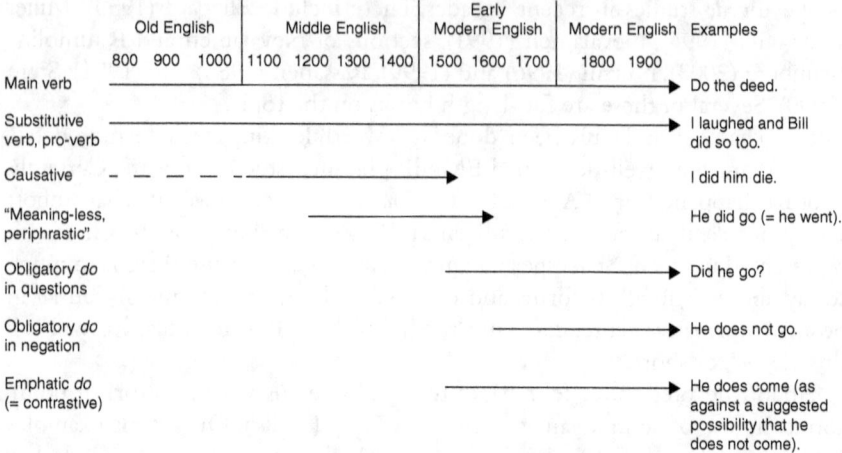

Figure 6.1 Survey of uses of *do*. From Stein (1990), p. 12, adapted from Traugott (1972), p. 199

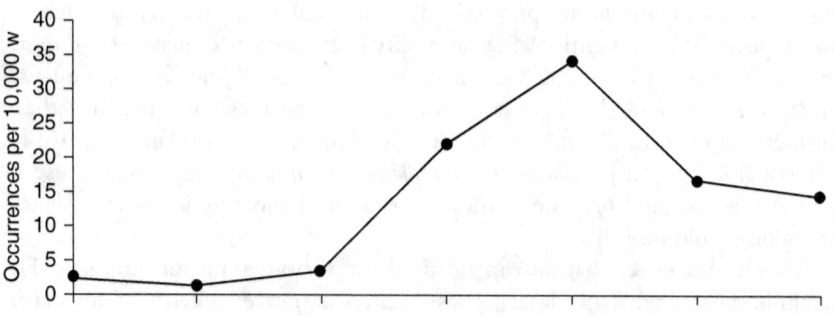

Figure 6.2 Occurrences of *do* in affirmative statements. From Nevalainen and Raumolin-Brunberg (2003), based on Nurmi (1999)[4]

Recent studies have also explored the specific linguistic contexts in which PA *do* was used in EModE. As we have seen, Abbott drew attention to similar-sounding verb forms like *eat* and *ate*. There are other examples, like *set*, *put*, and *cast* where present and past base forms are the same; ambiguity can be avoided by using *do* or *did* to indicate tense (*do set* versus *did set*). Phonotactics – the rules governing possible phonetic sequences in a language – can account for some uses of *do* to avoid awkward phonetic sequences. Rissanen suggests that *dids't endeavour* was favoured over awkward *endeavourest* for this reason, and this is perhaps why you find *didst banish* in Shakespeare, but not *banishest*.[6] *Do* is also more commonly used in sentences with adverbs. The adverb becomes 'associated with' the auxiliary *do*. Rissanen's example is from Elyot: *Helias the holy propheyt of god dyd* [by] *his own hands put to death the priests of the idol Baal.*

Another context where PA *do* occurs is when a sentence has a long subject and a short verb, and its use has the effect of lengthening (and hence giving more salience to) the verb phrase. Rissanen's exemplifies with: *thou must take heed how thy hens, ducks and geese do ley.*[7] Discourse functions are also mentioned, where the purpose is to draw attention to important points, or to signal the beginning of a new topic.[8]

Differences in register are also discussed in various accounts. Rissanen identifies 'formal spoken' as a register where PA *do* is often found. He specifically mentions court cases. One of his examples, from a trial text, is *I confess I did mislike the Queenes Mariage*. Even today PA *do* can commonly be found in legal contexts: here is an arrest being described in a recent novel: 'Brian Daniel Bishop, you are charged that … you did unlawfully kill Katherine Margaret Bishop.'[9] This is the 'PA *do* of arrest.'

There are also differences to do with gender and place. Nevalainen and Raumolin-Brunberg (following Nurmi, 1999) find that PA *do* was more common among men than women in the last two decades of the sixteenth century. Figure 6.3 gives information about regional use.

So EModE PA *do* has been well and truly documented, and it is natural that what has been studied should make its way into discussions about Shakespeare's syntax. A number of the sources mentioned contain Shakespearean examples. Barber, for example, uses the description of Clarence's murder in *Richard III* (1.4) to illustrate the various uses of all *do* forms. He uses Clarence's statements from that scene – *Where eyes did once inhabit*, and *Your eyes do menace me* – to show that 'in affirmative declarative sentences auxiliary *do* was normally unemphatic' (1997: 194).

Between Abbott's 1869 *Grammar* and the beginning of the twenty-first century, there was no comprehensive Shakespearean grammar produced, except for Wilhelm Franz's *Shakespeare-Grammatik* (1900). Then, in the early twenty-first century, two Shakespeare Grammars appeared in quick succession: Blake (2002) and Hope (2003). We will look at these grammars in detail in the next

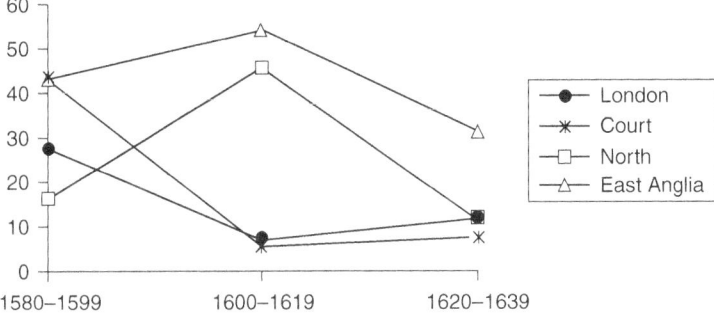

Figure 6.3 Regional distribution of *do* in affirmative statements. From Nevalainen and Raumolin-Brunberg (2003:175), based on Nurmi (1999:177)[10]

section. They too draw on the kinds of studies we have been considering, and many of the PA *do* points we have drawn attention to are mentioned in their descriptions. Thus Hope uses a passage from *Titus Andronicus* to exemplify the various uses of *do*, relating it to the general EmodE 'richness of variant forms' we have spoken of. He illustrates the 'formal spoken' use of PA *do* with Falstaff's pompous comments on pitch (black tar; 1H4 2.4.406): *This pitch – as ancient writers do report – doth defile*, and he speaks about the discourse-marking function of *do*, 'highlighting the crucial verb in a narrative, or marking a shift in topic' (2003: 141). As this, and many other examples in this section show, treatments of Shakespeare's grammar have truly benefited from the amount of recent work in historical syntax.

6.2 Two new Abbotts: Blake and Hope

At the end of the brief witches' scene that opens *Macbeth*, the three 'weird sisters' chant:

> *Padock calls anon: faire is foule, and foule is faire:*
> *Houer through the fogge and filthie ayre.*

(1.1.9, First Folio)

The word *hover* needs some explanation. Is it a verb or a noun – there was a noun in use in Shakespeare's lifetime, and it could here mean 'the state of hovering (in the air).' If it is a verb, is it an imperative, and if so who are the witches commanding? Or is it a first person plural present ('we hover')? This could also have an imperative meaning: 'let us hover.' Blake discusses the passage in the Introduction to his *Grammar* and argues that 'whichever grammatical interpretation one chooses has a significant implication for an understanding of the tone and purpose of this scene.'[11] Examples like this lead Blake to the conclusion that 'it is time that [Shakespeare's] language was given more attention than it currently receives; and this is one purpose behind this grammar.' The study of grammar is, he is arguing, important to the understanding of Shakespeare. Language needs to be higher in the scholastic 'pecking order' (to use the phrase from 5.7).

Blake's *Grammar* is a detailed reference book, at 400 pages slightly shorter than Abbott's. It has five main chapters: The Noun Group; The Verb Group; Adverbials, Interjections, Conjunctions and Prepositions; Concord, Negation, Ellipsis and Repetition; Clause Organization and Sentence Structure. There is an introductory chapter entitled 'The Linguistic Background' which includes a lengthy discussion of punctuation and spelling, and there are final chapters on Discourse and Register, Pragmatics. So Blake is using the term grammar in a broad sense.

In his review of the book, Vickers is appreciative of the fact that Blake chronicles some linguistic differences between quarto and folio texts.[12] This can be seen in his treatment of the different ways of expressing our PDE *yes* – *ay* (sometimes written *I*) and *yea* on the one hand, and *yes* on the other. There was a tendency in EModE to use *ay/yea* in answer to positive questions or statements, and *yes* in relation to negative ones. Blake's examples are both from the same scene in *The Two Gentlemen of Verona*, and concern a letter Silvia has received from Valentine:

> Valentine: ... Madam, they [the lines] *are for you.*
> Silvia: *Ay, ay; you writ them, sir, at my request*
>
> (2.1.118–9)

Just three lines before we find:

> Valentine: *What means your ladyship? Do you not like it?*
> Silvia: *Yes, yes; the lines are very quaintly writ.*
>
> (2.1.115–6)

We have lost this distinction in PDE, but there is a similar one in French between *oui* and *si*: the way the Harrap dictionary puts it is that *si* is 'used in answer to a negative question.' But Blake uses differences between quarto and folio versions to show that the *ay/yes* distinction was not always followed in Shakespeare. One of his examples is a line from *Richard III* (2.3.3). Quarto 1 has *I, that the King is dead*, while the First Folio is *Yes, that the King is dead*. The suggestion is that *ay/yea* was on the way out.

Blake's section on prepositions shows just how thorough his coverage is. It is 23 pages long. The prepositions are listed alphabetically, with subdivisions for the various meanings, and for each meaning one or more Shakespeare examples are given. To choose an example at random, he has 31 lines for *at*, identifying eight categories of meaning (and one of these is the umbrella category of 'various others'). In contrast Onions' dictionary (1986) has just one line, and Crystal and Crystal (2002) four, though, as you might expect, the *OED* coverage far outstrips any of these, with 59 separate meanings, and Shakespeare cited in relation to 25 of them. Most of the meanings Blake lists have some equivalents in later stages of the language. For example, EModE *at* can be used to indicate 'value especially after verbs of buying or selling.' He gives an example from *Coriolanus* (5.6.46): *At a few drops of women's rheum ... / ... he sold the blood and labour.* The present-day reader might pause momentarily over the meaning here, but the *OED* does have as one of its senses: 'of price or value' – an 1849 example being from Macaulay: 'Wheat was at seventy shillings the quarter.'

Hope's *Shakespeare's Grammar* was commissioned by the Arden Shakespeare to replace Abbott's. In his 'Introduction,' Hope discusses why the time was ripe for a replacement. The nineteenth-century grammar consisted, Hope points out, of a series of sections set out alphabetically – dealing with grammatical categories and moving from 'A' for Articles to 'V' for Verbs. No real attention was given to relating the sections and hence to providing a coherent account of the language. Hope aims to rectify this. Like Blake, he is able to use advances in historical linguistics to provide more explanatory comment than Abbott could.

Part 1 of Hope's *Shakespeare's Grammar* covers the Noun Phrase (NP), and Part 2 the Verb Phrase (VP). Hope's aim to present an overall picture, plus his desire to provide a resource for stylistics, lead to his inclusion of 'stylistic overview' sections in each of these two parts. They give, in his own words, 'an account of the stylistic and literary effects' associated with the element of structure being considered.[13] For example, the 'stylistic overview' of the NP section uses passages from *Macbeth* and *The Winter's Tale* to illustrate the range of NP choices available to Shakespeare. One parameter of choice is degree of pronoun replacement, and Hope shows how Shakespeare begins the final scene of *Macbeth*, Act 1 with a series of 'it's with unclear referents, giving the sense of 'overhearing someone in the middle of thought': *If it were done when 'tis done, then 'twere well/ It were done quickly* (1.7.1).[14] Another parameter is degree and type of modification. Sometimes the modifying phrase comes before the noun, as in *the Lady Paulina's steward* (WT 5.2.26). Sometimes it comes after, as in the very next line: *This news, which is called true*. A further choice is whether to use Latinate or Germanic vocabulary. Hope argues that Macbeth's utterances are sometimes abstract and reveal a 'kind of insubstantiality,' for which Latinate vocabulary is suitable:[15]

> *If the assassination*
> *Could trammel up the consequence, and catch*
> *With his surcease success.*
>
> (Mac 1.7.3)

But then, two lines later he shows another side of his character, down-to-earth and Germanic:

> *that but this blow*
> *Might be the be-all and the end-all! – here,*
> *But here, upon this bank and shoal of time,*
> *We'd jump the life to come.*
>
> (Mac 1.7.5)

One way in which Abbott and Hope are similar is that both have a pedagogic dimension. As we saw in 3.4, Abbott's *Grammar* had a 'Notes and Questions' section towards the end, intended for student use. As well as providing useful information to editors and linguistic specialists, Hope's *Shakespeare's Grammar* also aims to inform the non-linguist, and the book contains much basic linguistic information. The NP section, for example, goes into some detail about the linguistics of the structure, explaining what heads, pre-heads, and post-heads are. Hope's book is about half the length of Blake's *Grammar*, and under half the length of Abbott's work. Since it is more focused on main syntactic areas, it is less comprehensive than Blake's.

6.3 A fascinating wealth of detail

As we have seen in relation to PA *do*, a good deal of detailed work has been done on EModE grammar. There are several collections of papers, all already mentioned in this book, which focus just on Shakespeare and provide a fascinating wealth of detail for anyone interested in the nuts and bolts of Shakespeare's language. One is the 1987 Salmon and Burness collection, which has a section entitled 'Shakespeare and Elizabethan grammar.' The section's contents.

Kakietek's first paper in the collection will give an example of the type of detailed grammatical discussion found in small-scale studies of this sort. It is entitled 'The perfective auxiliaries in the language of Shakespeare.' In PDE, perfective aspect is expressed by use of *have* + past participle – as in 'I have opened,' 'he has seen.' But in EModE, and Shakespeare, *be* is sometimes used instead of *have*. Kakietek lists some of the verbs that use *be*, including *go*, *come*, *arrive*, and *walk*. Thus right at the beginning of *Henry IV, Part 2* (1.1.4), the Porter says: *His Lordship is walked forth into the orchard.* There are some verbs found with both *be* and *have*. Hence in the same play, Falstaff announces: *his highness is fallen into this same whoreson apoplexy* (2H4, 1.2.107), while in *Measure for Measure* (2.4.178)

Table 6.1 Chapters dealing with grammar in Salmon and Burness (1987)

Author	Area covered	Observations
Vivian Salmon	sentence structure	focusing specifically on colloquial English.
Celia Millward	pronominal case in imperatives	*Get thee to a nunnery* (Ham 3.1.121) or *Get thou to a nunnery*?
Piotr Kakietek	perfect auxiliaries	see below.
Piotr Kakietek	*may* and *might*	uses are different from PDE.
Y. M. Biese	ingressive auxiliaries	auxiliaries meaning 'become.' E.g. *come* and *get* in *How came it yours?* (Cym 5.5.131) and *How to get clear of debts* (1.1.134).
Rajendra Singh	multiple negation	*nor understood none neither* (LLL 5.1.144).
Estelle Taylor	*–eth* and *–es*	Sometimes one and sometimes the other: *It blesseth him that gives and him that takes* (MV 4.1.184).
Estelle Taylor	*–s* ending for *do* and *have*	though these verbs continued to use the *–eth* longer than other verbs, you do find *does* and *has* in Shakespeare.

Table 6.2 'Small words' discussed in Adamson (2001)

Words	Examples	Comments
and (an) = PDE 'if'	*Zounds ... I'll make one; an I do not, call me villain* (1H4 1.2.100).	
his/it = 'its'	*The hardest knife ill-used doth lose his edge* (Sonn 95).	
may = ability	*May you stead* [help] *me?* (MV 1.3.7).	Also used for 'permission' or 'likelihood,' as in PDE.
shall = 'bound to' or 'must'	*He hath been out nine years, and away he shall again* (KL 1.1.31).	
that (this, thus and *there)* used deictically, often with gestures	*Take this from this, if this be otherwise* (Ham 2.2.156).	In one interpretation, Polonius here points to his head and shoulders.

Isabella says of her brother that *he hath fall'n by prompture of the blood*. The use of *have* in this example may perhaps be because, as Kakietek also notes, there is an adverbial in the sentence: adverb of place, time, manner, duration, frequency tend to be accompanied by *have*. Incidentally, some have suggested a slight difference of meaning signalled by the choice of *be* or *have*. The latter focuses attention on the action itself, while *be* emphasizes the state resulting from the action.[16] So, 'I had come' may emphasize the action of travelling, while 'I was come' is suggesting 'and here I am.'

Adamson et al.'s (2001) collection contains one chapter (Adamson, 2001) focusing on what she calls 'small words,' all of them monosyllables. Some are false friends to the modern reader – in use today, but with different meanings. Here are the words she looks at (with the exception of *thou* and *you* which will be discussed in 7.3).

Some comments on the first of these: the use of *and* (or *an*) for 'if' was more common in ME than in EModE, but you do find it in Shakespeare where it is, Adamson notes, particularly common among lower-class speakers. Hence Bottom in *A Midsummer Night's Dream* (1.2.47): *An I may hide my face, let me play Thisbe too.* Adamson also mentions the use of *so* in the same way, as in Iago's: *So they do nothing, 'tis a venial slip* (Oth, 4.1.9). *But* is also used in conditionals, to mean 'if not.' Hence Brabantio's reluctant agreement to allow Othello Desdemona's hand (1.3.191):

> *I here do give thee that with all my heart*
> *Which, but thou hast already, with all my heart*
> *I would keep from thee.*

6.4 Grammar with a sociolinguistic dimension

'Common among ... lower-class speakers,' Adamson says. One of the major changes that took place in linguistics in the second half of the twentieth century was a shift towards interest in sociolinguistic dimensions of language use. The sociolinguist Hymes criticized Chomsky for his 'Garden of Eden' view of language, concerned only with its internal structure and not with the way it is used by people in real situations.[17] Hymes' notion of 'communicative competence' opened the way for the exploration of 'language in use.' This new perspective led, *inter alia*, to the development of 'variational sociolinguistics,' an approach which gives a valuable new dimension to the study of historical grammar. It looks at variables of use – like region, class, and gender – and by studying how language develops in relation to these, provides a rich and detailed account of how some forms disappear, while others become established.

We have already seen (6.1) how Nevalainen and Raumolin-Brunberg consider these variables in relation to PA *do*. It is worth looking at their approach in more detail. Like most variational studies, their book *Historical Sociolinguistics* relies on a corpus for data. In their case it is the *Corpus of Early English Correspondence* (CEEC), a 2.7 million-word collection of 6,000 letters written between 1417 and 1681. They investigate 14 areas, one of which is PA *do*. Another is the third-person singular present tense verb endings –*s* and -*th*. As this passage from Portia in *The Merchant of Venice* shows (and as was mentioned in Table 6.1), we find variation in Shakespeare:

> *The quality of mercy is not strained,*
> *It droppeth as the gentle rain from heaven*
> *Upon the place beneath. It is twice blest,*
> *It blesseth him that gives and him that takes.*
> *'Tis mightiest in the mightiest, it becomes*
> *The thronèd monarch better than his crown.*
>
> (MV 4.1.182)

Sometimes (as with *droppeth*) there can be metrical reasons for the choice, but not always. One of the parameters Nevalainen and Raumolin-Brunberg consider is time. As Figure 6.4 shows, the diffusion of –*s* took place in two waves, in the latter half of the fifteenth century, and then more strongly about a century later. By the 1680s, -*th* had more or less disappeared:

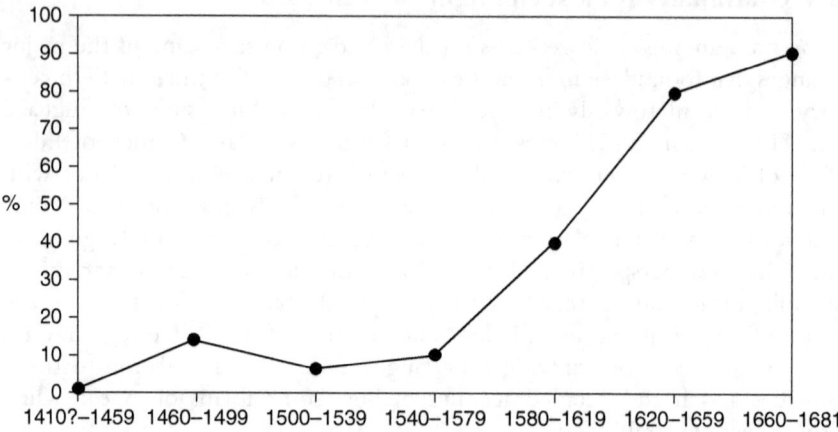

Figure 6.4 The replacement of the third-person singular suffix –*th* by –*s*. Percentages of –*s*. From Nevalainen and Raumolin-Brunberg (2003: 68)[18]

Table 6.3 Third-person singular indicative suffix -*s* vs. – *th*. Percentages of -*s*. From Nevalainen and Raumolin-Brunberg (2003:140)[19]

	1520–1559				1640–1681			
	-TH	-s	%	Total	-TH	-s	%	Total
Royalty	17	0	0	17	0	55	100	55
Nobility	58	13	18	71	10	158	94	168
Gentry	274	25	8	299	45	635	93	680
Clergy	86	4	4	90	35	217	86	252
Social aspirers	177	5	3	182	23	170	88	193
Professionals	56	1	2	57	36	200	85	236
Merchants	304	33	10	337	8	107	93	115
Other non-gentry	30	42	58	72	3	39	93	42
Total	1002	123	11	1125	160	1581	91	1741

As regards region, the -*s* form travelled southwards, starting in the north and moving downwards. It began to catch on in London in the mid-1500s, and its use increased in all regions thereafter, though in rural East Anglia the process was slow.

There were also social class differences, as Table 6.3 shows.

The movement towards –*s* was led by the lower classes. In Table 6.3, the numbers on the left, dealing with 1520–1559, show that in the corpus data only those in the 'other non-gentry' category were using -*s* more than -*th*. The nobility were overwhelmingly using -*th*, and royalty avoided -*s* completely. By

1640–1681 royalty and the higher social classes had changed their third-person behaviour dramatically.

Nevalainen and Raumolin-Brunberg also look at gender differences. They find that in the early rise (late fifteenth century) men used more *-s* forms than women (though this might, they say, be the result of skewed data). In the second, more dramatic rise, women are quicker to adopt the form. Nevalainen and Raumolin-Brunberg's consideration of other forms sometimes shows the same phenomenon, with men tending to prefer localized forms, while women often pick up new ones with more general distribution.[20]

The extent to which these variational features are reflected in Shakespeare does not seem to be fully known yet. The pattern of class use may contribute to a perception that *–th* was the more formal of the two, and indeed in Shakespeare, the *-th* form is found mainly in verse, and *–s* nearly invariably in prose.[21] But we do not know how *-s/-th* usage relates to male/female characters in Shakespeare.

6.5 How to do things with grammar

As we have seen, the new sociolinguistic perspective of the late twentieth century was concerned less with a language's structures, and more with how they were used. A book that helped spark that change has a title that captures the new perspective very well. It is the philosopher John Austin's *How to Do Things with Words*, published in 1962. The new emphasis falls on the purposes to which language is put, and on how they are achieved. In terms of Shakespeare's grammar, this would mean looking at how he 'did things with grammar,' rather than on how the grammatical system was structured. Part of Hope's book *Shakespeare and Language* (2010) is concerned with how Shakespeare 'does things with grammar.' One chapter, for example, is entitled 'Agency and uncertainty in Shakespeare's syntax.' One of Hope's arguments is that 'Shakespeare is generally interested in activating inanimate things,' and he links this *inter alia* to Shakespeare's preference for *-ing* participles in certain contexts. His example relates to these lines in the Prologue of *Henry V* (26):

> *Think, when we talk of horses, that you see them*
> *Printing their proud hoofs I'th' receiving earth*

The phrase *receiving earth* presents the earth as an active agent, which a phrase like *pierced earth* would not do. Shakespeare, Hope says, 'seems to have a need to animate, and activate, almost everything he mentions, however inactive or inanimate we might think.'[22] He also notes an increasing use of non-restrictive *which* relatives in later plays. Often such relatives express a personal subjective comment. One of Hope's examples is from *The Winter's Tale* where the Third Gentleman reports the King's reaction to the finding of his lost daughter who, it transpires, has been brought up by a shepherd: *now he thanks the old shepherd, which stands by like a weather-bitten conduit of many kings' reigns* (5.2.53). Hope says: 'we are not simply being told what happened: we are being told what the speaker's emotional reaction to the events was.'[23] He concludes that a feature of Shakespeare's developing style is its 'tendency to depict the process of thought by extending certain sentence elements, and using a set of additive subordination strategies.'[24] These include post-head modification, apposition of NPs, and adverbial clauses.

6.6 Towards pragmatics

Here is a non-Shakespeare example of 'how to do things with grammar.' It is described by two American linguists with anthropological interests, Edward Keenan and Elinor Ochs, in a chapter entitled 'Becoming a competent speaker of Malagasy,' (Keenan and Ochs, 1979). They speak of a situation in which a European enters a village in Madagascar, and asks some women in the courtyard for one of his friends. The friend's wife says her husband is not there. The European asks when he will return, and the wife says: 'Well, if you don't come after dinner you won't catch him.' Keenan and Ochs note that this use of a double negative would be interpreted as uncooperative in Western society; the wife is not being as helpful as she could be. But, Keenan and Ochs say, she is in fact just being non-committal, something which is important in Malagasy society. Her reply makes it clear that even if the European comes after dinner, the friend will not necessarily be there. So if the European comes then and does not find the friend, he cannot feel he has been given incorrect information.[25]

Keenan and Ochs' observations involve a grammar point – double negatives. But their prime focus of interest is on a functional use of language (a 'speech act'): 'how to give information' in Malagasy. They are exploring an area of linguistics which came to the fore with the new sociolinguistic perspective. It has become known as 'pragmatics,' defined in the *OED* as 'the study of the use of linguistic signs (esp. sentences) in actual situations.' Pragmatics has much to say about grammar, but its main concern is not with the grammar system, but with how language (including grammar) is used to achieve communicative aims. This is the topic of the following chapter.

Notes

1 It is often difficult to be certain when an emphasis was intended, and this applies to the example here.
2 Rissanen (1999), p. 187.
3 Abbott (1870), sect. 304.
4 The frequency is per 10,000 words, and the data were collected from the 1998 CEEC, briefly described in 6.4.
5 Johnson (1755), p. 67.
6 Rissanen (1999), p. 242.
7 From Anthony Fitzherbert's *Book of Husbandry*.

8 Rissanen (1999), p. 241.
9 James (2008).
10 Frequency and data as in Table 6.2. See note 4.
11 Blake (2002), p. 12.
12 Vickers (2005), p. 145.
13 Hope (2003), p. 4.
14 *Ibid.*, p. 14.
15 *Ibid.*, p. 14.
16 Rissanen (1999), p. 213.
17 Hymes (1972), p. 271.
18 Figures exclude uses with *have* and *do*. Data from CEEC and Supplement.
19 Figures exclude uses with *have* and *do*. Male informants.
20 Nevalainen and Raumolin-Brunberg (2003), p. 112.
21 Lass (1999), p. 163.
22 Hope (2010), p. 142.
23 *Ibid.*, p. 158.
24 Hope (2010), p. 168.
25 Keenan and Ochs (1979), p. 150.

7 Shakespearean 'rules of use'
Pragmatics

7.1 Speech acts, and some Shakespeare examples

An Englishman who has been in China for a short while, but who speaks some of the language, meets a Chinese acquaintance in the street. The acquaintance greets him by saying, *Have you eaten? Yes, I have*, the Englishman replies. But he is puzzled. Why such a strange question? Is the acquaintance perhaps asking him out for a meal? The answer is no: the question is not an *invitation* but a *greeting*; the acquaintance is showing concern by enquiring whether the Englishman has satisfied his hunger. The question is roughly equivalent to the English *How are you?* used when two people meet. This is generally not a *request for information* either. If you treated it as such and provided a report on your health, you would be regarded as odd. You would not be following an important 'rule of use' which says that in the meeting context *How are you?* (and *Have you eaten?* in parts of China) are fulfilling the speech act of *greeting*.[1]

There are many linguistic ways in which utterances like *Have you eaten?* can be analysed. A phonetician might draw attention to the final vowel sound in *eaten* (/ə/, the vowel sometimes called 'schwa'). A grammarian's analysis could focus on the perfective aspect (*have* + past participle), pointing out the irregular participle of the verb *eat*. The sentence could also be analysed in terms of word significations. On this semantic level, the meaning of *eat* would be identified as something like 'put in the mouth and consume,' while *you*, the subject of the sentence, is referring to a person being addressed. Note that none of these analyses gives any information about the sentence's possible use as a greeting. For that we need an analysis focusing explicitly on the performance of speech acts and the rules of use associated with them. This is the concern of pragmatics. The growth of interest in this area happened partly because it was realized that it existed as a separate level of analysis, but also because it is important for effective communication. As Hymes famously put it: 'There are rules of use without which the rules of grammar would be useless'; and if you do not know these rules, communication will suffer.[2]

The *Have you eaten?* example reveals that how speech acts are expressed is not universal. In parts of China this may be an appropriate greeting form. In Tagalog (a language of the Philippines) the form can be *Where are you going?*

The appropriate answer will not be a truthful account of your movements, but a formula like *Only there*, akin to the English formulaic *Fine, thanks* in response to *How are you?* And though *How are you?* is common in Britain, there are geographical differences. *Are you all right?* is the standard greeting in some areas. There are historical differences too. Two common greeting forms today are *hi* and *hello*. These are in fact comparatively new. The first instance given in the *OED* for *hello* used in this way is dated 1827, and for *hi* it is 1862. *How are you?* makes no appearance at all in Shakespeare. Facts like these provide convincing justification for the historical study of speech acts; and understanding EModE rules of use is important if we are to understand what Shakespeare's characters are saying.

Crystal and Crystal (2002) provide plenty of detailed information on the expression of some speech acts in Shakespeare. For 'greetings,' for example, they note that a common way is to enquire about health or well being. *How fares my Kate?* asks Petruchio in *The Taming of the Shrew* (4.3.36). Odder to the modern ear yet still identifiable as a greeting is Claudius' *How, sweet Queen!* (Ham 4.7.162). 'Divine invocation' is an alternative way. *The Merchant of Venice* has *God bless your worship!* (2.2.110), and you find *God save you, Signor Gremio* in *The Taming of the Shrew* ((1.2.160). There are also 'time of day' greetings. These exist today too (*Good morning* etc.), but some Shakespearean ones are strange to us. *King Lear* has *Good dawning to thee, friend* (Oswald to Kent, KL2.2.1), and in *Timon of Athens* there is *The good time of day to you, sir* (3.6.1). Crystal and Crystal offer similar coverage for other speech acts, like 'farewells' and 'swearing.'

An important component of greeting, as well as of other speech acts, is addressing someone correctly, and in the sixteenth century there were numerous etiquette books offering guidance on the topic. Replogle (1973) is an early pragmatics study, and it focuses on forms of address in Shakespeare salutations. The etiquette book she cites is William Fulwood's 1568, *The Enimie of Idlenesse: Teaching the maner and stile how to endite, compose, and write all sorts of Epistles and Letters: as well by answer, as otherwise.* One of Fulwood's messages is: 'If we speak or write of or to our superiors, we must do it with all honour.' This will involve the use of many superlatives (*most mighty, most loyal, most worthy* and so on), while for equals these would be inappropriate. Replogle shows that the conventions can be very specific. *Dread*, for example, when applied to a person, is generally restricted to monarchs – almost always the case in Shakespeare.

As with greetings, and speech acts in general, the conventions governing how to give the correct form of address have changed over time. Hence looking back to Shakespeare from today 'we have seen insults where there are none,' Replogle says, 'and have ignored them when they exist.'[3] One of Replogle's examples illustrates how easy it can be for the modern reader to miss an insult, as well as how important forms of address were regarded. It occurs in *Henry VI, Part 2* when the rebel leader and commoner Jack Cade meets aristocratic Sir Humphrey Stafford. Cade's insult is to use *sirrah* as a form of address, a term generally used to inferiors – *Go to, sirrah*, Cade rudely tells Stafford (2H6 4.2.147).

Cade, who has given himself the pseudonym Mortimer, then decides that he is important enough to be addressed as 'Lord Mortimer.' A soldier is put to death for daring to call him just 'Jack Cade' (4.6.9), and thereafter his followers are understandably careful to refer to him as 'my lord.' On one occasion, Dick the butcher approaches Cade and says *I have a suit unto your lordship*. Cade's reply: *Be it a lordship, thou shalt have it for that word* (4.7.3).

Modern readers cannot but be aware of inappropriate forms of address used by Falstaff to Prince Hal – heir to the throne – in *Henry IV, Parts 1* and *2*. Falstaff most commonly uses the familiar *Hal*, though other (even more familiar) forms like *sweet wag* also occur. When, at the end of *Henry IV, Part 2*, Prince becomes King, Falstaff persists with his inappropriate address forms, using *King Hal, my royal Hal*, and *my sweet boy*. Critics have argued that the subsequent rejection of Falstaff by the new King is cruel. Replogle comments that it is 'a lack of understanding of the symbolic ramifications of salutations [that] has made this famous rejection scene seem to many to be precipitate, unmotivated, and even cruel.'[4]

Replogle's work is a relatively early study of historical speech acts in English. Interest in this area has increased since, and in 2008 Jucker and Taavitsainen's *Speech Acts in the History of English* appeared. Among the issues the book considers are 'promising' in Middle English (Pakkala-Weckstrom), 'requesting' in the nineteenth-century commercial community (De Lungo Camiciotti), and 'apologies' through the history of English (Jucker and Taavitsainen). One chapter dealing specifically with Shakespeare is by Busse. He focuses on directives, particularly as they occur in *King Lear*. Status is an important determiner of how directives are given, Busse shows, and the play is one in which the status of the main character – and others – goes through a number of transformations. The first part of Busse's chapter looks at the uses of the imperative for directives. Based on Blake's (2002) analysis, he notes the various imperative forms, some of which differ from PDE. Sometimes, for example, a second-person pronoun can be used. As we saw in Table 6.1, this may be the subjective form – in *Richard III* for example, when Clarence says to the Second Murderer *Come thou on my side* (1.4.269). But there are roughly an equal number of cases where the objective form is used, as in Hamlet's directive to Ophelia: *Get thee to a nunnery* (3.1.121). Another form strange (but not unknown) to modern ears is the use of a perfect auxiliary, as in Antipholus of Syracuse's directive to Dromio of Ephesus in *The Comedy of Errors* (1.2.72): *Come on, sir knave, have done your foolishness*. Busse also looks at politeness markers, noting that *please* on its own was not used in Shakespeare's time. *(I) pray (you)* and *prithee* were the most commonly found markers, and others include *an(d) it please you* and *if it please you*. In the second part of his chapter, Busse lists the directives used in some key scenes in *King Lear*. In the opening scenes, he notes, royal Lear tends to use the unadorned imperative, as befits a king to subjects. Thus we find: *Give me the map there* (1.1.37), and, to his daughters: *Tell me, my daughters* (1.1.48), then *Our eldest-born, speak first* (1.1.54). Lear's status changes over time as he moves from king to 'foolish, fond old man.' His directives become correspondingly more polite and request-like: *Pray you now forget, and forgive. I am old and foolish*, he says to Cordelia (4.7.83).

7.2 Politeness and impoliteness

'Directives' are speech acts where politeness is a particularly important concern. 'Being polite' is a major area of interest to pragmatics as a whole, including historical approaches. One study that focuses on Shakespeare is Brown and Gilman (1989), which looks at politeness strategies in *Othello, Hamlet, Macbeth*, and *King Lear*. Their study is based on the theory of politeness developed in Brown and Levinson (1987). Two main concepts used by them are positive and negative face. A working definition of positive face is that it relates to a person's desire to be appreciated. Negative face is the desire to be free of undesirable consequences, and negative politeness tries to mitigate the negative consequences of something that is said or requested. Brown and Gilman classify the positive and negative strategies Shakespeare uses in the four plays. One of their 15 positive strategies is 'noticing admirable qualities,' as when the First Senator calls Othello *brave Moor* (Oth 1.3.288), or Desdemona speaks of *thrice-gentle Cassio* (3.4.118). Another more complex strategy is to 'give reasons why [the] speaker wants what he or she does so that it will seem reasonable to the hearer.' Their *King Lear* example is when Regan says to Oswald: *Our troops set forth tomorrow: stay with us*. She adds an explanation to her request, making it sound reasonable: *The ways are dangerous*, she says (4.5.16).

One of Brown and Gilman's categories of negative politeness is not to assume that the hearer must or will comply to a request; making it seem that whether or not they comply is their choice. For example, when Hamlet's mother asks Rosencranz and Guildenstern to stay at the court for a while, her request might be regarded as tantamount to a directive – she is the Queen, after all. But she phrases it as if they have choice: *If it will please you / To show us so much gentry [courtesy] and good will / As to expend your time with us awhile* (Ham 2.2.21). Another category involves stating any potentially 'face threatening act' as an instance of a general rule, to soften the offence by making it sound less personal. So when Gloucester tells Lear that Regan and her husband are not available to speak to the former king, he says: *My dear lord, / You know the fiery quality of the Duke, / How unremovable and fixed he is / In his own course* (KL 2.4.87). 'It is nothing personal,' Gloucester is saying – 'the Duke is difficult with everyone.'

In the latter parts of their paper, Brown and Gilman consider three factors which, according to Brown and Levinson, control the degree of politeness shown in a given situation:

(a) The power relationship (P) holding between speaker and hearer. If the speaker is socially superior to the hearer, he is likely not to bother much with politeness, and might even go for the brusque imperative (much as Lear does in early parts of *King Lear*). But if the hearer is socially powerful and the speaker not, then a more polite approach will be required.

(b) The distance relationship (D) between speaker and hearer. If they know each other well and are friends, then you might expect a more informal, less polite, interaction. But if the two are strangers, politeness may be required.

(c) Ranked extremity (R). This is the degree of imposition (the 'size') of what is being considered. If you are just asking someone to lend you a pen for an hour, a large amount of politeness is not required. But if you are a young adult asking your parents to lend you several thousand pounds towards your first house purchase, then all your politeness skills will be brought into play.

Brown and Gilman's purpose is to find out whether these factors – (P), (D) and (R) – are the important determiners of politeness in the plays they are considering. Their method is to assign 'scores' to utterances according to how polite they are. So the brusque imperative would score low, and a request using *I humbly beseech you* would score high. They then identify pairs of utterances in the tragedies which differ in terms of just one of the three factors. For example, in some pairs both the distance between the interactants (D), and the (R) that is involved, are roughly the same. The only difference is the (P). In other pairs the difference will be between (D) but not (P) and (R), and so on. This enables them to see how degree of politeness (as measured by their 'scores') is related to (P), (D) and (R).

To exemplify the method used, Brown and Gilman take an exchange from *King Lear* in which Edgar, disguised as a mad beggar, meets Goneril's husband, the Duke of Albany. Edgar wishes to converse:

> Edgar: *If e'er your grace had speech with man so poor,*
> *Hear me one word.*
>
> (5.1.38)

The request is an indirect one, *your grace* shows deference; *man so poor* is self-abasing, and *one word* minimizes the imposition. So the utterance is given a high 'politeness score.' Albany's response is curt, and receives a low score: *Speak*, he says (5.1.39). In this example, the same speakers are involved, so D and R are unchanged, but the P values are very different: Edgar is a mad beggar, with no power, while Albany is a Duke, married to the King's daughter.

Brown and Gilman's results show that for the factors (P) and (R) the Shakespearean characters act as Brown and Levinson's theory predicts. Both factors are seen to be important. As regards (D), the theory predicts that more distant interactants will be more polite with each other. In fact Brown and Gilman find that 'the more the speaker likes the hearer, the greater the concern with the hearer's face and so the more polite the speech; the less the liking, the less the concern and also the politeness.'[5] Sometimes people are more polite to friends than to strangers.

The study makes an interesting observation concerning 'excessive politeness.' Sometimes, Brown and Gilman note, a character uses more politeness than a situation seems to require. In such cases, there is sometimes an 'off-record' element – something more important is being suggested than is being stated. An example is when Macbeth suggests to Banquo that they need to talk about something relatively unimportant, involving a small amount of (R). But in relation to it, Brown and Gilman say, Macbeth produces 'one of the politest speeches in the play':[6]

> *Yet, when we can entreat an hour to serve,*
> *We would spend it in some words upon that business,*
> *If you would grant the time.*
>
> (2.1.22)

The reason for this excessive politeness is that Macbeth is really asking Banquo, indirectly, whether he will be a part of the conspiracy which will involve murder. The (R) is in fact considerable.

Pragmatics is concerned with impoliteness as well as politeness. We have already seen, in 4.3.1, that Shakespeare was something of a master of abuse. In a 1996 paper, Culpeper aims to produce what he calls an 'anatomy of impoliteness,' and he uses some Shakespearean examples. One he develops at length is from *Macbeth*, where the hero thinks he sees Banquo's ghost. Lady Macbeth tries to bring him to his senses with a series of impolite remarks attacking his manhood. *Are you a man?* she says (3.4.57); *... these flaws and starts – / ... would well become/A woman's story at a winter's fire* (3.4.62); and later: *What! quite unmann'd in folly?* (3.4.72). Culpeper shows how such statements flout various politeness norms. His paper also discusses ritualized 'banter,' a form of impoliteness where superficial rudeness is often intended to reinforce group solidarity. Again Culpeper has Shakespearean examples, one being from *Romeo and Juliet* (2.4) where Mercutio and Romeo exchange insults in a contest of wits. He views such exchanges as a vestige of 'flyting' – a form of competitive ritual insulting that was common in Old Norse. Culpeper later produced a book on impoliteness (2011a), though the main emphasis there is not historical.

7.3 *Thou* and *you*

George Fox (1624–1691) was a religious dissenter, and one of the founders of the Quaker movement. As he travelled round the country preaching his dissenting views, he was often met by opposition and violent persecution. His *Journal* described what happened one December day in 1651:

> [I] came at night to an inn where was a company of rude people. I bid the woman of the house, if she had any meat, to bring me some; but because I said 'Thee' and 'Thou' to her she looked strangely on me. Then I asked her if she had any milk; and she said, No.

The woman, Fox discovered, was not telling the truth, and an altercation followed. The result was that:

> I walked out of the house and went away till I came to a stack of hay, and lay in the hay-stack that night in rain and snow, it being but three days before the time called Christmas.[7]

The reason why the woman looked strangely on Fox, and probably why she did not help him, was that he used the *thou* forms of address, instead of the *you* normally used between strangers. He was, in the woman's eyes, being impolite.

In fact Fox was acting out of principle, at a time when religious dissenters like him felt that everyone should be treated equally, and hence addressed equally too. The *you* form, used to strangers and to those regarded of high status, was seen by Fox as discriminatory and wrong. Indeed, with colleagues John Stubs and Benjamin Furley he wrote, in 1660, a pamphlet attacking the use of *you* showing (in the words of its title) *how emperors and others have used the singular word* [thou] *to one, and how the word 'you' came first from the Pope*. The use of *you*, in other words, was a wicked Papist invention.

Fox was acting on principle, but others would flout proper usage in order deliberately to insult. Thus in *Twelfth Night* (3.2.43), Sir Toby Belch is trying to goad Sir Andrew Aguecheek into having an argument with Cesario. Belch's advice: *If thou thou'st him some thrice, it shall not be amiss*; 'call him *thou* a few times,' he is saying, 'and that should do the trick.'

Clearly the uses of *thou/you* involved issues of politeness. They have indeed been much studied. Mulholland (1967), Barber (1981) and Calvo (1990) focus just on Shakespeare, and there are other studies, like Wales (1983) and Hope (1994) which look at EModE in general. Indeed, most descriptions of EModE have sections dealing with the distinction; particularly noteworthy ones being Barber (1997) and Lass (1999). Brown and Gilman (1960 and 1989) look at the pronouns in terms of sociolinguistic theory.

Mulholland (1967), along with many others, points out that it is only when one person is being addressed that the *thou/you* choice comes into operation. *You* is unequivocally the form used in the plural, when more than one person is being referred to. Mulholland looks at two plays, *Much Ado About Nothing* and *King Lear*. As we shall see later, *thou* and *you* can also express 'temporary' feelings, but Mulholland is interested in uses which show 'permanent connections between people.'[8] Social class and gender are the variables that mainly concern her. She finds 'that *you* is the generally accepted majority form of the pronoun in use in the upper classes.'[9] In the plays she looks at, she does not find evidence for *thou* prevailing between lower classes.

Brown and Gilman (1960, 1989) – who are not solely concerned with Shakespeare – use the concept of 'power' in their discussion. The word can be used to describe different social rankings between people, but also, in a family context, different statuses. Barber (1981) too looks at power, focusing on some scenes in *Richard III*. One is Act 1, Scene 4, where Clarence is murdered in the

Tower. The murderers address their social superior Clarence as *you*, while he, when talking to them singly, uses *thou*. Similarly in a family context. Crystal (2008) exemplifies with the way Lear (with the powerful status as father) addresses Goneril and Regan (less statusful as daughters). Asked to express the extent of her love for her father, Goneril says *Sir, I love you more than word can wield the matter* (KL1.1.55). Lear's response:

> *Of all these bounds, even from this line to this,*
> *With shadowy forests and with champains riched,*
> *With plenteous rivers and wide-skirted meads,*
> *We make thee lady. To thine and Albany's issues*
> *Be this perpetual.*
>
> (KL 1.1.64)

Gender is also a relevant factor. Mulholland finds find men using *thou* to women, (reflecting a perception of high to low status current at the time) while women use *you* back (as perceived low to high). This applies even with married couples. Hence in *Henry IV, Part 1* (2.3.76), we find Lady Percy saying *But hear you, my lord*, to her husband, Hotspur. His reply is *What sayest thou, my lady*. Barber (1997) states that this usage is found through the EModE period in general.

Brown and Gilman (1960, 1989) use another concept – of 'solidarity' – in their analysis. This refers to the feeling of sameness between people, emphasizing elements that they have in common. Solidarity leads to speakers using the same pronouns with each other – a reciprocal use of *thou* or *you*. As we have seen, Mulholland finds reciprocal *you* among statusful individuals. She does not find *thou* consistently used between lower-class speakers, but there are others who do. Barber, for example, notes that Clarence's murderers use *thou* to each other.

Table 7.1 shows a rather oversimplified account of *thou/you* use in relation to the status dimension.

Barber (1997), who is looking at EModE in general, also notes other special uses.

Here are some:

- to ghosts: *Go on, I'll follow thee* Hamlet says to his father's ghost (Ham 1.4.79).
- to spirits: in *Richard III* (1.2.7), Lady Anne addresses the body of her dead father-in-law thus: *thou bloodless remnant of that Royal blood*. And when Lady

Table 7.1 Use of thou/you in relation to status

high → low	*thou*
low → high	*you*
high → high	*you*
low → low	*thou*

Macbeth evokes the spirit of the night (Mac 1.5.48) she says: *Come, thick night, / and pall thee in the dunnest smoke of hell.*
- to inanimate objects: in *The Merchant of Venice* (2.9.34) the Prince of Aragon talks to the silver casket he is about to open: *Why then [I turn] to thee, thou silver treasure-house.*
- to gods: Coriolanus' friend Menenius is delighted when he hears the former is returning home: *Take my cap, Jupiter, and I thank thee* (Cor, 2.1.100).

One of the most penetrating analyses of the *thou/you* distinction is Wales (1983). She finds Brown and Gilman's account in terms of solidarity inadequate, and her treatment is particularly useful in relation to a further set of dimensions. As mentioned earlier, Mulholland confined herself to 'permanent connections between people.' There are of course other languages that have forms similar to EModE *thou* and *you*. Examples are *tu* and *vous* in French, *du* and *Sie* in German. Often the convention in these languages is to use these forms in a relatively 'stable' way: you tend to use *du* or *Sie* with a person for a protracted length of time. Change from *Sie* to *du* (and *vous* to *tu*) does happen, but this often represents a meaningful change in relationship. Indeed in both German and French there are verbs: *duzen* and *tutoyer* ('to give the *thou*') which mark the rite of passage. In English the change could be less long-lasting. As Wales (1983:114) puts it: 'in English usage, right from the beginning, there was always considerable fluctuation between ... [*thou*] and [*you*] ... forms in the singular; whereas in French and German, even today, momentary shifts are rare.' Brown and Gilman (1989:178) use the phrase 'easy retractibility' in relation to the English use of *thou*.

Many who write about the *thou/you* distinction in EModE concentrate on these fluctuations. They can mark moments of intimacy. Barber (1981) illustrates in Act 1, Scene 2 of *Richard III*, where Richard is wooing Anne, despite the fact that he killed her husband-to-be. He begins with the *you* form: *Lady, you know no rules of charity, / Which renders good for bad, blessings for curses* (1.2.68). But as Richard feels that his wooing is getting somewhere, he changes to *thou*: *Curse not thyself, fair creature* (1.2.132), he says; and, *I would I were, to be revenged on thee* (1.2.133). Other plays where there is romantic intimacy (*Romeo and Juliet*, *The Taming of the Shrew*) show similar periods of *thou* use, with 'easy retractability' – permitting a return to *you* at some point.

Amorous intimacy is not the only emotion that evokes *thou*. As Barber (1981) shows, Anne responds to Richard's *you* in his 'rules of charity' lines above, with a *thou*: *Villain, thou know'st nor law of God nor man*, she says (1.2.70). This is what Barber (p. 169) calls the '*thou* of anger and contempt.' Interestingly, when Anne begins to be persuaded by Richard, her anger and contempt lessen, and she switches to the respectful *you* form: *put up your sword*, she says (1.2.196).

Barber illustrates another example of anger and contempt in *Richard III* (1.4), when Clarence is murdered. As we saw earlier, the murderers address Clarence as *you*. But at some point they become angry with him and start to use *thou*:

> 2nd Murderer: And that same vengeance doth he hurl on thee
> For false forswearing and for murder too:
> Thou didst receive the sacrament to fight
> In quarrel of the house of Lancaster.
> 1st Murderer: And like a traitor to the name of God
> Didst break that vow, and with thy treacherous blade
> Unrip'st the bowels of thy sovereign's son.
>
> (1.4.204)

Barber also talks about a 'sardonic or contemptuous *thou*.'[10] His example is again from *Richard III*. In the first scene, Richard uses *you* to Clarence, but in his immediately following soliloquy he switches to *thou* in this chilling speech:

> *Go, tread the path that though shalt ne'er return.*
> *Simple, plain Clarence, I do love thee so*
> *That I will shortly send thy soul to heaven*
>
> (R3, 1.1.117)

Barber also discusses a 'mock polite or ironical *you*,' while Brown and Gilman (1989) give an example of a 'grateful and affectionate *thou*.' In *Macbeth*, Malcolm usually addresses Macduff with *you*. But there is a point in Act 4 (3.135) where he wants to show gratitude that Macduff has revealed himself truly against 'devilish Macbeth.' He says: *but God above/ Deal between thee and me! For even now/I put myself to thy direction.*

To what extent can shifting emotions explain changes from *you* to *thou* and vice versa? There are other, 'unemotional' factors sometimes involved. Mulholland (1967) and Barber (1997) are among those to note that *thou* and *you* are associated with different types of verb. Barber, for example, says that *thou* 'tended to be favoured before auxiliaries, and *you* before lexical verbs.'[11] It has also been suggested that the *thou/you* distinction can have a textual function. Calvo (1990) discusses this in her study on fool-master discourse in Shakespeare – one which also touches on a number of other issues discussed in this chapter. She argues that 'switching from one pronoun to another is one of the textual markers available to a speaker wanting to indicate to the addressee that their interaction is taking a new direction.'[12] Her example is from *Much Ado About Nothing*. At the beginning of 5.2 Beatrice and Benedick are flirting in their own inimitable way. Beatrice addresses Benedick with *you* and Benedick uses *thou*. But at the end of one episode of philosophical and amatory banter, Bendick abruptly changes the topic, and with it his choice of pronoun:

> *Benedick:* And now tell me, how doth your cousin?
> *Beatrice:* Very ill.
> *Benedick:* And how do you?
> *Beatrice:* Very ill too.
>
> (MA 5.2.80)

Calvo comments that in such examples,

> it is not the use of one particular pronominal form or another in a precise context that is meaningful but rather the *shift* from one pronoun to another. The shift, and not each pronominal form *per se*, performs a signalling function in the global organisation of the dramatic dialogue.[13]

Wales (1983) advocates caution in the search for emotional correlates to *thou/you* changes. Her conclusion is that from the thirteenth century onward *you/thou* shifts may 'occur within the same sentence, so that contextual changes are often hard to justify.'[14] Thus while, as we saw earlier, Lady Percy uses *you* to husband Hotspur in *Henry IV, Part 1* (2.3), she also uses over ten *thou* forms in her first speech to him in that scene (2.3.39–66). Such shifts, Wales suggests, may do no more than indicate a change in register (*you* being more formal, *thou* more informal). Wales' argument is a warning: though on some occasions there may be credible emotional explanations for the 'unstable,' retractable use of *thou*, we come to grief if we try to account for all uses in these terms.

Another conclusion Wales reaches is that overall *you* is the unmarked form, and *thou* the marked one. This is suggested by some statistics Wales gives, related to the drama of the time. They show that:

- *thou* forms are far outnumbered by *you* forms;
- momentary shifts from *you* to *thou* are more frequent than shifts from *thou* to *you*.

7.4 Implicature, and 'flouting maxims'

In his introductory book *Pragmatics*, Yule (1996) considers the sentence *The President is a mouse*. The person hearing this sentence may first try and interpret it literally – that the President is a small mammal that squeaks. The immediate conclusion is that this is not what the speaker intended. Because this literal interpretation cannot be true, the hearer is forced to search for alternative interpretations. In Yule's words: 'if someone says ... something that is literally false, the hearer must assume the speaker means to convey more than is being said.'[15] The term 'conversational implicature' is used to define the 'additional unstated meaning that has to be assumed' if a conversation is to progress.[16] One of the main areas of pragmatics is to study how conversational implicatures 'work' – how speakers and hearers attach meanings to sentences which go beyond what the words actually say.

The linguistic philosopher Paul Grice considered conversational implicature in terms of what he called the 'Cooperative Principle.' This is a statement of assumptions which participants in a conversation follow if communication is to proceed smoothly. It is stated in terms of a number of 'maxims' (Grice, 1975):

- Maxim of Quantity: be as informative as required – no more no less;
- Maxim of Quality: do not lie;

- Maxim of Relation: be relevant;
- Maxim of Manner: be perspicuous (brief, orderly, unambiguous, clear).

'Flouting maxims' is the mechanism by which we alert hearers to the presence of possible implicatures.[17] Shakespeare is discussed in the implicature literature. Here is an example which Thomas (1995) gives from *The Taming of the Shrew*.[18] Petruchio has come to ask Baptista for his daughter's hand in marriage. The daughter is the shrewish Katherina. Petruchio asks her father:

> Petruchio: And you, good sir. Pray have you not a daughter
> Called Katherina, fair and virtuous?
> Baptista: I have a daughter, sir, called Katherina.

(2.1.42)

Petruchio is asking whether Baptista has a daughter called Katherina, and also, indirectly, whether she is fair and virtuous. Baptista's reply confirms the daughter's name, but makes no mention of fairness and virtue. He therefore flouts the maxim of quantity, providing less information than requested. Petruchio will notice this of course, and it will lead him to seek implicatures. The one he will doubtless pick up is that Katherina is neither fair nor virtuous.

Coulthard (1985) looks in more detail at Shakespearean conversational implicature, particularly in relation to the remarkable scene in *Othello* (3.3) where Iago manages over the space of a few lines to persuade Othello that his wife Desdemona is being unfaithful with Cassio. At the beginning of the scene, 'Othello is perfectly happy in his marriage; at the end he has decided to murder Desdemona and Cassio.'[19]

Iago has a pragmatic problem. He wants to suggest to Othello that his wife Desdemona is being unfaithful with Cassio, whom Othello regards as a friend. Since Othello is Iago's boss, he must tread very carefully, working in very indirect ways – particularly so because Othello loves his wife dearly, and very much trusts Cassio. Iago has to rely heavily on implicature to achieve his wicked aim. One of his major strategies is a more dramatic extension of what Baptista does in *The Taming of the Shrew* example above – he fails to provide full answers to questions asked, leaving hearers to seek answers for themselves. Here, for example, Othello and Iago see Desdemona and Cassio finishing a conversation together. Perfectly innocent, perhaps, but Iago wished to suggest alternative interpretations. He does so by answers which flout the maxim of quantity:

> Iago: Ha! I like not that.
> Othello: What dost thou say?
> Iago: Nothing, my lord; or if – I know not what.
> Othello: Was not that Cassio parted from my wife?
> Iago: Cassio, my lord? No, sure, I cannot think it
> That he would sneak away so guilty-like,

>   *Seeing you coming.*
> Othello: I do believe 'twas he.

(Oth 3.3.35)

Desdemona and Othello then have a conversation in which it becomes clear that it was indeed Cassio she was talking to. A few lines later, Iago asks a question to which we, and Othello, know he already knows the answer – a further strategy for causing suspicion. This is followed by a series of questions asked by Othello, none of which Iago answers:

> Iago: My noble lord –
> Othello: What dost thou say, Iago?
> Iago: Did Michael Cassio,
>   When you wooed my lady, know of your love?
> Othello: He did, from first to last. Why dost thou ask?
> Iago: But for a satisfaction of my thought –
>   No further harm.
> Othello: Why of thy thought, Iago?
> Iago: I did not think he had been acquainted with her.
> Othello: O yes, and went between us very oft.
> Iago: Indeed!
> Othello: Indeed? Ay, indeed. Discern'st thou aught in that?
>   Is he not honest?
> Iago: Honest, my lord?
> Othello: Honest? Ay, honest.
> Iago: My lord, for aught I know.
> Othello: What dost thou think?
> Iago: Think, my lord?
> Othello: Think, my lord! By heaven, he echoes me,
>   As if there were some monster in his thought
>   Too hideous to be shown. thou dost mean something.

(3.3. 92-107)

Iago, and Shakespeare behind him, is clearly a master at the art of implicature.

Gilbert (1997) looks at 'how Shakespeare exploits the social conventions of speech to dramatic effect.'[20] He considers Grice's Maxims in detail, and shows how on many occasions Shakespeare makes his characters flout them for dramatic effect. He introduces his discussion on the maxim of quantity by saying that 'there must be an upper and lower limit to the amount of details anyone wants in a conversation.'[21] Baptista's answer to Petruchio's question, considered earlier, is 'lower than the low limit' (it says less than might be expected) and hence sets up the search for implications. In *Macbeth* 1.3, the witches' responses, or lack thereof, are similarly low in information. *Stay, you imperfect speakers, tell me more*, Macbeth implores as the witches vanish (1.3.70). Their aim, Gilbert says, is to arouse Macbeth's ambition by saying too little. One of Gilbert's examples of 'saying too much' occurs in *A Midsummer Night's Dream* when Snug, acting the Lion in the *Pyramus and Thisbe*, play feels compelled to reveal his real identity (not really a lion) so as not to frighten the ladies. He says:

> *Then know that I as Snug the joiner am*
> *A lion fell, nor else no lion's dam,*
> *For if I should as lion come in strife*
> *Into this place, 'twere pity on my life.*
>
> (5.1.219)

Unnecessary information. 'Perhaps this breach of the maxim of quantity,' Gilbert says, 'is part of the theme of reality and illusion in the play.'[22] A further example is from *Henry IV, Part 1*, when Falstaff appears for the first time, emerging from a drunken slumber. *Now, Hal, what time of day is it, lad?* are his first words. The maxim of quantity suggests a reply stating what the time is. Instead, Hal launches into a lengthy diatribe about Falstaff's character and drunken behaviour. Hal's flaunting of the maxim of quantity not only tells us a lot about the new character we have just met (Falstaff). It also touches on a number of the play's themes. Gilbert (1997) looks at Grice's other maxims and provides similar examples of Shakespearean characters flouting them.

7.5 Pragmatic noise

In 5.5 we mentioned Culpeper's proposal for a 'new dictionary,' one feature of which was that it would include items that have tended to be omitted from previous Shakespeare dictionaries. One category of such items are related to what Culpeper (2012) and Culpeper and Kytö (2010) call 'pragmatic noise.' Examples are words like *ah*, *ha*, *oh*, *um*, and *fie*. An important characteristic of pragmatic noise items is that they are not 'normal' words being used in a special context (so interjections like *dear me* and *heavens* would not count). Also they do not 'behave grammatically' – taking inflections, or having fixed positions in sentences, for example. Often they act as discourse markers, expressing what the speaker or writer's feeling or attitude is towards what they are saying. Table 5.2 showed Shakespearean examples for the word *ah*.

It may seem like an anti-climax to end the chapter with mention of words like *ah*, so devoid of 'conventional' meaning; unlike words such as 'chair,' 'house,' 'love,' 'come,' 'go,' they do not have clear referential meanings. But these '*ah*-words' are just those that pragmatics was partly set up to handle. Indeed, they may be considered as extremely important words, carrying so much information about what people are feeling and want to say. Pragmatic noise is, you could argue, right at the heart of language behaviour.

Notes

1. This example, and some of the following discussion, is taken from Johnson (2013).
2. Hymes (1972), p. 278.
3. Replogle (1973), p. 101.
4. *Ibid.*, p. 111.
5. Brown and Gilman (1989), p. 193.
6. *Ibid.*, p. 198.
7. Parker (1905), p. 62.
8. Mulholland (1967), p. 158.
9. *Ibid.*, p. 160.
10. Barber (1981), p. 170.
11. Barber (1997), p. 155.
12. Calvo (1990), p. 17.
13. *Ibid.*, p. 26. This example is used in another interesting paper on the *thou/you* distinction: Fanego (1996).
14. Wales (1983), p. 114.
15. Yule (1996), p. 128.
16. *Ibid.*, p. 128.
17. A more accurate term is 'non-observance' which, according to Grice, may be done in various ways: flouting, violating, infringing, opting out of, suspending. These are discussed in Thomas (1995), p. 64 on.
18. Thomas (1995), p. 69.
19. The quotation is from Muir (1968), and is cited by Coulthard (1985), p. 185.
20. Gilbert (1997), p. ix.
21. *Ibid.*, p. 67.
22. *Ibid.*, p. 72.

8 Original pronunciation
'Pronounced out of Ireland'?

8.1 Puns: amusing … and revelatory?

In the list of *Dramatis personae* for *As You Like It*, Jaques is sometimes described as 'a melancholy gentleman,' or 'a melancholic traveler.' He is not much prone to jollity. Wandering in Act 2 through the Forest of Arden, he meets the court jester, Touchstone. Something Touchstone says makes Jaques laugh for a whole hour – no mean feat given Jaques' dour nature. Why? What is the joke? Here is Jaques' description of the meeting; the *he* in the first line is Touchstone:

> *And then he drew a dial from his poke,*
> *And looking on it, with lack-lustre eye,*
> *Says, very wisely, 'It is ten o'clock'.*
> *'Thus we may see', quoth he, 'how the world wags:*
> *'Tis but an hour ago since it was nine,*
> *And after one hour more 'twill be eleven,*
> *And so from hour to hour we ripe, and ripe,*
> *And then from hour to hour we rot, and rot,*
> *And thereby hangs a tale.'*
>
> (2.7.20)

The joke? Kökeritz (1953) observes that the word *hour* would have been pronounced like our present-day *oar*, which would also be the way the word *whore* would have been pronounced. If you read the passage again, replacing *hour* with *whore*, it takes on a quite different, and humorous, air (and perhaps the word *tale* assumes a new dimension too).[1]

This example suggests that knowing something about how Shakespeare was pronounced (the 'original pronunciation,' or OP) can reveal wordplay that the modern reader would miss, in this case because the words *hour* and *whore* are no longer homonyms. The study of OP has become a topic of interest in recent times, but the subject also has a history, beginning more than a century ago. There are various short accounts of early work on Shakespeare's pronunciation: an entire paper on the subject (Crystal, 2013), and sections in longer books.[2] Accounts invariably make mention of an 1864 article by Noyes and

Pierce called 'Shakespearean pronunciation' which appeared in the *North American Review*. In 1865, another American, Richard Grant White, produced a version of a speech from *Hamlet* with spellings which reflected how he thought it would have been pronounced. His prediction of the readers' reaction was interesting: 'They will imagine Hamlet exclaiming "A *baste* that wants *discoorse* of *rayson*/Would *haive moorn'd* longer!" and overcome by the astonishing effect of the passages thus spoken, they will refuse to believe that they were ever thus pronounced out of Ireland.'[3] The perception that OP sounded like English with an Irish accent is a common one, and indeed Kökeritz (1953) puts forward the theory that the English brought their language to Northern Ireland, where it was not subject to sound changes that later occurred in England: hence today's Irish pronunciation of English retains features found in English Elizabethan pronunciation. A few years later (1869–89), Alexander Ellis produced his *On Early English Pronunciation*, and this included a lengthy section on Shakespeare (Ellis was the English philologist identified by Bernard Shaw as the prototype of Professor Henry Higgins of *Pygmalion*). Another scholar with an interest in OP was the German, Wilhelm Viëtor. In 1906 his *A Shakespeare Phonology* appeared. It included a comprehensive rhyme list, 150 pages long, with rhymes classified according to final sounds. Thus there is, for example, a section on /-ɪŋs/, including *brings* and *kings*, and another on /-oi/ which has *annoy* and *boy* as examples. At about the same time, the phonetician Daniel Jones' attention was also on OP. In 1909 he gave a public presentation at University College London entitled 'Scenes from Shakespeare in the original pronunciation.' A review in *The Observer* newspaper declared the effect of the pronunciation 'very pleasing,' and associated it, not with Irish, but with the 'rich dialect of the West of England, with a strong admixture of the Lancashire speech.'[4]

It might be said that the recent surge of interest in OP began with the work of Helge Kökeritz. He was a Swede, born in Gotland in 1902. He studied and worked at Uppsala University, then went to America, eventually to Yale. His interest in OP had practical outcomes, and in 1954 he coached a cast of actors at Yale for an OP performance of *The Merry Wives of Windsor*. He also made a recording of Shakespeare excerpts read in OP. His book *Shakespeare's Pronunciation* – a major landmark in the field – appeared in 1953. To map out other recent OP landmarks: four years later, the Oxford scholar Eric Dobson's two-volume *English Pronunciation 1500–1700* appeared. Though far from being focused on Shakespeare alone, it contributes significantly to our knowledge of OP, as too do other historical phonology studies of wider scope, like Lass (1999b). In 1981 the Italian scholar Fausto Cercignani produced *Shakespeare's Works and Elizabethan Pronunciation*. David Crystal is the doyen of the most recent OP studies. His substantial work in the area includes an account of how he, working with the Globe Theatre in London, helped towards an OP production of *Romeo and Juliet* (Crystal, 2005). His 2008 book on Shakespeare's language in general includes a short but informative and very accessible chapter on pronunciation. Then, in 2016, came an entire dictionary: his *Oxford Dictionary of Original Shakespeare Pronunciation*.

8.2 Why study OP

As Kökeritz's *hour/whore* example suggests, one motivation for the study and use of OP is to reveal wordplay now lost. Another revealing example which Kökeritz and others discuss involves the words *loins* and *lines*. One of the meanings of the latter word refers to 'family descent.' In OP /ɔɪ/ can be used in both words, making them homophones, pronounced /ləɪnz/. The pun gives an extra dimension to these words from the Prologue to *Romeo and Juliet*:

> *From forth the fatal loins of these two foes*
> *A pair of star-crossed lovers take their life*
>
> (Prologue, 5)

Kökeritz does not have much else to say about the motivations for OP, but there are others who do. Brook (1976) claims that the 'validity of an emendation' can be evaluated with reference to information about pronunciation, while Cercignani (1981) points out that it is not just puns, but rhymes and spellings too that can be explained by OP.[5] The Introduction to Crystal (2016) includes a discussion of motivations, and some of his examples also relate to textual details. He notes, of example, that in the First Folio, the name of the country is usually spelled *France*, and pronounced /frans/. But there are a few cases, Crystal notes, where the spelling is *Fraunce*.[6] This is often used when French is being read aloud, or when the speaker is French, suggesting that the form reflects a French native-speaker pronunciation, which Crystal gives as /frɔːns/. When, in *Henry V*, the king is wooing French Katherine, he repeats something she has just said with: *It is not a fashion for the maids of Fraunce to kisse before they are married, would she say* (5.2.262). The *Fraunce* spelling suggests that he is gently teasing her because of her French accent.

Both Brook and Crystal mention what the latter calls 'phonaesthetic effects' – 'phonaesthetics' being 'the study of the aesthetic properties of sound' (Crystal, 2008a). Crystal (2016) cites William Empson on the importance of the 'phonic dimension of text.' Shakespeare, Empson claims, was able more than any poet to 'exploit ... sensitivity to the sounds of language.'[7] OP reveals many otherwise-lost phonaesthetic effects, particularly in *The Sonnets*. One of Crystal's examples is from Sonnet 55:

> *When <u>wasteful war</u> shall statues over<u>turn</u>,*
> *And broils root out the <u>work</u> of masonry,*
> *Nor <u>Mars</u> his sword nor <u>war's</u> quick fire shall <u>burn</u>*
> *The living record of your memory.*

In RP (today's British 'Received Pronunciation'), there are four different vowel values to the underlined syllables in *wasteful*, *war*, *overturn/work* and *Mars*. But in OP *war* and *Mars* have the same vowel (/ɑː/). The vowels in *waste*, *turn* and *work*

(/a/, /ɐ/ and /ɔ:/) result in what Crystal calls 'a sequence of /a/-like vowels that adds an insistent urgency to the first and third lines.'[8]

8.3 Thirty years of OP

As we have seen, the period from 1953 till 1981 – less than 30 years – saw the publication of three major works in the field, by Kökeritz, Dobson, and Cercignani. How do these compare? One of Kökeritz's major contentions is that Shakespeare's pronunciation is closer to today's than to Chaucer's. This is because between Chaucer and Shakespeare came the Great Vowel Shift, changing the pronunciation of many vowels. After the Shift, between Shakespeare and today, no similarly major pronunciation alterations occurred. Thus anyone who thinks that Shakespeare's pronunciation was close to Chaucer's will, Kökeritz says, 'have to reconcile themselves to the fact that they would be able to understand Shakespeare ... with little effort.'[9] He also sees Shakespeare's pronunciation as advanced for its time – another reason for putting it comparatively close to today's educated southern English. Dobson and Cercignani disagree. The Great Vowel Shift had, Dobson argues, not fully run its course in the sixteenth century, so Shakespeare is not as close to RP as Kökeritz would have it. As for the advanced nature of Shakespeare's pronunciation, Dobson also shows 'that this assumption is untenable.'[10]

One of the strengths of Dobson's book is 'the extraordinary extent to which he reckons with variety in the pronunciation of early Standard English.'[11] Since it covers a far wider period than the other two books, it is has naturally less to say about Shakespeare alone, though the wider historical perspective is valuable. Cercignani's work shows the influence of Dobson; in the words of one reviewer, it is memorable for its 'rigour in examining every shred of evidence.'[12] But what kind of evidence is admissible? How do we find out what OP was like? How these important questions are answered differentiates the works we have been considering.

8.4 How we know: 'internal' evidence for OP

According to Cercignani (1981:2), 'the seeds of the major controversy between the upholders of internal evidence and the supporters of external testimony are to be found in the earliest studies.' White (mentioned in 8.1) used 'internal' evidence, from within the texts themselves – puns, spellings, rhymes and metre. But Noyes and Peirce (also mentioned in 8.1) regard such information as 'unreliable.' They concentrate on evidence external to the texts, based on what orthoepists and spelling reformers writing in the sixteenth century have to say (the *OED* gives as one definition of 'orthoepist,' 'any of a group of 16th- and 17th-century writers who sought to establish a standard pronunciation of English and usually to reform the spelling system in accordance with it'). We will look at these various types of evidence in turn. As we shall see, the internal versus external conflict continues into recent times.

8.4.1 Puns

Kökeritz's *hours/whores* and *loins/lines* examples reveal that the study of OP can expose puns otherwise hidden. OP can clearly illuminate puns. But can puns illuminate OP? Can identifying what looks like a pun say something about how Shakespeare was pronounced? An example that Kökeritz and others give is related to the word *jakes*, meaning 'latrine.' It was pronounced /dʒɛ:ks/. There are several occasions in Shakespeare where the context suggests the word is being used as a pun for two names: Jaques, and Ajax. For example, in *Love's Labour's Lost* Costard says: *Your lion, that holds his pole-axe sitting on a close-stool, will be given to Ajax* (5.2.574). Mention of *close-stool* ('chamber pot') – not to mention *pole-axe* – leads Kökeritz (1953) to comment that 'no Elizabethan would have missed this pun.'[13] It provides some evidence for /dʒɛ:ks/ as the pronunciation of 'Jaques,' and /ə dʒɛ:ks/ of 'Ajax'.

The extent of Kökeritz's interest in puns leads him to include in his book a 71-page chapter listing Shakespeare's homonymic puns. Table 8.1 gives a taste of some of these. These examples all involve words no longer homonyms in today's RP.

Both Dobson and Cercignani are critical of Kökeritz's excessive use of puns, while Schäfer describes them as 'Kökeritz's fatal Cleopatra.'[14] He shows 'unqualified enthusiasm' for them, Cercignani says, citing these lines from *The Comedy of Errors*:[15]

Table 8.1 Some Shakespearean puns. From Kökeritz (1953), Part 2

Words	Example	Pronunciation
stale/steal	Falstaff: *Tut, never fear me: I am as vigilant as a cat to steal cream.* Hal: *I think, to steal cream indeed, for thy theft hath already made thee butter.* 1H4 4.2.56	/ste:l/
ache/H	Scarus: *I had a wound here that was like a T, But now 'tis made an H.* AC 4.7.7	/tʃ/
Arden/harden = a coarse cloth	Touchstone: *Ay, now am I in Arden, the more fool I. When I was at home I was in a better place, but travellers must be content.* AYL 2.4.13	silent 'h'
Rome/room	Cassius: *Now is it Rome indeed, and room enough, When there is in it but one only man.* JC 1.2.156	/u:/
wards/words	Costard: *It is not for prisoners to be too silent in their words, and therefore I say nothing.* LLL 1.2.158	/wɔ:r/ (possibly dialectal)

> Dromio of Syracuse: Marry, sir, besides myself I am due to a woman. One that claims me, one that haunts me, one that will have me.
> Antipholus of Syracuse: What claim lays she to thee?
> Dromio of Syracuse: Marry, sir, such claim as you would lay to your horse; and she would have me as a beast – not that, I being a beast, she would have me, but that she, being a very beastly creature, lays claim to me.
>
> (3.2.81)

Kökeritz finds many puns here: *have/heave; a beast/abased; bastly/baste; claim/cleam (smear); horse/whores.* This is too much, says Cercignani.[16]

A major problem with puns as evidence is that it is often difficult to be sure that a pun is intended. Sometimes, it is true, 'plausibility in a given context' can strongly suggest the presence of a pun.[17] For example, in *The Two Gentlemen of Verona* we find the lines:

> Speed: Sir, your glove.
> Valentine: Not mine. My gloves are on.
> Speed: Why then, this may be yours, for this is but one.

This is partial evidence for /oːn/ as the pronunciation of 'one.' But often there is no certainty that a pun is there, and it may well be that Shakespeare intended a phonaesthetic effect to be created by 'partial antithesis rather than complete identity.'[18] Cercignani considers, for example, these lines from *The Taming of the Shrew*:

> That is, to watch her, as we watch these kites
> That bate and beat and will not be obedient.
>
> (4.1.181)

Here, *bate* and *beat* do not have to have the same vowel to be effective. 'Genuine homophonic puns,' Cercignani adds, 'are in reality comparatively rare.'[19] Kökeritz has 71 pages of them.

8.4.2 Occasional spelling

Another source of evidence about OP is orthographic, involving 'occasional spellings.' This is where a word is sometimes spelled in a particular way which may suggest its pronunciation; the adjective 'occasional' is used rather than 'erroneous' because spelling at the time was so varied that clear rights and wrongs could not always be identified. For example, in RP the words *century, torturing* and *ventur'd* all use the sound /tʃə/ while, Kökeritz says, the Elizabethan pronunciation was /əɹ/.[20] The spellings *centery, tortering* and *venter'd* are part of his evidence, because they suggest this pronunciation. Another example relates to variations in spelling between 'd' and 'th.' In the First Folio you find *fadom* ('fathom'), but also *fathomles; burden* as well as *burthen*, and *murder* alongside *murther*. The suggestion is that the consonant could be pronounced either /d/ and /ð/, sometimes according to phonetic context.[21]

All acknowledge that occasional spellings have associated problems. Distinguishing between significant spellings and mere misprints can be impossible. Also, there is often no way of knowing who is responsible for the occasional spelling, and hence whose pronunciation it may be reflecting.

8.4.3 Rhymes

Along with 71 pages of puns, Kökeritz (1953) also has a 96-page appendix entitled 'An index of Shakespeare's rhymes.' In these lines, for example, from *The Comedy of Errors*, *love* and *move* are rhymed:

> Adriana: With what persuasion did he tempt thy love?
> Luciana: With words that in an honest suit might move.
>
> (4.2.13)

There are, Kökeritz says, 16 *love/move* rhymes in Shakespeare, and plenty of other similar ones (like *come/doom* and *son/afternoon*).[22] The suggestion is that, unlike in today's RP, the words use the same vowels. Crystal (2016) transcribes it as /ɤ/, a sound slightly more closed than the RP [ʌ]. Another example from Kökeritz's rhyme list is *far* (/fɑːɹ/) and *war* (/wɑːɹ/). This rhyme from *All's Well that Ends Well* uses these words:

> Write, write, that from the bloody course of war
> ...
> Bless him at home in peace, whilst I from far.
>
> (3.4.9)

Both Dobson and Cercignani have more faith in rhymes as evidence than in puns. 'I have often cited rhymes,' Dobson says, 'since the intention to rhyme is usually a matter of objective fact.' But, he adds, 'there is sometimes room for doubt whether an exact rhyme was achieved.'[23] There are various sorts of 'inexact rhymes' which suggest the need for caution.[24] Eye-rhymes are where words look similar on the page, but do not rhyme, like RP *cough* and *though*.[25] Then there are half-rhymes, where words share common phonological features but need not be proper rhymes. Crystal has *dish* and *cash* as examples. Poets certainly make use of such rhyme types, but how common were they in Shakespeare's time? According to Cercignani and Crystal they were rather rare; particularly eye-rhymes because poetry in the Renaissance was largely (though by no means entirely) a matter of oral performance.

8.4.4 Metre

Metrical evidence is particularly useful for gathering information about stress. Thus Kökeritz shows that (unlike today) words ending in the suffixes *-able* and *-ible* were stressed on the first syllable, examples being *delectable* and *detestable*. This is suggested by the metre in lines like:

> Making the hard way sweet and delectable.
>
> (R2 2.3.7)
>
> And I will kiss thy detestable bones.
>
> (KJ 3.4.29)

8.5 How we know: 'external' evidence for OP

Though Kökeritz does not entirely dismiss 'external' evidence, he voices doubts about what the ortheopists have to say. They are, he says, 'inclined to recommend and describe theoretical and archaic pronunciations.'[26] On occasions he also takes pains to uncover the regional origins of ortheopists, claiming that they spoke dialects unrepresentative of standard pronunciation, and were hence unqualified to make judgements about pronunciation. Dobson's approach to sources of evidence is quite different. He does not ignore the 'internal,' but when Kökeritz was asked to produce a review of Dobson's book, he is scathing about how Dobson handles such evidence. He says: 'no writer on the history of English sounds, probably, has known less about phonetics than Dobson.'[27] External evidence is Dobson's main source. His massive work started life as a review of English writers in the 1500–1700 period concerned with spelling and pronunciation. Volume 1 is entirely dedicated to describing their work. It includes lists of grammars of foreign languages, books of shorthand systems, and rhyming dictionaries. Volume 2 is the nuts and bolts: a 'systematic phonology' of the language over the period.

John Hart was one of Dobson's external sources. He died in 1574, and was a spelling reformer whose best-known work was *An Orthographie* (1569). He is one of those whom Kökeritz dismisses as regional, claiming that his English was 'nothing but a modified form of his native Devonshire dialect' and hence not representative of the kind of English Shakespeare knew.[28] Dobson could not disagree more. For him, Hart's was well and truly the English of London.

It is worth taking a closer look at Hart's work, to illustrate the kind of sources Dobson uses. For him, Hart 'deserves to rank with the greatest English phoneticians and authorities on pronunciation.' Otto Jespersen (the celebrated Danish linguist, mentioned in 5.2.1) shared this admiration, and in 1907 produced a monograph about Hart. *An Orthographie* argues the need for spelling reform, analyses English sounds, and proposes letters/symbols to represent each orthographically. The latter part of the book is written using his own symbols and letters, and according to Dobson, 'it is this long continuous passage of phonetic writing that gives the *Orthographie* its particular value.'[29] Hart produced what Dobson calls the 'first really systematic description of the sounds of English.'[30] Here, as an example of his phonetic prowess, is his description of diphthongs:

> a joining of two vowels in one syllable keeping their proper sound, only somewhat shortening the quantity of the first to the longer quantity of the

last: which is the only diversity that a diphthong hath, from two vowels coming together yet serving for two syllables.³¹

Hart was the first to use a number of symbols. One is /ʃ/, used for the sound at the beginning of today's pronunciation of 'she.' The word was pronounced the same way in Shakespeare's day, and Hart writes it 'ʃi.' On one occasion in *An Orthographie* (as it happens a few lines before the word 'ʃi' occurs), Hart spells the words 'observation' and 'derivations' as *observasion* and *derivasions*. In RP today, we use the same 'sh' (/ʃ/) sound in these words. The fact that Hart does not write the words with a /ʃ/ suggests that the *-tion* suffix could then be pronounced /sɪən/ rather than /ʃən/. The example shows how orthoepistic evidence can be useful to determine OP. Another example from Hart is how he writes *teim tu teim* for our 'time to time.' This suggests that the pronunciation of 'time' was /təim/, and indeed this is how Crystal renders it in his 2016 *Dictionary*.

A further example from Dobson of how contemporary linguistic description can help establish OP relates to how the letter 'r' was pronounced in Shakespeare's time. Jonson's 1640 book *English Grammar* describes [r] as the 'dog's letter,' because it sounds like a growl (the Latin term was *littera canina*). Jonson provides a detailed description of how to make the sound, with 'the tongue striking the inner palate, with a trembling about the teeth. It is sounded firm in the beginning of words, and more liquid in the middle, and ends; as in *rare* and *riper*.' Here Kökeritz (1953: 314) is for once attentive to orthoepistic evidence, saying that Jonson's comments were the first hint that initial [r] was different from medial and final. Jonson is describing, Kökeritz says, 'what may well have been a trilled initial *r* sound.' Dobson (1957:326) also mentions Jonson's description, though he points out that Jonson had taken it from another source, the sixteenth-century French humanist philosopher Pierre de la Ramée (Petrus Ramus). Whatever the source, the description contributes to our knowledge of OP.

Dobson gives details of more than 50 orthoepists who provide guidance on pronunciation. A good number are after Shakespeare's time. Here are brief details of three who are near Shakespeare contemporaries:

> **William Bullokar** (c. 1520- c. 1590), born in west Sussex, produced a detailed proposal for spelling reform – his *Booke at Large Booke at Large for the Amendment of Orthographic for English speech …* (1580). He also wrote a *Bref Grammar for English* (1586) which can lay claims to being the first published grammar of English.

A problem which all spelling reformers faced was that proposals often involved the introduction of many unfamiliar letters or symbols, to differentiate sounds. Bullokar's proposals involved the use of many diacritics, which detracted from the popularity of his new system.

> **Richard Mulcaster** (1531–1611). He was born in Carlisle, and studied at both Cambridge and Oxford. He became a teacher, and eventually headmaster at Merchant Taylors' School (Middlesex), then St Paul's School

(London). His book, *The First Part of the Elementarie* (1582), discussed the subject matter suitable for elementary education, looking in detail at the topics of reading and writing. He also wanted to contribute to attempts to elevate English to the status of Latin.

Mulcaster was, Dobson says (117), 'one of the greatest English pedagogues.' He tries to lay down standard spellings, and he develops a spelling system that did not involve the introduction of new symbols. But the book was long and hence expensive – it includes a list of 8,000 'hard words' – and this restricted its success.

Alexander Gil (1565–1635) was born in Lincolnshire, and studied at Oxford. He became a schoolmaster, then headmaster at St Paul's School London (following on from Mulcaster). Milton was one of his pupils. His main publication was *Logonomia Anglica* (1619). It was written in Latin with the aim of teaching English to foreigners. There was a section on grammar, as well as a phonetic system of spelling. This system had the advantage of not departing too much from standard orthography, though he did revive the Old English letters ð and þ for the two sounds of 'th.' He also used the symbol /ŋ/.

Dobson (p. 131) comments: 'Of all the reformed systems of spelling which were suggested in the sixteenth and seventeenth centuries none deserved to succeed more than that of Alexander Gil.'

8.6 Some Shakespearean sounds

What do these various forms of evidence show? What was Shakespearean pronunciation like? Just a few (and by no means all) salient features are here described, with the focus on areas where there are differences from today:

Vowels and diphthongs:

- Today's /ʌ/ (as in RP 'love': /lʌv/) was pronounced with the more closed vowel /ɤ/. So 'love' was /lɤv/.
- Some sounds which are diphthongs in RP were pronounced as long vowels:

RP vowel	example word	OP vowel	OP word pronunciation
/eɪ/	'say'	/e:/	/se:/
/əʊ/	'both'	/o:/	/bo:θ/
/ɪə/	'here'	/i:/	/i:ɹ/
/ɛə/	'fair'	/ɛ:/	/fɛɹ/
/aʊə/	'hour'	/o:/	/o:ɹ/ The same pronunciation as in 'whore,' as discussed in 8.1.

- But OP was not diphthong free. The common first element was the central vowel /ə/. Thus both RP /aɪ/ and RP /ɔɪ/ were /əɪ/ in OP. So 'lines' and 'loins' were both /ləɪnz/. Other diphthongs:

  Today's /aʊ/ was /əʊ/. So our 'now' was /nəʊ/
  Today's /ɔɪ/ was /əɪ/. So our 'boy' was /bəɪ/.

Consonants

- There is uncertainty about the pronunciation of 'r.' Before a vowel it was pronounced rather as today, though a trilled version was possible. The phonetic symbol is /r/. In RP it is not pronounced after a vowel ('car': /kɑː/). In OP this post-vocalic 'r' is pronounced rather as today in the English West Country or in America. The phonetic symbol used is /ɹ/. A word which shows both forms is /rɛːɹ/ ('rare').
- Today /h/ can be dropped in unstressed, but not in stressed, positions. OP could have it dropped in stressed positions also. Hence /iːɹ/ ('here'), and /and/ ('hand').
- Some speakers pronounced our /ʃ/ as /sɪ/, in words like 'suspicious' and 'pensioner.' Crystal (2016) renders these /səspɪsɪəs/ and /pɛnsɪənəɹ/.
- Like Scottish speakers today, words beginning with 'wh' were pronounced with an initial aspiration. This is written phonetically as /ʍ/ or /hw/. Thus 'which' is /ʍɪtʃ/, and 'what' is /ʍɑt/.

8.7 OP performances

We have seen that even the early writers on OP, like Richard Grant White and Daniel Jones, put their OP thoughts into practice through public performances. Kökeritz's 1954 performance of *The Merry Wives of Windsor* at Yale has already been mentioned. Crystal (2016) lists other early performances. A major performance milestone was the opening of London's reconstructed Globe Theatre in 1997. Its ethos supported original practices of many kinds – costumes, sets, acting styles; so 'original pronunciation' was in tune with its objectives. In 2004, The Globe staged an OP production of *Romeo and Juliet*, in which Crystal was centrally involved. It had a run of just three days, in a season which also included non-OP performances of the play. A full-length run of OP *Troilus and Cressida* followed. Then America became interested. There was a 2010 *Midsummer Night's Dream* in Kansas, a 2011 *Hamlet* in Nevada, a 2012 *Cymbeline* in Oregon, followed by *Julius Caesar* in Texas, *Twelfth Night* in Minneapolis and *The Merchant of Venice* in Baltimore. OP returned to the London Globe in 2014 with a *Macbeth*, and a 2015 *Henry V*.[32] OP recordings have also been produced, including Ben Crystal's 2012 *Speeches and Scenes Performed as Shakespeare Would Have Heard Them*.

Crystal (2005) provides an informative and entertaining account of the 2004 production of *Romeo and Juliet*, including a chapter summarising evidence sources. He describes how the project came into existence, how the play was rehearsed, how performed, how received by audience and actors. Here are some of his observations:

In rehearsal

- Actors were not looking forward to the experience, and displayed 'varying symptoms of panic.'
- The sound causing most difficulty was the OP /oː/ as in /noːn/ ('none'). /əɪ/ was also troublesome; /ləɪk/ tended to come out as Irish 'loike.'
- As actors became familiar with OP, they occasionally used it to communicate with each other outside the script. Crystal: 'When people start to play with an accent or dialect, then they truly can be said to own it.'[33]

In and after performance

- The audience seemed to like the performance, and applause at the end was more than on other days (when the non-OP performance took place). Particularly encouraging was the enthusiasm of children in the audience, possibly because the speech was less 'formal' that the usual RP they associated with Shakespeare performances.
- Because of features like an increase in elisions, the OP performances were about 10 minutes shorter than the non-OP ones. The faster rhythm affected interactions between characters.
- Characters like the Nurse and Juliet felt that the pronunciation 'toughened them up' and made them sound more down-to-earth. Crystal is unable fully to explain this. Possibly the departure from formal-sounding RP?
- Shakespeare's word play came across less as an intellectual exercise, and more as a pleasure. Said one actor: 'It was more about enjoying making sounds – sounds that complicated one another, echoed one another, matched one another.'[34]

8.8 Crystal's 2016 *Dictionary*

Crystal's *Oxford Dictionary of Original Shakespearean Pronunciation* (2016) is without doubt the crowning glory of the recent OP movement. Focused on one electronic edition of the First Folio (the Bodleian Library edition), it was ten years in preparation. It provides a useful resource to anyone interested in the field, but is mainly directed at those aiming to stage OP performances.

Entries provide various sorts of information, going well beyond what 'normal' dictionaries contain. To illustrate, Figure 8.1 gives the entry for a word we considered in 8.1: *hour*. The example shows that entries list inflected forms (~'s, ~s and ~s' in this case). Pronunciations are then given, including alternatives. One of the pieces of information which, Crystal says, took a long time to collect, relates to the frequencies of various spellings ('sp' in Figure 8.1); in this case the numbers show that *houre* is the most frequent. Then come rhymes ('rh'), with locations given for the occurrence of each. Puns are also listed – and for *hour*

hour / ~'s/ ~s/ ~s' *n*
ɔːɹ, ɔːəɹ [/ *syll*] / -z
  sp houre²⁴⁵, hower⁸, howre⁴³,
  howr's [hour is]¹ / houres⁹, howres²
  / houres⁹⁷, hours³, howers¹,
  howers²³ / houres²
  rh bower *MND 3.2.8*; deflower,
  power *Luc 347*; flower, power *LC 72*;
  flower *AY 5.3.27, PP 13.6, TN 2.4.39*,
  VA 1187; Glendower *1H4 1.3.99*;
  power *3H6 4.1.147, S 126.2, Tim*
  3.1.63, WT 4.1.8; sour *S 57.5*; four *LLL*
  5.2.368; sycamore *LLL 5.2.90* /
  flowers *LLL 4.3.355, PP 14.26, S 16.5*;
  powers *Luc 297*; showers *S 124.10*;
  towers *Luc 944*
  pun *AY 2.7.24ff* whore
  > half-, marriage-hour; after-hours

Figure 8.1 The entry for the word *hour* in Crystal (2016)

this makes mention of the homophone *whore* that made gloomy Jaques laugh so much. The final line in Figure 8.1 shows cross references to words with the same pronunciation, in this case, all compounds involving the headword *hour*. The book also has a lengthy Introduction giving information on types of evidence used, plus a history of OP. There is also an associated website, accessible to those who have a copy if the book. Again, the resources provided are impressive. There are audio files pronouncing all entries in the dictionary, including inflected forms. There is also a complete list of rhymes and half-rhymes. Access to the Bodleian Library First Folio, used in producing the *Dictionary*, can also be gained through the site.

In the book's Introduction, Crystal mentions that presentations have already been made of period texts other than by Shakespeare, including John Donne. The work of composers like John Dowland and William Byrd have also been performed in OP.³⁵ Crystal was doubtless wise to restrict his *Dictionary* to Shakespeare's First Folio, but it does seem likely that in the future the scope of OP will extend further to include a greater number of writers and composers. Then there are, of course, the OPs of other ages to be explored. It seems likely that the study of past pronunciations has a healthy future.

Notes

1 Kökeritz (1953), p. 58.
2 Including Kökeritz (1953) and Cercignani (1981). The account in this section owes much to the Introduction in Crystal (2016).

3 Cited in Crystal (2016), p. xxxii.
4 *Ibid.*, xxxv.
5 Cercignani (1981) p. viii.
6 *Ibid.*, xxxi.
7 Empson (1930), p.88, cited in Crystal *Ibid.*, xxxix.
8 Crystal (2016), p. xxvii. This section considers just some of the motivations that have been discussed, in Crystal (2016) for example.
9 Kökeritz (1953), p. 6.
10 Cercignani (1981), p. vii.
11 Ekwall (1958), p. 305.
12 Schäfer (1985), p. 420.
13 Kökeritz (1953), p. 91.
14 *Ibid.*, p. 420.
15 Cercignani (1981), p. 11.
16 *Ibid.*, p. 12.
17 *Ibid.*, p. 12.
18 *Ibid.*, p. 14.
19 *Ibid.*, p. 14.
20 Kökeritz (1953), p. 271.
21 The /d/,/ð/ variation is discussed by Kökeritz, Dobson, Cercignani, and Crystal (2016). The examples are Cercignani's.
22 *Ibid.*, p. 242.
23 *Ibid.*, p. vii.
24 The phrase is from Crystal (2016), p. xxiii.
25 The examples are Crystal's.
26 *Ibid.*, p. 18.
27 Kökeritz (1961), p. 156.
28 Kökeritz (1953), p. 245. Cited by Dobson (1957), p. 87.
29 *Ibid.*, p. 63.
30 *Ibid.*, p. 73.
31 *Ibid.*, p. 74.
32 Information about performances is taken from Crystal (2016).
33 Crystal (2005), p. 117.
34 *Ibid.*, p. 146.
35 Crystal (2016), p. xii.

9 'Multifarious liberty and gay individualism'

Shakespeare in print

9.1 Variation in spelling and punctuation

This book is about William Shakespeare. Or is it Shackspeare? Or Shakspeare? Or Shaxpeare, Shakspeyr, Shackesper, Shagspere, Shaxspere, Shakysper, Shackspere, Shackespeare, Shakespear, Shakespere, Shaxper, Shakspere, Shackespere, Shexpere, Shacksper, Shaksper, Shaxpere, Shakyspere?

All these spellings of Shakespeare's name – and more besides – have been attested;[1] that which we call a rose by any other word would indeed smell as sweet!

Elizabethan spelling is nothing if not variable. The 'contents' page of the First Folio lists *The Tragedy of Hamlet*, while elsewhere in the volume the play is called *The Tragedie of Hamlet*. The first item under 'Histories' on the same contents page has *The Life and Death of King John*, but the second item prefers a lower case for *death* (while keeping it for *Life*): *The Life and death of Richard the ſecond*. In Act 2, Scene 1 of *The Merry Wives of Windsor* you find *in mee* in one line, and *boorded me* in the next. The first line of the celebrated sonnet 18 is *Shall I compare thee to a Summers* day; line 4 begins *And Sommers lease* ... Nor is Shakespeare's the only name to show spelling variation. In Act 1 of *The Two Gentlemen of Verona* we read about *Eglamoure*, while in Act 4 it is *Eglamore*. Crystal (2016) which, it will be recalled from 8.8, notes spellings as well as pronunciations, has our 'Machiavel' sometimes as *Macheuile*, sometimes *Macheuill* and sometimes *Machiuell*.

Punctuation is also variable. According to Salmon (1986), the way the ends of quatrains in the sonnets are marked vary according to the compositor (who arranged the type for printing) involved.[2] As we shall see later, exclamation and question marks were often interchanged, and colons as well as full stops could mark the ends of sentences. Though it may seem strange to compare dress fashions with commas and full stops, this is exactly what one Austrian Shakespearean scholar does. In Elizabethan times, Flatter (1948) says:

> people strutted about displaying bright colours in their doublet and hose, wearing feathers in their hats and rings in their ears: everyone who wanted to show his importance sported his own fashion and style not only in his

clothes but in everything else – and something of that multifarious liberty and gay individualism is mirrored in the Elizabethan punctuation.[3]

The idea is fanciful, and the reasons for variation are more mundane. One is that the language was in a state of flux, with conventions not yet established. Another is the number of hands involved in the transmission of texts – from author through scribe, prompter/producer, compositor, to editor. To maintain Flatter's fanciful image, we might indeed say that each of these characters had their own individual feathers in their hats and rings in their ears.

9.2 Spelling, and graphology

9.2.1 'Old-spelling' editions

As we have seen a number of times in this book, 'going back to originals' has been a recurring theme over the centuries. It is not surprising that the issue of 'original spelling' (or 'old-spelling' – OS – as it is sometimes called) should raise its head at some point. It was pushed to the fore by the Malone Society. Named after Edmond Malone (1741–1812; he was mentioned in 2.4 and elsewhere), the Society was founded in 1906 'for the purpose of producing accurate copies of the best editions of early plays.'[4] By the end of 1907, six editions had been produced, including plays by Peele and Greene. The number of volumes, all using OS, has increased annually.

Another source of OS texts are facsimiles, and these have grown in number since the invention of photography. Shakespeare's First Folio has been a common subject, and between 1866 and 1954 five photographic First Folios were produced. A problem which the production of photographic facsimiles faces is 'show-through,' where the letterpress for one side of a page comes through the paper and makes the other side of the page difficult to read. The American academic, Charlton Hinman, wrote a book entitled *The Printing and Proof-Reading of the First Folio of Shakespeare* (1963), and this made him an ideal person to produce another facsimile. His was a facsimile with a difference, because he had access to Washington's Folger Shakespeare Library, which owned no fewer than 82 copies of the First Folio (out of a total of 233 surviving). Hinman's was 'the first facsimile in which every page had been selected from among a large number of copies in an attempt to find a clean, clear example with a minimum of show-through.'[5] His facsimile (known as the Norton Facsimile after the publisher's name) was therefore a composite of various First Folios. It appeared in 1968, and there was a second edition in 1996.[6]

In the context of these developments – the Malone Society texts and the photographic facsimiles of the First Folio – debate regarding 'old versus modernized' spelling arose. It was started by an English scholar, John Russell Brown. He produced a modernized spelling version of Webster's works, and in a 1960 article, he attacked the OS versions of plays that were becoming increasingly popular. He distinguishes two types. There are the 'facsimile reprints' that we have been discussing. He describes in great detail a number of problems with these, including 'show-through,' pointing out that even with photographs it is often difficult to recognize what is truly original. But he reserves his full ire for what he calls the 'old-spelling critical editions,' where editors make judgements regarding what are *bone fide* old-spellings, sometimes with little justification: 'as soon as a reader of a modern old-spelling edition puts his faith in any single spelling as due to his author, he is making assumptions which cannot be warranted without recourse to further evidence …'[7] Particularly dangerous is an editor's desire to create that vaguest of things, a 'Renaissance flavour,' by introducing quaint and old-seeming spellings (of the 'Ye Olde Sweet Shoppe' variety). Such a practice, Brown says, 'can do no service to the original authors.' Given the many problems associated with attempting to recreate original old-spelling, Brown argues that it might be advisable to go for a modernized spelling text, a 'kind of edition which dispenses with the risky impression of the "real" thing.'[8]

Another Brown, Arthur this time, writes a rejoinder. He starts by declaring vested interests, as a member of the Council of the Malone Society and editor of an OS edition of the dramatist John Heywood. Not surprising then that his argument is in favour of 'old-spelling critical editions.' He accepts that no version, not even photographic facsimile, will produce reliable original spelling. Indeed, he says, 'photographic reproduction is … the most dangerous thing of all, for the very method of producing it and its "likeness" to the original lull him [the textual student] into a sense of false security.'[9] Total originality is impossible, and editorial intervention is almost inevitable in any attempt to produce OS. But in his view this does not decrease the value of attempts to capture its spirit. His final sentence is: 'I shall continue to rely on my Malone Society edition and my critical old-spelling editions, confident that in these I shall find editorial responsibility of a high order.'[10]

The general editor of the Malone Society publications, Walter Greg, puts the case for OS particularly robustly and succinctly. 'To print *banquet* for *banket*, *fathom* for *faddom*, *lantern* for *lanthorn*, *murder* for *murther*, *mushroom* for *mushrump* … is sheer perversion.'[11]

But for Stanley Wells, it is Greg who shows 'sheer perversion.' In 1978, Oxford University Press established a Shakespeare department to undertake the preparation of new Shakespeare editions. Wells was to be the General Editor, and the decision was made early on to modernize spelling (though as we shall see in the next section, an original-spelling edition was also produced). He was aware that little effort had previously been given to establishing principles which would guide how modernization should be managed. Thus in preparation for his editorial duties, he decided to articulate these principles. The result was Wells and Taylor's 1979 book, *Modernizing Shakespeare's Spelling*. In the first part of the book, Wells explains the decision to modernize, and argues against the 'conscious conservation of archaic and obsolete spellings,' which often appear simply eccentric and obscure.[12] He distinguishes different types of variation. One category, which he calls 'semantically indifferent variations,' are where two forms show no difference in etymology or sense. The examples given above from Greg – including *banket* and *blanket*, *fathom* and *faddom* – are of this type. Wells' view is that 'when there is no distinction in meaning, it seems right ... to use the standard rather than the archaic form.'[13] This holds even when an archaic form is thought to represent an original spelling: 'to retain some spellings simply because the editor regards them as aurally preferable,' he witheringly remarks, 'is like playing occasional notes of a Beethoven sonata on a fortepiano while the rest are played on a modern grand piano.'[14]

Wells also looks at 'semantically significant variants.' Sometimes modern variants like *metal/mettle* are used without distinction in Shakespeare. In such cases, Wells feels that the modern editor should reflect the PDE distinction. But there are also cases where Shakespeare has distinctions which are no longer made today. For example, he often uses the word *enow* as the plural of *enough*. Thus in *Anthony and Cleopatra* Lepidus speaks of Anthony having *evils enow to darken all his goodness* (AC 1.4.11). Here, Wells is in favour of using the modern form only, replacing *enow* with *enough*. Sometimes, spelling decisions can reflect important aspects of a play. Wells argues that according to some scholars, the location of *As You Like It* is 'more firmly in France than has been supposed.'[15] This might lead an editor to have *Ardenne* rather than *Arden*, and to speak of *de Bois* rather than *de Boys*.

Wells and Taylor (1979) also contain three papers by Taylor about the text of *Henry V*. Two versions of the text are available. The one editors usually use is in the First Folio of 1623. But there is also an earlier Quarto dated 1600. It is less full and accurate, and editors often ignore it. Taylor wishes to establish whether any attention should be given to the Quarto version. His essays are exemplaries of close textual analysis. They are not chiefly concerned with spelling differences, though sometimes, as with Wells' *As You Like It* example, Taylor shows how close attention to textual differences can have important consequences. For example, in both the Quarto and Folio of *Henry V* Act 3, Scene 5, the King of France orders some of his entourage to proceed to Agincourt. But he tells the Dauphin, in no uncertain terms, to stay with him in Rouen (3.5.64). In the Folio, the Dauphin in fact turns up in Agincourt (3.7). In the Quarto, on the other hand, it is not the Dauphin but the Duke of Bourbon who is at Agincourt, delivering the Folio's Dauphin lines. Taylor debates the 'Dauphin versus Bourbon' issue, one of the possibilities being that Shakespeare himself had a change of mind, deciding that it would be a good idea to have the Dauphin present at Agincourt. In his conclusion Taylor says that 'future editors of *Henry V* ... will have to decide whether Bourbon or the Dauphin appears at Agincourt.'[16]

9.2.2 The Oxford original-spelling edition

The major Shakespeare spelling event of the twentieth century was doubtless the original-spelling edition of Shakespeare's complete works. It appeared in 1986 under the general editorship of Wells and Taylor. Like Hinman, they use various sources in an attempt to arrive at the most reliably original copy. Sometimes this is the First Folio, in the case of *As You Like It* for example. On other occasions they use a Quarto, as for example for *The comicall History of the Merchant of Venice*. Often they have one main source, but add material from another. For example, their *The Tragedie of King Richard the second* is based on the 1597 first edition, with material also from the First Folio. In most cases the differences between various texts are small and local, but in one case, they are so great that Wells and Taylor include two versions of the play: *The Historie of King Lear* (based on the 1608 Quarto), and *The Tragedie of King Lear* (based on the First Folio).

Wells and Taylor's edition includes an essay by Vivian Salmon entitled 'The spelling and punctuation of Shakespeare's time' (1986). Even more detailed is Salmon's 1999 chapter 'Orthography and punctuation' in Lass (1999), covering the whole Early Modern English period, and not just Shakespeare. Chapters 3 and 4 of Crystal (2008) also provides detailed description, as do some (though by no means all) books dealing either with Early Modern English in general (like Görlach, 1991), or with Shakespeare in particular (like Blake, 2002).

Salmon's (1986) essay provides useful background to the historical position of English and how it contributed to orthographical variation. Until the fifteenth century, official documents, she says, were written in Latin or French. Henry V, who reigned from 1413 to 1422, did much to support English, and during his time the central Midland dialect became accepted as the norm, thus providing a degree of standardization. The introduction of printing – Caxton set up his printing press in 1476 – did much to foster standardization, but this took a long time to occur, one reason being that foreign compositors were brought over from the continent, and they were unfamiliar with English and its spelling conventions. Salmon describes other attempts at standardization. There was a 1530 spelling manual, existing now in fragments and involving the printer John Rastell. Later in the same century, there were the efforts (mentioned in 8.5) of spelling reformers like John Hart, William Bullokar and Richard Mulcaster.

9.2.3 *The First Folio, and some graphology*

What were the variations in spelling that occurred in Shakespeare texts, and how did Elizabethan writing differ from today's? Here is a passage that will help answer these questions. It is a celebrated speech of Prospero's, from the First Folio of *The Tempest*. It contains examples of a good number (though not all), of the writing points we shall be considering:

> Pro.Ye Elues of hils, brooks, stãding lakes and groues,
> And ye, that on the ſands with printleſſe foote
> Doe chaſe the ebbing-*Neptune*, and doe flie him
> When he comes backe: you demy-Puppets, that
> By Moone-ſhine doe the greene ſowre Ringlets make,
> Whereof the Ewe not bites: and you, whoſe paſtime
> Is to make midnight-Muſhrumps, that reioyce

> To heare the ſolemne Curfewe, by whoſe ayde
> (Weake Maſters though ye be) I haue bedymn'd
> The Noone-tide Sun, call'd forth the mutinous windes,
> And twixt the greene Sea, and the azur'd vault
> Set roaring warre: To the dread ratling Thunder
> Haue I giuen fire, and rifted *Ioues* ſtowt Oke
> With his owne Bolt: The ſtrong baſs'd promontorie
> Haue I made ſhake, and by the ſpurs pluckt vp
> The Pyne, and Cedar. Graues at my command
> Have wak'd their ſleepers, op'd, and let 'em forth
> By my ſo potent Art. But this rough Magicke
> I here abiure: and when I have requir'd
> Some heauenly Muſicke (which euen now I do)
> To worke mine end vpon their Senses, that
> This Ayrie-charme is for, I'le breake my ſtaffe,
> Bury it certaine fadomes in the earth,
> And deeper then did euer Plummet found
> Ile drowne my booke.   *Solemne muſicke.*
> *Heere enters Ariel before: Then Alonſo with a franticke geſture, attended by* Gonzalo. Sebaſtian *and* Anthonio *in like manner attended by* Adrian *and* Franciſco: *They all enter the circle which* Prospero *has made, and there ſtand charm'd: which* Proſpero *obſerving, ſpeakes.*
>
> (5.1.33–55)

Here are some of the passage's graphological points discussed in Salmon (1986) and elsewhere; one of the *OED* definitions for 'graphology' is 'the study of written and printed symbols and of writing systems':

ſ and s – Both 'long s' (ſ) and 'short s' forms are used. The former is like our letter 'f' but without the 'nub' (crossbar) on the right-hand side; in italics it appears as *ſ*. It comes from the informal handwriting system used in ancient Rome, called 'old Roman cursive,' where its form was *ſ*. In general this 'long s' was not found at the ends of words, where the *s* form was used (hence *brooks* in the Prospero passage), as it was also for a capital (the passage has *Sences*). Occasionally the short *s* does occur medially (within a word), next to an f or as the second element of a double 's.' So instead of ſſ you occasionally find ſs (*baſs'd* in the Prospero passage). This was to do with the printer's necessity to adjust the spaces between letters (called 'kerning'). The long 's' disappeared from English printing in around 1800, though it continued to be used in handwriting for some time thereafter.

u and v – In classical Latin, *u* and *v* were orthographic variants, and either could be used to represent both the consonant and the vowel. The convention developed of using *v* at the beginnings of words, and *u* elsewhere. This is what our passage shows (*vp* versus *Elues*). The consonant/vowel distinction which we have today first occurred in the 1630s. Thus in the last published play with a

'Liberty and individualism' 139

Shakespeare contribution, *Two Noble Kinsmen* (1634), you find *under* (2.2.619), while in the 1623 First Folio, in *A Midsummer Night's Dream* for example, you find *vnder*. But even at the time of Johnson's *Dictionary* (1755), there is no head-letter *U*, and words beginning with *u* (like *use*) are included under the head-letter *V*. So the entries for *uttermost* and *vulgar* appear on the same page.

i **and** *j* – Today *i* and *j* also show a vowel/consonance distinction. *j* is not found in classical Latin, although (for reasons of legibility) it was used as a Roman numeral when the last element in a sequence of 'i's; so three was iij. *j* was rare in Early Modern English. In Shakespeare there is one example of the 'Roman numeral' use: in the First Folio version of *Love's Labour's Lost* (1.2.35) you find *I haue promis'd to study iij yeres with the Duke*. There are no other *j*s in the Folio, except for the expression *Scotch ijgge* that occurs twice in as many lines in *Much Ado About Nothing* (2.1.65–6), both in Folio and Quarto. Elsewhere the word is written *iigge* (in *Love's Labour's Lost* 3.1.10 for example). As our passage shows, we otherwise find *i* for our *j* – *Ioues* for *Jove's* for example. As with *u/v*, our *i/j* distinction came in the seventeenth century, and in the late-published *Two Noble Kinsman*, you do find it occurring. There, you have *judgement* (1.1.200), while in the First Folio *Midsummer Night's Dream* (1.1.57) the word is *iudgement*. Again as with *u/v*, *i* and *j* appear under the same head-letter ('I') in Johnson's *Dictionary*.

~ and & – The tilde (~) is often used by printers as a space-saving device. It indicates a following missing letter, usually an *m*, or *n*, and occurs only over the vowels *a*, *e*, *o*, and *u*. Generally it is found in lines where there is a reason to save space – commonly a 'justified' line. Its use goes back at least as far as the 1068 Domesday Book, and it went out of fashion in the mid-seventeenth century. Occurrences in the First Folio are rare, but our first line contains one: *stãding*. The same line also has an ampersand (meaning 'and'), much more common in Elizabethan texts.[17]

9.2.4 Some spellings

There are differences between Elizabethan and modern spelling, but there is also much overlap. According to Crystal (2008), roughly 70 per cent of spellings in the First Folio are as in modern English.[18] There are just five old-spelling features that, he says, because of their frequency, may make spelling in Shakespeare texts seem alien to the modern reader. Here are four of them; the fifth – the use of an apostrophe to replace an *e* – will be discussed later under punctuation (9.3.4):

(a) The presence or absence of a final –e.

In just the first four lines of our Prospero passage, there are four examples of words ending in *e* which would have no final *e* in modern English – *printleſſe*, *foote*, *doe* and *backe*. In her discussion of the final *e*, Salmon (1986) notes that it is often functionless. Sometimes, she says, it is a remnant from an earlier form of the language. The Middle English verb *walken* ('to walk'), for example, over time became *walke*. The final *e* was pronounced until about 1400, then it disappeared from speech but remained in the spelling. On many occasions, there is no linguistic reason at all for the final *e*, and this applies to some words in our passage. Salmon notes that sometimes a final *e* is added to words that would otherwise be just two letters long, and she speaks of 'a preference for a minimum of three which still survives in Modern English.'[19] The passage has *doe*; others, common in Shakespeare texts, are *bee*, *hee*, and *mee* for our *be*, *he*, and *me*.

There is a further use of final *e*, Salmon says, that is far from functionless, and it came into use in the sixteenth century. The letter can indicate that a preceding vowel should be pronounced as a long vowel or a diphthong. It still does this today: compare our *hat* with *hate*, *mad* with *made*, *not* with *note*, *strip* with *stripe*. Because of its effect on the nature of the preceding vowel, modern-day spelling teachers sometimes talk about the 'magic *e*.' The *e* in EModE could be equally magical, and in fact two of the word-pair examples above (*mad/made* and *strip/stripe*) are also given by Mulcaster, whose description of the *e* comes close to calling it magic. It is, he says, a 'letter of maruellous vse in the writing of our tung' because it 'sometime altereth the vowell.'[20]

(b) The use of double instead of single consonants

Another spelling feature which sometimes has a similar function to the 'magic *e*' is the doubling of consonants, common in Shakespeare texts. Salmon's examples include *sitt*, *pitty* and *dogge*.[21] There are no examples in the Prospero passage, at least of words where you do not find similar doubling in modern English. This doubling came to mark the preceding vowel as short, a function that can be seen in modern-day pairs like *sitting* with *siting*. Notice that above we used *mad* and *made* as examples of the 'magic *e*.' If there were a word *madde* in modern English, we would doubtless pronounce the vowel as short (as in *mad*), despite the final *e*. This would be because of the double consonant. But, as with the *e*, consonant doubling was often functionless, particularly at the end of words, like *satchell* and *woefull*. This unnecessary repetition was lamented by reformers like Mulcaster. He complains about 'the dubling of consonants at the end of a word ... and a thousand such ignorant superfluities.' Mulcaster's rather quaint theory claimed that it was 'the swiftness of the pen sure, which can hardly stay upon the single ending *l*, that causeth this doubling'; the pen just cannot stop.[22] Lass (1999a) says the doublings were often just 'typographical decorations.'[23]

There is another kind of consonant doubling that does occur in our passage, in *Magicke* and *franticke*. According to Salmon, such *c+k* sequences continued until the early nineteenth century.[24] They are still found today in words ending with *c*, before inflections beginning with a vowel. Thus modern English *frolic*, but *frolicking*.

(c) The use of *ie* instead of *y* at the end of words

Using *ie* for our final *y* was very common in EModE. There are two examples in the Prospero passage: *flie* and *promontorie*. Once again Mulcaster has something to say about it: 'When ... *i* is it self the last letter ... it is qualified by the *e*, as *manie, merie* ... where the verie pen, will rather end in the *e*, then in the naked *i*.'[25] Of course, there are occasions in modern English when we add a suffix to a word ending in *y*, which then becomes *ie*. So we 'change' *y* to *ie* when we add an *s* to it. Thus *history* becomes *histories*. We do the same when a verb takes a final *s*: we write *to deny*, but *he denies*.

(d) The use of ie or ee for vowels with an 'ee' phonetic quality

There is just one word in the passage – *heere* – where you find *ee* that is not in PDE. There are plenty of other examples in Shakespeare texts, including *neere*, *trophee*, and *atcheeve*. These examples show that *ee* was used to cover various modern spellings associated with *i*-related sounds.

9.2.5 Spelling and 'edication'

The nineteenth-century American humourist, Artemus Ward, had something to say about spelling – a skill that he himself failed to pick up. 'No man has a right to be a lit'rary man onless he knows how to spel,' he said. 'It is a pity that Chawcer, who had geneyus, was so unedicated. He was the wuss speller I know of.'[26] For many people today, poor spelling does indeed indicate slovenly writing and lack of 'edication.' The accusation can be levelled because today spelling has become largely standardized. But there was, as we have seen, little standardization in the Elizabethan period, so Ward's comments would be as unfair for Shakespeare as they were for 'Chawcer.' We have also seen that there were attempts to create norms, particularly through the work of spelling reformers like Hart and Mulcaster. One might argue that in many ways, English spelling today remains largely 'unreformed.' But it is at least standardized.

9.3 Punctuation

9.3.1 Some twentieth-century punctuation studies

Twentieth-century interest in Elizabethan punctuation began long before Flatter talked about feathers and rings. In 1911, the Oxford literary scholar, Percy Simpson, wrote *Shakespearean Punctuation*. He was one of the first to give importance to the spelling and punctuation in early versions of printed texts. The approach came to be known as the 'New Bibliography.'

Alfred Pollard was an important character in the New Bibliography. He wrote a number of books about Shakespearean texts, arguing, like Simpson, for the value of early texts which, he felt, were sometimes close to what Shakespeare actually wrote. His *Shakespeare's Fight with the Pirates and the Problems of the Transmission of His Text* was published in 1917. Then there was the critic John Dover Wilson. In his later years, he produced an edition of Shakespeare. Indeed it came to dominate his life from 1921 to 1966. Volume 33 of *The Cambridge Dover Wilson Shakespeare* was *The Tempest*, and his edition contains an introductory 'Note on Punctuation.' It gave details of the principal Elizabethan punctuation marks and their uses.

The 1960s saw several publications related to punctuation. We have already mentioned Salmon's introductory chapter to the 1986 Wells and Taylor *Original-Spelling* edition of Shakespeare. Twenty-four years earlier she wrote a paper on early seventeenth-century punctuation. Partridge's 1964 book on Elizabethan orthography deals largely with colloquial contractions, but it contains two chapters on punctuation. The American Fredson Bowers produced a number of books (including, intriguingly, *The Dog Owner's Handbook*). Canine interests aside, he was best known as a bibliographer, and in 1968 produced his *On Editing Shakespeare*.

Thereafter, there is Treip (1970). Her book is about Milton's punctuation, but it contains a chapter dealing with the Elizabethan period. In 1982 Graham-White wrote a paper comparing the punctuation in different versions of the anonymous comedy drama written in the 1550s, *Gammer Gurton's Needle*. He later produced a book on punctuation in Shakespeare (1997). As in many other spheres, the Salmon and Burness (1987) collection makes a significant contribution; there is a section dedicated to punctuation, with two papers, by McKenzie, and Warren. Also as in other spheres, Crystal has much to say. His (2008) book on Shakespeare has a chapter on punctuation, while Crystal (2015) gives an entire history of English punctuation.

9.3.2 Whose punctuation?

In her 1962 paper, Salmon says that two major issues have dominated twentieth-century discussion on Shakespearean punctuation. One is: whose punctuation it in fact was; the other, what its functions were. On the first of these issues, Simpson (1911) argued that the punctuation of the First Folio could be trusted – either it came from Shakespeare, or from compositors who were following accepted practices. Dover Wilson's view was similar. He claimed that the punctuation in the plays was so good that it must have been Shakespeare's own. As evidence he cites Act 1, Scene 2 of *The Tempest*. 'If the reader,' he wrote, follows 'the pause effects in the exquisite dialogue between Miranda and her father ... [he] will become a complete convert to Shakespearean punctuation.'[27] There is just the smallest piece of evidence of how Shakespeare himself might have punctuated. It occurs in a collaboratively written play called *Sir Thomas More*, which appeared in the 1590s. Five distinct handwritings are involved, referred to as Hand A-E, and there is a suggestion that Hand D was Shakespeare's. The short passage in Hand D is lightly punctuated, using mainly commas: in 69 lines of blank verse, there are 24 commas, plus only three semicolons and six full stops.[28] This suggests that possibly Shakespeare's punctuation was not as careful as Dover Wilson claims. Partridge (1964) argues that such light punctuation was the norm for Elizabethan playwrights. He describes the comma as the 'stop-of-all-work' and says that the dramatists' sole aim was to punctuate just enough to avoid misunderstandings. The exception was Jonson, who took great care over his punctuation – one reason doubtless being that he was writing at a slightly later date, when plays were beginning to be read, not just performed.

As with spelling, there are many who were in a position to modify punctuation during the performance and text-production processes. Theatre prompters and producers, Partridge argues, will have added punctuation of their own to guide actors. So too will the scribes, and McKenzie (1959) speaks of the 'far from negligible role' of compositors. All these agents will have added variation to the punctuation – using their own preferred practices. McKenzie provides some numbers. There were, he says, five compositors involved in the First Folio, each with their own punctuation habits. To illustrate the variations, he compares the First and Second Quartos of *The Merchant of Venice*. He finds no fewer than 3,200 changes. Most are 'inconsequential variants in spelling.'[29] Some 715 are to do with punctuation, and over half involved adding commas. The effect was to increase the amount of punctuation – to make it 'heavier.'

Bowers, writing in 1966, expresses a common view: no one, he says,

> is so foolish any more as to argue that the punctuation—now demonstrated to be mainly compositorial—is Shakespeare's own … But such as it is, it is the most authentic that we have, and it is usually well suited to clarify the casual Elizabethan syntax.[30]

With this in mind, Bowers advocates that modern editors should be cautious about making punctuation changes to early texts, a view which, much later, Atkins (2003) also puts forward.

Bowers' advice to editors is appropriate since they themselves have played a major part in changing the punctuation of Shakespearean texts over the centuries, making it fit into the conventions of their own time. A comparison of two versions of a celebrated speech from *Romeo and Juliet* (2.2.1) will show how much heavier punctuation became.[31] The first is from the First Folio, the second from a Victorian version edited by Singer and dated 1875. The Victorians were particularly guilty of heavy Shakespearean punctuation, and this example shows the major role that exclamation marks and dashes play in this. Note in passing the two different spellings of 'sun' (*Sunne* and *Sun*) in lines 3 and 4; also *Veſtal*, an example of an adjective with a capital letter:

The First Folio:

Rom. He ieaſts at Scarres that neuer felt a wound,
But ſoft, what light through yonder window breaks?
It is the Eaſt, and *Iuliet* is the Sunne,
Ariſe faire Sun and kill the enuious Moone,
Who is already ſicke and pale with griefe,
That thou her Maid art far more faire then ſhe:
Be not her Maid ſince ſhe is enuious,
Her Veſtal liuery is but ſicke and greene,

And none but fooles do weare it, caſt it off:
It is my Lady, O it is my Loue, O that ſhe knew ſhe were,
She ſpeakes, yet ſhe ſayes nothing, what of that?
Her eye diſcourſes, I will anſwere it.

Singer's version:

Rom. He jests at scars, that never felt a wound.—
But, soft! what light through yonder window breaks?
It is the east, and Juliet is the sun!—
Arise, fair sun, and kill the envious moon,
Who is already sick and pale with grief,
That thou her maid art far more fair than she:
Be not her maid, since she is envious;
Her vestal livery is but pale and green,
And none but fools do wear it; cast it off.—
It is my lady; O! it is my love:
O, that she knew she were!—
She speaks, yet she says nothing. What of that?
Her eye discourses, *I will answer it.*

The First Folio passage has 20 punctuation marks. If '–' is counted as two marks, then Singer's version has 30. As we are about to see, 'heavier' punctuation can have a deleterious effect on such passages.

9.3.3 Punctuation rhetorical and grammatical

The second issue Salmon mentions is the function of punctuation. According to many, there was a major difference between punctuation then and now. Today, Simpson (1911) says, 'we base our punctuation … on structure and grammatical form.'[32] Hence one use of commas, semicolons, colons, and full stops is to mark off phrases, clauses, sentences. 'Grammatical punctuation' became common in the seventeenth century (with an increase in reading, where grammatical punctuation can play an important role). Its development was rapid. In fact Graham-White (1982) claims that there was more grammatical punctuation in Shakespeare Folios than in the earlier quartos.[33] But – Simpson again – 'the old system was guided by the meaning.'[34] Punctuation had a rhetorical function, to aid those involved not in silent reading, but in theatrical performance. 'In Shakespeare's day …,' Pollard writes, 'all the four stops, comma, semicolon, colon and full stop, could be … used simply and solely to denote pauses of different length irrespective of grammar and syntax.'[35]

Writers on Shakespearean punctuation from Simpson on make reference to sixteenth-century texts which discuss this 'rhetorical' function of Elizabethan punctuation. These include John Hart's *An Orthographie*, dated 1551, Richard Mulcaster's 1582 *Elementarie* (both mentioned in 8.5), and George Puttenham's

The Arte of English Poesie, 1588 – a book which Shakespeare doubtless knew. A particularly detailed account of punctuation practices at a slightly later date is given in Simon Daines' 1640 *Orthoepia Anglicana*.

Hart uses a musical analogy to describe the functions of stops to indicate pause lengths. The comma, he says, is like a crotchet, and the colon like a minim – so perhaps the full stop would be a semibreve. In his *Arte of* Poesie, Puttenham refers to these punctuation marks as *cefure* (a 'caesura' being a kind of pause), describing how they allow 'eafment to the breath.'³⁶ Mulcaster's description is longer, and it shows that alongside the rhetorical, we also find grammatical uses like today's.³⁷ Here for example is how he describes the comma. It is 'a small crooked point, which in writing followeth some small branch of the sentence, and in reading warneth vs to rest there, and to help our breth a little.' The first use he mentions – 'in writing' – is a grammatical function. But the second use ('in reading') is rhetorical; it says something about how the sentence is to be uttered. Mulcaster makes this writing/reading distinction in relation to a number of punctuation marks, with the 'writing point' to do with grammar, and the 'reading point' with 'elocution.' This is part of what he says about brackets, for example:

> parenthesis is expressed by two half circles, which in writing enclofe fom perfit [self-contained] branch ... not fullie coincident [of the same value] to the fentence ... and in reading warneth us, that the words inclosed by them, ar to be pronounced with a lower and quikker voice ...

The rhetorical use of punctuation marks helped actors deliver their lines. As Dover Wilson put it in 1921: 'the stops, brackets, capital letters in the [Shakespeare] Folio and Quartos are in fact stage-directions, in shorthand. They tell the actor when to pause and for how long, they guide his intonation, they indicate the emphatic word.'³⁸ Sixty years later, Graham-White (1982) explores this in his *Gammer Gurton's Needle* study. He too notes that the marks help actors pace their speeches by giving information about pause lengths. His claim is quite extreme, that 'it would not be too much to say that an actor can find his sub-text in such a farce as *Gammer Gurton's Needle* and in other Elizabethan plays, implied in the punctuation.'³⁹ Those involved in theatrical performance today seem to have taken on board the message that punctuation is worthy of careful attention. Crystal (2008), for example, tells how in 2005 he attended rehearsals of the Globe Theatre's production of *Troilus and Cressida*. 'I can affirm,' he says, 'that there were many discussions between director and actors over precisely how much value to attach to a comma.'⁴⁰

One of Graham-White's conclusions is that early versions of plays need to be consulted for guidance on rhetorical punctuation. His study compares an early (1575) version of *Gammer Gurton's Needle* with a modern (1963) one, containing much 'grammatical punctuation.' He concludes that the added punctuation is 'unhelpful' to the actor, showing a 'lack of sensitivity to the dramatic situation.'⁴¹ He compares one passage where the character is talking in 'a dramatic and excited burst.' The early version captures this through few punctuation marks, allowing the actor to deliver in a breathless manner. The later version slows down the pace with continual punctuation marks indicating grammatical structure.

Graham-White's book on punctuation in Shakespeare (1995) makes the same point. Light punctuation is able to give a sense of 'tumbling' movement, which disappears if heavy punctuation is added. But at the same time Graham-White shows that though later punctuation is usually heavier, Shakespeare could himself use heavy punctuation to indicate hesitancy and a lack of fluency. Warren (1987) gives some examples. He selects three Shakespeare soliloquies as they appear in the First Folio, and compares their punctuation with five editions appearing in the late 1960s and early 1970s. One of the soliloquies is from *Julius Caesar* (2.1.18), where Brutus is trying to justify to himself his part in the conspiracy to kill Caesar. He is being very hesitant, and the high number of commas in the First Folio increases this sense of hesitancy:

> *Th' abuse of Greatnesse, is, when it dis-ioins*
> *Remorse from Power: And to speake truth of Caesar,*
> *I haue not knowne, when his Affections sway'd*
> *More then his Reason.*

Warren points out that some modern editors make the punctuation here lighter, losing the hesitant tone of the lines.[42]

9.3.4 Some punctuation details

When it comes to detailed use of punctuation marks, Crystal (2008), along with Salmon (1986) and (1999), gives many concrete examples of usage in Shakespearean texts. These sources are used in the following brief descriptions of some Elizabethan marks:

Exclamation mark[43]

The exclamation mark first appeared in English in the 1590, and so was very new when Shakespeare was writing. One theory is that it derives from the Latin word *io*, meaning 'joy.' Mediaeval copyists, the theory runs, wrote *io* at the end of sentences to show happiness (a form of in-text commentary comparable perhaps – though with different meaning – to the modern use of 'lol'). Over time the 'I' came to be written over the 'o,' which became a dot. Partridge (1964) is among many sceptical of this theory.

Initially in English, the exclamation mark indicated emphasis, though there was a 'joyful' association from early days: in his *Orthographie*, John Hart calls it 'the wonderer,' and Jonson associates it with sentences 'pronounced with an admiration.'[44]

'Liberty and individualism'   147

In its early use, exclamation and question marks were sometimes confused. Part of the reason, Dover Wilson suggests, was that printers had small stocks of exclamation marks, so used question marks instead.[45] Whatever the stock levels, exclamations and questions can sometimes be difficult to distinguish. Both then and now, a word like *how* can be used both to exclaim (*How beautiful it is!*), and to interrogate (*How much did it cost?*). Hence perhaps these First Folio lines from *Hamlet* (1.2. 132):

> O God, O God!
> How weary, ſtale, flat and vnprofitable
> Seemes to me all the vſes of this world?
> Fie on't?

The confusion can also occur the other way round, with an exclamation mark where there should be a question mark:

> Dem: O Helen, goddeſſe, nymph, perfect, diuine,
>   To what my, loue, ſhall I compare thine eyne!
>
> First Folio MND (3.2.137)

Sometimes, Crystal points out, there is no exclamation mark where we might expect one, as for example in this exhortation from *Henry V* (First Folio 3.1.34):

> King: Cry, God for Harry, England, and S George.

Crystal (2008) looks at the distribution of exclamation marks over the Shakespeare canon, and finds no real developmental pattern. There are none in the early plays, but none either in the late *The Winter's Tale*. The vast majority occur in lines beginning with an interjection, most often *Oh* or *O*, though there are plenty of interjection sentences without the mark. Different compositors use the exclamation mark in different ways. Crystal find their usage in *Much Ado About Nothing* and *A Midsummer Night's Dream* particularly sophisticated, where they occur after *what* and *how*, and even after an imperative (not, that is, so exclusively after *Oh* or *O*).

Apostrophe

A common use of the apostrophe in modern English is to mark possession: hence *the boy's desk* and *the boys' desk*. There are no uses of the possessive -*'s* in the Prospero passage, though there is one point where it would be used in modern English: *Ioues* where we would have *Ioue's* ('Jove's'). The possessive apostrophe was not unknown in Shakespeare's time, but it was found irregularly. This passage from the original-spelling edition (Wells and Taylor 1986) of *Antony and Cleopatra* (2.2.5) has the possessive apostrophe in one line, but not two lines before:

> *Let Anthony looke ouer Caesars head,*
> *And speake as lowd as Mars. By Iupiter,*
> *Were I the wearer of Anthonio's Beard,*
> *I would not shaue't to day.*

These lines also contain an example of an apostrophe used to replace a missing letter: *shaue't* for *shave it*. The word 'apostrophe' comes from the Greek *apostrophos* meaning 'the turning away or rejection of a letter.'[46] There are plenty of examples of this use in the Prospero passage, including *bedymn'd, azur'd, op'd*. There is also one example which shows the irregular way in which apostrophes (like other punctuation marks) are used: in line 22 we find *I'le*, and in 25 *Ile* without the apostrophe. As a general rule, letters which are pronounced very lightly are the ones that are dropped. Common contexts for this are: the vowel sound of an *-ed* verb ending, some lightly pronounced medial vowel, letters in a preposition, a pronoun or the definite article, parts of common verb sequences, particularly using the verbs *do, be,* or *have* – here either part of the pronoun or part of the verb goes. Some examples:

o'my life	*do's*	*'tis*	*desp'rate*
wil't	*sland'rous*	*sh'adulterates*	*th'ther day*
o're	*for't*	*auis'd*	*reueng'd*
y'haue	*thou'rt*	*w'are*	

Some Shakespearean contractions sound distinctly odd to the modern ear. Twice in *As You Like It* (3.3.68 and 5.4.53) you have *God'ild*, a corruption of 'God yield you' meaning 'God reward you.'[47]

The common use of *-'d* for *-ed* deserves particular attention. Words, like *crooked*, which in modern English have two syllables can sometimes be monosyllabic, and this is indicated by the use of *-'d*. Hence in Wells and Taylor's *Henry VI Part 3* (5.6.79) we find *Let Hell make crook'd my Minde to answer it.* But in *Cymbeline* (5.5.478) we find *And let our crooked Smoakes climb to their Nostrils.* These examples suggest how metre can play a role: a monosyllabic *crook'd* is required in the first instance, and a disyllabic *crooked* in the second. Metrical considerations can also explain variable pronunciation of the *-ed* verb ending, reflected in the spelling by use of *-ed* or *'d*. In these First Folio lines from *Richard III* (1.1.6), the iambic metre requires *bruiſed* to be disyllabic (in modern English we might write it *bruiséd*), while *chang'd* needs to be a monosyllable:

> *Our bruiſed armes hung vp for Monuments;*
> *Our ſterne Alarums chang'd to merry Meetings.*

Capital letters

In EModE, capital letters are used at the beginning of each line in blank verse. As in modern English, the letter following a full stop is always a capital, but sometimes in EModE colons or semicolons were used where today we might have a full stop, and there you will also find a following capital. Examples in the Prospero passage are *To* in line 12, and *Then* in line 26, both after a colon. The passage also shows words which have a capital even though not at the beginning of a sentence or a blank verse line. Sometimes in Shakespeare texts they are adjectives. We saw an example in 9.3.2 of *Veſtal* in the *Romeo and Juliet* passage. Blake's (2002) example is from *Henry V*, when the King says *the traitors receyu'd the Golden Earnest of Our death*. He hypothesizes that *Golden* is capitalized to suggest the noun 'gold,' while the capital on *Our* suggests royalty. But mostly, as in the Prospero speech, the capitalized words are nouns. Yet not all nouns have capital letters – in the passage *brooks*, *paſtime*, and *vault* do not. Salmon (1999) lists some of the attempts to explain the use of capitals.[48] Butler (1633), for example, suggests that 'important' nouns should receive capitals, 'vulgar' ones not.[49] But why should *brooks* be more vulgar than *Oke*? Another theory is that animate objects have capitals. *Art* and *Muſicke* provide counter-evidence, and certainly there are animate nouns (like *ſleepers*) which do not have capitals. Though it is often difficult to find any rhyme or reason in the use of capitals, some modern actors do follow the 'important nouns' view. Crystal (2008) cites the British actor Philip Voss who says: 'the punctuation of the First Folio, and particularly the capitalization of nouns, has been very influential on the way I stress some of the sentences.'[50] At the same time it is difficult to avoid the conclusion that English was moving towards the eighteenth-century situation when capitals were used for nearly all nouns, 'vulgar' as well as 'important' ones.

Italics

Italics can be used today, as in as in Elizabethan times, wherever there is a desire to make a piece of text stand out in some way. Their use for emphasis is particularly common. Here are some other uses, though it needs to be remembered that Elizabethan conventions are variable, so counterexamples can always be found:[51]

- for stage directions: in the Prospero passage: *Heere enters Ariel before* …;
- for foreign words: Shallow, in 2H4, refers to a *bona roba* (3.2.200);
- for names of people: in the Prospero passage: *Ioues*;
- for the words of songs: at the end of TN (5.1.386): *When that I was a little tine boy* …;
- for proverbs or maxims: Cressida in TC (1.2.292):

    Therefore this maxim out of loue I teach,
    '*Atchiuement is command: vngained beseech*'

- in prologues or epilogues: as in the first line of TC: *In Troy there lyes the Scene:* …

Comma, semi-colon, full stop

These punctuation marks are the ones today used to mark off grammatical divisions. They were, as we have discussed, earlier associated with pauses. In general the gradation in terms of pause length was comma → semi-colon → colon → full stop, though this gradation was often not observed.

As well as indicating a pause, the comma was also sometimes used in place of a hyphen in compounds. Today, many editors use hyphens in these lines from 1H4 (5.1.89):

> I do not think a braver gentleman,
> More active-valiant or more valiant-young

But the original-spelling version (Wells and Taylor, 1986) reads:

> I do not thinke a brauer Gentleman,
> More actiue, valiant, or more valiant yong

Jonson calls the semi-colon a 'subdistinction,' and for Daines it was a 'comma-colon.' It came into frequent use after about 1580, and though it was thought of as indicating a pause shorter than the colon, the two were often used interchangeably. Jonson used the semi-colon as a logical, rather than as a temporal marker.[52] As with much punctuation, there was considerable individual variation: according to Salmon, one compositor of the First Folio shows a definite preference for the semi-colon.[53]

As we have seen, a colon could often stand for a modern full stop. In line 12 of the Prospero passage, a following capital letter reinforces the sense of a sentence ending: *Set roaring warre: To the* …

A full stop (called a 'period' till the nineteenth century) was defined by Hart as marking the end of a sentence.

Hyphen

This was coming into common use in the 1570s. As today, one use was at a line end, when the second half of a word appears on the next line. Sometimes our modern conventions were followed, dividing a word at midpoint. Thus in the First Folio of *The Comedy of Errors* (4.4.19), we have:

> L. Dromio: Nay 'tis for me to be patient, I am in aduer-ſitie.

But just three lines before (4.4.16), there is a less elegant break:

> E. Dromio: To a ropes end ſir, and to that end I am re-turned.

Another example occurs in the Prospero passage, where the word *geſture* is on two lines, with the hyphen after the *ge-*.

Though as we have seen, a comma could stand for a hyphen in a compound, the latter was commonly used. Thus we find (CE 5.1.83) *life-preſeuing reſt*. Sometimes (but not always) a hyphen occurs after a prefix like *a*-. So again in *The Comedy of Errors* (2.1.78): *Backe ſlaue, or I will breake thy pate a-croſſe.*[54]

Inverted commas (and brackets)

These started to appear in the 1590s, but were not common till the late eighteenth century. In Shakespeare texts you often find the 'opening' commas, but not the 'closing' ones. Belarius in Cymbeline (4.2.26, in the original-spelling version) says: *"Cowards father Cowards, and Base things Syre Bace;/ "Nature hath Meale, and Bran; Contempt, and Grace.* Here each line of the 'saying' has opening but not closing marks. Inverted commas were used commonly for proverbs and maxims. Brackets too could be opened but not closed, acting like a comma or a dash.[55] Salmon takes her example from *Cymbeline* (5.5.54), where Cornelius says:

> *In fine*
> *(When she had fit you with her craft, to worke*
> *Her Sonne into th' adoption of the Crowne*

Modern editions sometimes replace the bracket with a dash here.

9.4 Punctuation's 'new age'

Our brief look at some Elizabethan punctuation marks reveals just how many of them were only starting to appear in Shakespeare's lifetime. It was less than a hundred years before Shakespeare's birth that Caxton set up his printing press (1476). The punctuation resources available to him were few, and he relied mostly on the *punctus* (full stop), and the *virgules* – a comma which had the form of a slash: /. The Caxton-Shakespeare comparison reveals that punctuation was indeed entering a new age in the Elizabethan period; and this in turn explains the amount of variability and the lack of standardization. Much of it was so very new.

Notes

1. Different spellings of Shakespeare's name have been collected together by David Kathman and can be seen in a paper available online: http://shakespeareauthorship.com/name1.html
2. Salmon (1986), p. liv.
3. Flatter (1948), p. 136.
4. Stated in the Society's website, http://malonesociety.com.
5. Blayney (1996), p. xxvii.
6. As noted in the Preface, Hinman's First Folio is the one used throughout this book.
7. J. R. Brown (1960), p. 60.
8. J. R. Brown (1960), p. 61.

9 A. Brown (1960), p. 70.
10 *Ibid.*, p. 76.
11 Greg (1942), p. li.
12 Wells and Taylor (1979), p. 4.
13 *Ibid.*, p. 10.
14 *Ibid.*, pp. 7–8.
15 *Ibid.*, p. 34.
16 *Ibid.*, p. 164.
17 For more information about the Elizabethan use of tildas, see Hill (1959).
18 Crystal (2008), p. 61.
19 Salmon (1986), p. xiv.
20 Mulcaster (1582), p. 111; cited by Salmon (1986), p. xlv.
21 Salmon (1986), p. xlv.
22 Mulcaster (1582) p. 121.
23 Lass (1999a), p. 11.
24 Salmon (1986), p. xlvi.
25 Mulcaster (1582), p. 114, cited by Salmon (1986), p. xlvi.
26 Ward (1867), p. 44.
27 Dover Wilson (1921), p. lvii.
28 Rokison (2013), p. 288.
29 McKenzie (1959), p. 362.
30 Bowers (1968), p. 177.
31 The comparison is taken from Johnson (2013), p. 248.
32 Simpson (1911), p. 16.
33 Graham-White (1982), p. 96.
34 Simpson (1911), p. 16.
35 Pollard (1917), p. 90.
36 Puttenham (1589), p. 88.
37 Mulcaster (1582), p. 148.
38 Dover Wilson (1969), p. xxxvii.
39 Graham-White (1982), p. 98.
40 Crystal (2008), p. 69.
41 Graham-White (1982), p. 99.
42 Warren (1987), p. 463.
43 The exclamation mark examples are taken from Crystal (2008).
44 Jonson (1909), p. 146.
45 Dover Wilson (1969), p. lix.
46 Partridge (1964), p. 185.
47 Dusinberre (2006).
48 Salmon (1999), p. 38.
49 Butler (1633), p. 4, cited in Salmon (1999), p. 38.
50 Smallwood (2003), pp. 17–18, cited in Crystal (2008), p. 521.
51 Crystal, Blake, and Salmon are the sources for this list.
52 Partridge (1964), p. 190.
53 Salmon (1999), p. 40.
54 The examples in this section are taken from Crystal (2008).
55 Salmon (1986), p. lv.

10 Verse and prose
Changing a 'sorry bed'

10.1 IPs: Procrustes' 'sorry bed'?

The early scenes of *Richard II* are dominated by a dispute between Mowbray and Bolingbroke. It is decided that the dispute should be settled by a duel. But just before it begins, King Richard intervenes. He throws down his 'warder' (truncheon), to stop the action. As the Lord Marshall announces (1.3.118):

Stay! The King hath thrown his warder down.

The line has troubled editors in the past, because it is not a complete iambic pentameter (IP). A syllable is missing at the beginning. Instead of IP's deDUMdeDUMdeDUMdeDUMdeDUM, you have DUMdeDUMdeDUMdeDUMdeDUM. In such cases, past editors have often assumed that something was missing. Pope's solution for this line was to add the word *but*: *But stay! The King hath thrown his warder down* – deDUMdeDUM … The example is taken from Groves (2011), who notes that others more recently have found other solutions. The second edition of Arden, for example, suggests that the form *throwen* – the spelling of *thrown* in Q1 – should be used; this makes up for the lost syllable, though the resulting metrical sequence is highly odd.

Groves discusses these 'short pentameter' lines at length, and his example suggests that when past editors have come across metrical irregularities, they have tended to regard them as 'mistakes,' and have duly 'corrected' them. The IP pattern was seen as a framework into which lines had to fit. Sicherman (1984: 180) uses a classical image to describe this framework. It is like, he says, the 'sorry bed' of Procrustes – the figure in Greek mythology who cut up people to make them fit into an iron bed.[1] The same 'mistakes to be corrected' view could be applied to Shakespeare's use of verse forms other than the IP. Samuel Johnson, for example, has a comment on a scene in Act 4 of *Henry VI, Part 1*, where Young Talbot is mentioned, and Shakespeare starts to use rhyme. For Johnson, its use 'strengthens the suspicion that these verses were originally part of some other work, and were copied here only to save the trouble of composing new.'[2] Johnson seems to be suggesting the use of verse is a 'mistake.'

Such attempts to view metrical variations as the results of 'compositorial botching, metrical license or authorial inadvertence' were replaced in the twentieth century by the view that they were instead often deliberate 'choices within the signifying system of the metre.'[3] This shift in perception is one of the major ways in which studies in verse and prose from the mid-twentieth century on differ from earlier approaches. The number of metrical studies has been rather small in comparison with some other linguistic areas. Derek Attridge's publications in the field are an important contribution, particularly his *The Rhythms of English Poetry* (2014). As far as Shakespeare is concerned the field is dominated by George Wright's *Shakespeare's Metrical Art* (1988); and for prose, Brian Vickers' *The Artistry of Shakespeare's Prose* (1968) is, according to one reviewer, 'likely to remain the most searching, detailed and comprehensive account of Shakespeare's prose that we have.'[4] Others have provided useful overview accounts, sometimes going into considerable detail. These include Wright (2001), McDonald (2003), and Crystal (2008, Chapter 9). Other more exploratory studies include Koelb (1979) – one of a number of generative grammar approaches to the topic – Tarlinskaja (1983), Ingham and Ingham (2011), and Groves (2011 and 2013).

Sicherman (1984) is one of those who argues for a 'choices' rather than 'botching' explanation. She talks of the prejudice of eighteenth-century editors against short lines. Her study focuses on short lines in *Julius Caesar*, a play in which Shakespeare appears to be experimenting with verse forms, and one which has a particularly large number of short lines. Sicherman shows how such lines can be used as stage directions, or to add rhetorical emphasis, or often to reveal nuances of character. For example, she discusses Brutus' lines (2.1.61):

Since Cassius first did whet me against Caesar,
I have not slept.
Between the acting of a dreadful thing ...

Sicherman claims that the missing feet in the second line 'represent Brutus' struggle towards an articulation of his state of mind.'[5]

Like most issues to do with Shakespearean metre, short lines are discussed at length in Wright (1988). His comprehensive analysis places emphasis on the great variety of verse and prose lines used by Shakespeare in the plays; indeed, 'miscellaneousness' is the word he uses.[6] He gives examples from *Hamlet* and *King Lear*. Thus in Act 4, scene 3 of the former, the King speaks iambics all the time, but not always in pentameters. Then, two scenes later, the King and Queen speak iambs, 'while mad Ophelia sings and speaks prose in their presence.'[7] To make the point for *King Lear*, Wright takes figures from E. K. Chambers' 1930 tome, *William Shakespeare: A study of facts and problems*, a great source of statistical information. An Appendix in Volume 2 contains a series of 'metrical tables,' providing statistics for rhyming lines, and blank verse lines with their different variations. Chambers' figures for *King Lear* show 191 short lines, 131 lines with extra syllables at the caesura break, 64 Alexandrines,

580 feminine or triple endings, all out of a total of 1079 blank verse lines.[8] Miscellaneousness indeed.

10.2 'Miscellaneousness' in blank verse

Blank verse was a comparative newcomer to English, making its first appearance in 1539 in works by Howard, Earl of Surrey. The form quickly gained a central place in Elizabethan drama. McDonald (2003) describes it as Shakespeare's 'default metre.'[9] But, he adds, over his career, Shakespeare 'utterly transformed the sound of the pentameter line' through the use of many types of variation.[10] It is a question of 'dissimilitude within similitude': a constant 'IP base' containing many variations.

When Katherina in *The Taming of the Shrew* is suffering particularly at the hands of her husband Petruchio, she complains that her father treats beggars better. The first line of her complain is (4.3.4):

> *Beggars that come unto my father's door.*

The line illustrates one of the most common types of IP variation found in Shakespeare. It is a pentameter, and most of the feet are iambs. But the first foot is a trochee (/x). One way of considering the trochee is as an 'inverted iamb': inverted from x/ to /x. When a trochee is followed by a normal iamb, the sequence is /xx/. This 'trochaic inversion,' as it is called, is – Wright says – particularly common at the beginnings of lines in Renaissance poetry, and it gives 'a metrical flourish that could enliven the usual pattern.'[11]

Wright's study provides a useful categorization of Shakespeare's departures and deviations from the IP norm. He identifies three categories. The first are non-blank verse lines, using prose or rhyme. We shall deal with these in 10.4 and 10.5. Category 2 contains lines which are iambs but not pentameters, while Category 3 lines are pentameters but not iambic. Table 10.1 lists and exemplifies some (though not all) of Wright's Categories 2 and 3.

As Shakespeare's style developed, the number of 'irregular' lines increased, and certainly exceeded those of his contemporaries. Lines with more than the IP expected number of syllables (sometimes called 'hypermetrical') were uncommon in the early plays, but 'by the end of his career every third line is hypermetrical.'[13] Similarly with short lines. Wright has an Appendix giving line lengths of the plays, and in some of the later plays more than 20 per cent of the lines are short.

As Table 10.1 shows, the parameters of variation in Shakespeare's metre are many, and we shall here concentrate just on short lines. If, as Wright argues, the departures and deviations from IP are not 'mistakes' due to carelessness, but deliberate manifestations with underlying intentions, what purpose do they fulfil? General reasons which Wright (and others) cite are: to avoid the tedium of plodding similitude, to make dialogues 'sound more convincing,'[14] to provide 'opportunities to be terse, curt, swift, ominous, surprising.'[15]

Table 10.1 Some of Wright's departures and deviations from standard IP lines. Based on Wright (1988)[12]

II. Deviations from Pentameter		
A. Short lines		
Short lines	Fewer than 5 stresses	2nd line in: *I can be patient, I can stay with Regan/I and my hundred knights* (KL 2.4.225)
B. Long lines		
Hexameters	6 stress lines (Alexandrines) (can be used for special statements)	*To have what we would have, we speak not what we mean* (MM 2.4.118)
Heptameter	7 stress lines (bizarre, used by characters like Pistol)	*Rouse up revenge from ebon den with fell Alecto's snake* (2H4 5.5.27)
III. Deviations from Iambic		
A. Extra unstressed syllables		
Feminine	An extra unstressed syllable often at the end of a line	*To be, or not to be, that is the question* (Ham 3.3.56)
Epic caesura	An extra unstressed syllable before the midline pause (so a kind of midline feminine ending)	*His acts being seven ages. At first the infant* (AYLI 2.7.144) (ages. At = /xx)
Triple endings	2 unstressed syllables at line end	*What's Hecuba to him, or he to Hecuba* (Ham 2.2.559) (last word = /xx)
B. Omitted syllables		
Headless	Unstressed syllable missing at beginning of line	*Stay! The King hath thrown his warder down* (R2 1.3.118) – Groves' example discussed in text
Broken-backed	Missing syllable after midline pause	*The curtained sleep. Witchcraft celebrates* (Mac 2.1.43) x/x/ (x) /x/x/
Monosyllabic feet	Unstressed syllable missing other than at line-beginning or after midline pause	*Youth, beauty, wisdom, courage, all.* (AW 2.1.181) /(x)/x/x/x/

Wright lists three specific situations in which short lines occur. 'More and more,' he says, 'Shakespeare ended his impressive speeches (eventually, almost any speech) with strong short lines.'[16] We met an example of this in 9.2.3, where Prospero's celebrated speech ended (Tem 5.1.57) with the half-line *I'll drown my book*. Here the short line gives a sense of 'dramatic conclusion.'

A second use is in what Wright calls the 'anomalous short line.' This often signifies pithy exchange, sometimes suggesting indignation. For example, in the opening scene of *Julius Caesar* (1.1.51), Marullus castigates the crowd for praising Caesar. Here are four lines. The third is indignantly short:

> *And do you now strew flowers in his way,*
> *That comes in triumph over Pompey's blood?*
> *Be gone!*
> *Run to your houses, fall upon your knees*

'Shared lines,' where more than one character speaks, are a special type of short line. They too became common in the later plays. Fredson Bowers (whom we met in 9.3.1) says that 'by the last plays [the use of shared lines] … was close to ten times the frequency of the early comedies.'[17] This early example is from *Henry VI, Part 1* (2.1.66):

> *Bastard: Mine was secure.*
> *Regnier: And so was mine, my lord.*

Notice that the two parts of the line together make an IP.

Sometimes a line is made up of a series of short statements. Crystal (2008) illustrates this well by laying out the constituent parts of the line across the page (which is not how it is normally printed).[18] The example is from *King John* (3.3.66):

> *King John: Death.*
> *Hubert: My lord.*
> *King John: A grave.*
> *Hubert: He shall not live.*

In this case the parts of the line taken together make up one of Wright's 'headless IPs.' A function of these shared lines is to 'accelerate the tempo of a conversation or a group scene.'[19] They also have the effect of 'tightening the dramatic relationship between people.'[20] In addition, he suggests that 'the shared line can be a means first of permitting speech to burst out of its usual constraints and then reaffirming its metrical ties.'[21] He exemplifies by a lengthy exchange between Jessica and Lorenzo in *The Merchant of Venice* (5.1.9), made up of a series of parallel speeches, each repeating the phrase *in such a night*. Here is part of it:

> *Lorenzo: In such a night*
> *   Stood Dido with a willow in her hand*
> *   Upon the wild sea banks, and waft her love*
> *   To come again to Carthage.*
> *Jessica: In such a night*
> *   Medea gathered the enchanted herbs*
> *   That did renew old Aeson.*
> *Lorenzo: In such a night*
>   …

The fact, Wright says, that the lines are shared suggest 'speech bursting out,' while the fact that they are joined together to form IPs 'reaffirms metrical ties.'

Groves (2011) is another who looks in detail at short lines and their significance. Far from being 'botches,' he regards them rather like the 'rhetorical punctuation' we looked at in 9.3.3 – 'a way of "pointing" performance for actors (and readers).'[22] He concentrates on 'short pentameters,' where there are fewer than the ten syllables, five feet that the standard IP requires. His starting point is the one we have seen, the Lord Marshall's announcement in *Richard II*: *Stay! The King hath thrown his warder down.* Groves talks about 'the surprise of the silent initial off-beat – performatively a little like treading in the dark on a step that isn't there' and 'it conveys the abruptness of the Marshall's injunction.'[23]

Groves has his own list of the various different effects that these short pentameters can produce. One of these he calls 'the jolt,' because it accentuates a break. It is often used, as in the *Richard II* example, for 'abrupt attention-seeking imperatives and vocatives.'[24] A further example he gives is *Go, take hence that traitor from our sight* (2H6 2.3.98). Though such headless constructions are, Groves notes, very common, they are not a Shakespeare innovation. Marlowe is among other dramatists who use them. What is new in Shakespeare is their use in other positions in the line, not just initially. An example is Lady Macbeth's *Under my battlements. ^ Come you spirits* (Mac, 1.5.40): ^ is the symbol Groves uses to indicate the silent off-beat in a 'jolt.' Another 'accentuation of a break' occurs when there is a new addressee. In these lines of Malcolm's from *Macbeth*, the addressee is Duncan, except for the last three words, where he is talking to the Captain. The change is indicated by a silent beat (1.2.4):

> Malcolm: This is the sergeant
> Who like a good and hardy soldier fought
> 'Gainst my captivity. [to Captain] ^Hail, brave friend!

The jolt can be a disagreement between two characters, as in these lines from *The Winter's Tale* where Hermione and Leontes are in conflict (2.1.100):

> Hermione: You did mistake.
> Leontes: ^No: if I mistake.

Groves uses the symbol ~ to indicate a silent off-beat associated with his second category, which he calls 'the drag.' His example is this line from Macbeth (3.1.102): *Not i'the worst ~ rank of manhood, say't.* Earlier editors like Furness note that a syllable 'is wanting' here, and has *most worst*, while others have *worser*.[25] Groves' silent off-beat (~) between *worst* and *rank* forces 'an emphatic accent on *worst*.'[26]

Before the twentieth century, there were, it is true, writers who identified the existence of metrical irregularities in Shakespeare. Abbott, for example, has a section discussing short lines,[27] and identifies some reasons why they occur, for example in 'passages of soliloquy where passion is at its height.' One difference between these and more recent accounts is the degree of attention that is given to these anomalies. This signals a more central difference: a perception that, as Wright points out, the anomalies need to be seen as 'integral elements in [Shakespeare's] verse technique.'[28]

10.3 'Fitting round': the 'art of congruence'

10.3.1 Caesurae, end-stopping and enjambment

Another form of variety which Wright discusses relates to the position of caesurae in metrical lines. Crystal and Crystal (2005) define the caesura as 'a rhythmical break in a line of verse, often in the middle.'[29] Wright shows that in poetry from Surrey to Sidney, the caesura traditionally came after a line's fourth syllable. Sometimes inexorably so, as in these lines taken from a poem known as *Tichborne's Elegy*, written by the poet Chidiock Tichbourne the day before his execution:

> *My prime of youth is but a frost of cares,*
> *My feast of joy is but a dish of pain,*
> *My crop of corn is but a field of tares*

And so Tichborne's lines trudge mournfully to his death. Shakespeare was one who contributed to the relaxing of the conventional caesura position. With time, he tended towards positioning them later in the metrical line. But these examples from Wright show just how much variation there could be. Often, though not always, there is punctuation which shows where the caesura falls:

Love! His affections do not that way tend	(Ham 3.1.163)
Love looks not with the eyes, but with the mind	(MND 1.1.234)
Why speaks my father so ungently? This	(Tem 1.2.445)
My thought whose murder yet is but fantastical	(Mac 1.3.138)
If music be the food of love play on	(TN 1.1.1)
Her father lov'd me oft invited me	(Oth 1.3.127)
Then trip him that his heels may kick at heaven	(Ham 3.3.93)
If you have tears prepare to shed them now	(JC 3.2.170)
I come to bury Caesar not to praise him	(JC 3.2.75)

When the position of the caesura was relatively fixed to line midpoint, poets had to show considerable ingenuity to make their words and sentences 'fit round' the prescribed pause points. As Wright puts it, 'early Elizabethan versification is essentially an art of congruence, a fitting of phrase to metrical pattern.'[30]

Nor was it just a question of accommodating caesurae: the iambic pentameter itself – that 'sorry bed' of Procrustes – was a relatively fixed pattern that needed to be 'fitted round.' In the work of dramatists like Marlowe, lines and syntactic units were made to coincide: the natural syntactic breaks occur where the lines end. This example is from *Dr Faustus* (1.3.1):

> *Now that the gloomy shadow of the earth,*
> *Longing to view Orion's drizzling look,*
> *Leaps from th'Antarctic world unto the sky,*
> *And dims the welkin with her pitchy breath:*
> *Faustus, begin thine incantations*

This procedure, known as 'end-stopping,' frequently occurs in Shakespeare's early comedies, as these lines from *The Taming of the Shrew* (4.3.2.) show:

> *The more my wrong, the more his spite appears.*
> *What did he marry me to famish me?*
> *Beggars that come unto my father's door*
> *Upon entreaty have a present alms,*
> *If not, elsewhere they meet with charity.*

Wright describes the Renaissance English playwrights' ingenuity at fitting the phrase to the line as 'dazzling.' 'Clearly,' he says, 'they mean us to hear two orders of language at once: a metrical order, in which the stresses alternate five times from weak to strong (with variations), and the order of the phrase or sentence ...'[31]

As the rules about relatively fixed caesura points loosened, so too did the need for end-stopping, and the practice of making the ends of grammatical units coincide with line-ends. The new variety provided ways of escaping from the strait-jacket of having to fit grammar into metrical line.

If we compare *The Taming of the Shrew* example with one from *As You Like It* – by no means a late play, written in fact just nine years after *The Shrew* – we already see a different pattern emerging:

> *And then the whining school-boy with his satchel*
> *And shining morning face, creeps like snail*
> *Unwillingly to school. And then the lover,*
> *Sighing like furnace, with a woeful ballad*
> *Made to his mistress' eyebrow. Then, a soldier,*
> *Full of strange oaths, and bearded like the pard,*
> *Jealous in honour, sudden, and quick in quarrel,*
> *Seeking the bubble reputation*
> *Even in the cannon's mouth. And then the justice*
> *...*

(2.7.146)

The full stops and nearly all the other punctuation marks come within lines rather than at their ends. The grammatical units do not coincide with the metrical lines. The technique is called enjambment (from the French *enjamber* meaning 'to stride over') – the syntax 'strides over' the line ending.

Wright identifies three configurations possible when lines and grammatical units do not coincide. The latter can run:

- from full line to in-line – starting at the beginning of a line and finishing before the end of another line;
- from in-line to in-line;
- from in-line to full line.

Here is a passage that shows the first two of these three possibilities. It is from a late play, *The Winter's Tale* (2.1.108):

> *I am not prone to weeping, as our sex*
> *Commonly are; the want of which vain dew*
> *Perchance shall dry your pities; but I have*
> *That honourable grief lodged here which burns*
> *Worse than tears drown. Beseech you all …*

The sentence as a whole (from *I am not prone* to *than tears drown*) is full line to in-line, and within this sentence there are clauses that run in-line to in-line – *as our sex/Commonly are*, for example. The passage also shows how caesura points can vary in position.

These lines from *King Lear* (1.4.279) are an example of in-line to full line:

> *If she must teem,*
> *Create her child of spleen, that it may live*
> *And be a thwart disnatured torment to her.*

Leech (1969) is another who discusses enjambment at length. He notes that sometimes Shakespeare's in-line to in-line sequences form IPs (or variations thereof) themselves. Hence in our *As You Like It* lines: the sequence from the caesura in line 2 to the caesura in line 3 forms an IP: *creeps like snail/Unwillingly to school*; so too (with some irregularity) is the sequence from line 4 to 5: *with a woeful ballad/ Made to his mistress' eyebrow*. Leech calls these 'ghost lines,' and others use the phrase 'straddled lines' for the same phenomenon.

The essence of enjambment is that syntactic and metrical units do not begin and end together. One might say that a 'tension' is set up between the structure of the verse (which deals in the unit of the line) and the syntactic structure, which cuts across that metrical unit. Leech talks about syntactic and verse 'finality,' where syntactic and metrical units end. He says that 'if either occurs without the other, some structural expectation is still unfulfilled; the reader has, as it were, arrived at a halting-place, not a destination.'[32] There is, in Wright's phrase this time, a 'counterpoint of line and sentence,'[33] where the two elements (verse and syntax) weave across and around each other, but do not coincide. Leech (1969) is about English poetry in general, and he considers this issue particularly in relation to the poet John Milton. He describes the aesthetic satisfaction which occurs when, in Milton's poetry, this counterpoint is resolved by metre and syntax finally coming together. He compares the effect to 'the perfect cadence at the end of a Bach fugue.' Occasionally this is also found in Shakespeare. The example Wright gives is of the Jaques speech we have been looking at. We focused on the second, third, and fourth 'ages of man.' The evocation of all the seven ages except for the second, Wright notes, begins in-line. But here is how the speech ends (2.7.164):

> *Last scene of all,*
> *That ends this strange eventful history,*
> *Is second childishness and mere oblivion,*
> *Sans teeth, sans eyes, sans taste, sans everything.*

Syntax and lines come together at the end, creating Leech's Bach-like perfect cadence. However, this type of ending is, in later Shakespeare, the exception rather than the rule. As we have seen, he more often prefers the effect of finishing on the half-line.

In Shakespeare, enjambment did indeed increase as time went on, and gradually became 'the rule rather than the exception.'[34] But it is possible to relate enjambment and end-stopping with certain dramatic situations, which may occur in plays early or late. Rokison's (2013), for example, relates enjambment (and varied internal line breaks) with this agitated speech of Juliet's, in the relatively early *Romeo and Juliet* (4.3.56):

> *O, look! Methinks I see my cousin's ghost*
> *Seeking out Romeo, that did spit his body*
> *Upon a rapier's point. Stay, Tybalt, stay!*
> *Romeo, Romeo, Romeo. Here's drink. I drink to thee.*

According to Rokison, end-stopping can be associated with 'public orations and measured summations,'[35] and her example is from *Coriolanus*. In Aufidius' summation – the very last speech of the play – there is, she says, 'a high incidence of end-stopping, and infrequency of line-breaks,' despite the lateness of the play (5.6.152):

> *Beat thou the drum, that it speak mournfully.*
> *Trail your steel pikes. Though in this city he*
> *Hath widowed and unchilded many a one,*
> *Which to this hour bewail the injury,*
> *Yet he shall have a noble memory. Assist.*

It is also possible to suggest, on occasions, an association between end-stopping and character. Perhaps it is his (under normal circumstances!) ordered military mind that makes Othello recount his ventures in this end-stopped way, despite the fact that *Othello* is a relatively late play:

> *Wherein I spake of most disastrous chances,*
> *Of moving accidents by flood and field,*
> *Of hair-breadth scapes i'th' imminent deadly breach,*
> *Of being taken by the insolent foe,*
> *And sold to slavery; of my redemption thence,*
> *And portance in my travels' history.*
>
> (Oth 1.3.133)

10.3.2 'Fitting round': subject-verb inversion

There have been a few other studies looking at the interaction between the nature of English and the exigencies of IP metre. Tarlinskaja (1983) was concerned with the relationship in Shakespeare between natural English stress patterns and the strong stress positions required by IP. More recently, Ingham and Ingham (2011) focus particularly on one syntactic structure: subject-verb inversion. A rule which came from Old and Middle English was that in some circumstances – for example after a clause-initial adverbial or direct object – the subject could be placed after the verb. Though the practice had largely died out by the end of the EModE period, it was still used in the sixteenth century. Two of Ingham and Ingham's examples are from Holinshed:

> *Then longed the duke sore to heare what he should haue said.*[36]

The inversion is a stylistic option, and on many occasions did not occur:

> *Then all the companies ware to him fealtie.*[37]

Ingham and Ingham investigate cases in Shakespeare where the subject is a pronoun. In normal circumstances, subject pronouns do not receive stress in English, so you would not expect to see them in a stressed position within an IP. What happens if the normal subject-verb order in an IP sequence were to involve placing a stress on a pronoun? Disruption of the metre could be avoided by a poet using the subject-verb inversion option. Hence in this line from *Richard II*, inversion ensures that the subject pronoun *I* is unstressed (1.1.128):

> *The other part reserved I by consent.*

Ingham and Ingham want to find out how often Shakespeare uses this device to preserve the metre; how much, in other words, he manipulates the syntax to fit the 'sorry bed' of the IP. They look at 15 non-comedy plays from *Titus Andronicus* to *Cymbeline*. They find that over his writing career, Shakespeare is four times more likely to position a pronoun in a non-stressed position. This suggests that he does indeed have a strong metrical sense; the IP is indeed his default. But how often does he manipulate word order (by subject-verb inversion) to achieve this? Their conclusion is that 'inversion did not constitute a device for managing compliance with iambic rhythm.'[38] Instead, inversion was seen as a 'freestanding stylistic variant used by the poet in order to achieve a high style effect, possibly even a monumental quality.'[39]

There are, nevertheless, occasions when Shakespeare does put a pronoun in a stressed position. Perhaps surprisingly, Ingham and Ingham find that this occurs more readily in early works. This partially contradicts Wright's view that disruptions in standard IP metre are associated with later rather than earlier works.

10.4 Other verse forms

Though IPs became Shakespeare's 'default metre,' a number of other verse forms are also found, some in abundance. Wright describes these in detail. Many use rhyme, which has associations *inter alia* with the theme of love, with songs, passages of moralizing, doggerel, and the supernatural.

There are three parameters along which verse can be analysed. Two of them we have already discussed. One is line length – the number of stressed syllables; in the case of the IP this is 5. The second is foot type. For the IP this is the iamb: x/.

The third parameter comes into play where there is rhyme, and it is rhyme scheme – what lines in a sequence rhyme with each other. One of the most common rhyme schemes in Shakespeare is the couplet. Using the conventional way of signalling rhyme schemes by using the letters of the alphabet, a pair of couplets would be *aabb*. The early plays are particularly full of couplets. There are more than 500 rhyming couplets in the early *Love's Labour's Lost*, and none at all in the late *The Winter's Tale*. In later plays, it was the convention often to end a scene with what is sometimes called a 'capping couplet.' At the end of 2.2. in *Hamlet*, for example, Hamlet has formed the idea of having a play performed which will expose the crime of his uncle, now king. The final words of the scene are (2.2.602):

> *The play's the thing*
> *Wherein I'll catch the conscience of the King.*
> Exit

According to Clemen (1951), capping couplets were a dramatic convention of the 1580s. This usage relates to the more general practice of employing couplets to impart words of wisdom – summarizing epigrams or adages – something that may happen at scene endings, as well as at other points in a drama. Another use, discussed in McEvoy (2006), is to give energy in rapid dialogue. Both of these reasons may be what causes the burst of couplets in the passage below from *The Comedy of Errors*. After this piece of quick-fire dialogue, the 'debate' continues with longer passages in couplets. Then, when other characters come on the scene, it is back to blank verse:

> Adriana: Why should their liberty than ours be more?
> Luciana: Because their business still lies out o' door.
> Adriana: Look when I serve him so he takes it ill.
> Luciana: O, know he is the bridle of your will.
>
> (CE 2.1.10)

The other major rhyme scheme in Shakespeare is the sonnet. In Shakespeare this is *ababcdcdefefgg*, with divisions into quatrians (*abab*, *cdcd* and *efef*) plus a final couplet: *gg* (which again with great frequency has a summarizing role). As with many sonnets, Shakespeare's sequence of 154 has love as a main theme. The sonnet's association with love is also shown in *Romeo and Juliet*. The play is written predominantly in blank verse and prose. But for the moment when the two lovers, Romeo and Juliet, first meet – and leading up to their first kiss – the pair produce a sonnet. Each has their own quatrain and the third quatrain is shared. They have a line each of the final couplet.

Attridge (2014), an important work on metre, provides some insightful analyses of specific works. One is Shakespeare's Sonnet 73, with its celebrated first quatrain:

> *That time of year thou mayst in me behold,*
> *When yellow leaves, or none, or few do hang*
> *Upon those boughs which shake against the cold,*
> *Bare ruined choirs, where late the sweet birds sang.*

The sonnet has, Attridge observes, received much critical attention (he mentions Nowottny 1962, Booth 1969, and Fowler 1975 in this regard). Attridge himself is concerned just with metre. He notes that the sonnets in general are more conservative than the plays in following the rules of the IP, and this is reflected in the first three lines above which are relatively straightforward IPs. The rhythmical shock comes in the fourth line's opening three words, *Bare ruined choirs*, each of which is stressed, 'suggesting an intensification of emotion' and 'helping to establish this as the dominant image of the quatrain,' which is of a 'bleak present.'[40] He notes that the line then returns to a 'happier past' *where late the sweet birds sang*. It is also a return to the IP. Attridge's sensitive analysis continues through the rest of the sonnet.

Other rhyme schemes, Wright reports, are occasionally found in Shakespeare. The rhyme royal – *ababbcc* – is used in *The Rape of Lucrece* and *The Lover's Complaint*. It came to be known as rhyme royal, probably because King James I of Scotland, something of a poet, used the form. One reason for the form's popularity was because there were several ways of grouping the lines by rhyme: thus you could have *aba* followed by two couplets, *bbcc*; or an *abab* pattern with a final *bcc*. Here is the sixth stanza of *The Rape of Lucrece* – *aba bbcc*:

> *Perchance his boast of Lucrece' sovereignty*
> *Suggested this proud issue of a king;*
> *For by our ears our hearts oft tainted be.*
> *Perchance that envy of so rich a thing,*
> *Braving compare, disdainfully did sting*
> *His high-pitched thoughts, that meaner men should vaunt*
> *That golden hap which their superiors want.*

Compare this with the eighth stanza (*abab bcc*):

> *When at Collatium this false lord arrived,*
> *Well was he welcomed by the Roman dame,*
> *Within whose face beauty and virtue strived*
> *Which of them both should underprop her fame:*
> *When virtue bragged, beauty would blush for shame;*
> *When beauty boasted blushes, in despite*
> *Virtue would stain that or with silver white.*

There is an interesting snatch of verse in *Much Ado About Nothing* where Beatrice, who has used prose throughout the first half of the play, bursts into rhyme when she hears Benedick loves her (3.1.107). The rhyme scheme she used is one of Spencer's: *ababcdcdee*.

The iamb is, as we have seen, the most common foot in Shakespeare, and indeed some have associated it with the natural rhythm of English. Its inversion, the trochee (/x) is occasionally used, often in shorter lines, and in incantations. Two examples are *Tell me where is fancy bred* (MV 3.2.63), and *Double, double, toil and trouble* (Mac 4.1.10). Spondees (//) are sometimes also used (*Cry, cry! Troy burns, or else let Helen go* – TC 2.2.113). Other feet like the dactyl (/xx) and the anapest (xx/) are rare.

The witches' line from *Macbeth* just mentioned shows a four-stress line, or tetrameter. Such short lines are characteristic of incantations. As well as the witches in *Macbeth*, they are also used by the fairies in *A Midsummer Night's Dream*: *Through the forest have I gone./But Athenian found I none*, says Puck, in trochaic tetrameters (2.2.73). Six-stress lines are called hexameters, or Alexandrines (so named because of their use in the twelfth-century French romance, the *Roman d'Alexandre*). They are occasionally found in Shakespeare as in this line of the Groom from *Richard II* (5.5.75): *To look upon my sometimes royal master's face*. It is a characteristic of Alexandrines that they can often be analysed into halves separated by a caesura, and for this reason they are sometimes regarded as pairs of trimeters (three-stress units). Hence the casket's inscription in *The*

Merchant of Venice 2.7.5) – *Who chooseth me shall gain what many men desire* – can either be seen as an Alexandrine or as two trimeters.

10.5 Prose

Act 2, Scene 3 of *Othello* is a long one. It begins with Iago manipulating Cassio into getting drunk, and finishes with Cassio being disgraced for doing so. The scene illustrates two differences in the situations when prose and verse are used. During the drinking, the characters speak prose – the appropriate medium for such a mundane activity, particularly one in which the discourse might not be entirely coherent. But Iago, when he soliloquizes, is very coherent. He 'retains his self-possession,' and shows just how much he is in control of the situation, by speaking in verse (2.3.45):[41]

> *If I can fasten but one cup upon him,*
> *With that which he hath drunk tonight already,*
> *He'll be as full of quarrel and offence*
> *As my young mistress' dog.*

The second situation comes later in the scene. Iago speaks prose when he is suggesting to the disgraced Cassio how he can get back into Othello's favour, via the favours of Desdemona (2.3.305):

> *You or any man living may be drunk at a time, man. I'll tell you what you shall do. Our General's wife is now the General …*

Then, at the very end of the scene, Iago again soliloquizes, and again it is in blank verse (2.3.360):

> *How poor are they that have not patience!*
> *What wound did ever heal but by degrees?*
> *Thou know'st we work by wit, and not by witchcraft,*
> *And wit depends on dilatory time.*

According to Vickers (1968), there is a 'contrast between prose for dissimulation with others and verse for direct self-revelation.'[42]

Vickers' study is very detailed, and in the case of *Othello* he devotes some 20 pages to observing how Iago moves in and out of prose in *Othello*. One of his major concerns throughout his book is to identify the rhetorical figures Shakespeare uses, and we will look at these in 11.5. Another concern is imagery. Here he is, as he acknowledges, following on from the work of Spurgeon and Clemen, whose work we considered in 4.2.1 and 4.2.2. But Spurgeon, Vickers claims, suffered from the desire to link imagery to 'Shakespeare's own personality and taste,'[43] while Clemen virtually ignores Shakespeare's prose. Vickers draws up his own taxonomy of images. It has seven categories, as shown in Table 10.2:

Table 10.2 Vickers' image categories (based on Vickers, 1968)[44]

Type	Characterization	Examples
thematic	beyond the immediate context but related to the development of the play	Disease imagery in Hamlet: *foul and pestilent congregation of vapours* (Ham 2.2.303); *vicious mole of nature* (1.4.24) etc.
situational	'dramatizes an important situation' within the play	In *Coriolanus*, the theme of 'reversal of values' is symbolized by mother Volumnia kneeling in front of son Coriolanus, rather than the other way round (Cor 5.3). Described in Jarka (1967).
stage	visual effects that meaningfully add to the drama	'Overhearing scenes' as in *Twelfth Night*, *Much Ado*, *Othello*. See following discussion.
atmospheric	creating a dramatic mood	The arrival of Duncan at Macbeth's castle: *The raven himself is hoarse / That croaks the fatal entrance of Duncan / Under my battlements* (Mac 1.5.36).
subjective	'a persona is individualized by his recurrent choice of a particular sort of image'	Clemen shows how the imagery used by Othello characterizes him, revealing what kind of person he is.[45]
objective	'a character is consistently described by other people in the same terms'	Richard III as a monstrous animal: *That bottled spider, that foul bunch-backed toad!* (R3 4.4.81).
forensic	manipulative; 'images to influence some other person'	Cade trying to stir up anger against Lord Say for an unpatriotic act: *for thereby is England mained* [maimed] *and fain to go with a staff, but that my puissance holds it up* (2H6 4.2.154).

Because Vickers is concerned with developing an overall framework for study, elements of what he says through his book relate to verse as much as prose. The same may be said for one of his major conclusions regarding Shakespeare's development. It is to show how verbal devices used initially in the early comedies become re-used – to very different effect – in the later tragedies. These are, in Vickers' own words, 'application to a tragic purpose of techniques evolved in comedy.'[46] One of his examples is the 'trapping of characters' device, where a character is made to believe something false, often by overhearing a contrived conversation. It is used to comic effect on Malvolio, Beatrice, and Benedick, among others. It is also found in *Othello*, when Iago arranges for Othello to overhear a conversation between himself and Cassio, apparently about how the latter wooed Desdemona (4.1). But the effect here is far from comic. This transference from comedy to tragedy also happens with concrete verbal devices. In *A Midsummer Night's Dream*, for example, Bottom confuses the senses – *I see a voice* he says at one stage (5.1.189), and *The eye of man hath not heard* at another (4.1.209). The same device is used in *King Lear*, when Lear says to blinded Gloucester (4.6.151): *A man may see how this world goes with no*

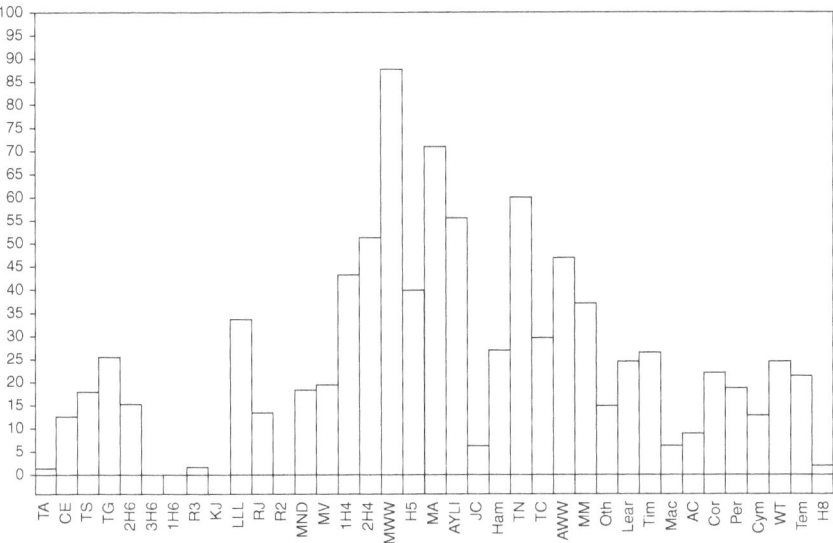

Figure 10.1 Percentage distribution of prose in Shakespeare's plays (from Vickers, 1968: 433)

eyes. Look with thine ears. These examples also show that though much of Vickers' book focuses on details in individual plays, he also has things to say about overall development.

Arguably the greatest value of Vickers' account is that he specifies the circumstances in which prose and verse are used, something that Crystal (2008) also does at length.[47] We have already seen two sets of circumstances at the start of this section, but there are many others. Some are shown in Figure 10.1.

The table shows that there is no gradual increase in prose with time, culminating in the late plays. The early plays tend to have little, with the exception of *Love's Labour's Lost*. It is with *Henry IV, Part 1* (written around 1596) that the use of prose really takes off, and if anything, the prose heyday is in the middle period. The highest point is *The Merry Wives of Windsor*, written almost entirely in prose, with just an occasional piece of verse. Thereafter there is some tapering off. Some plays like *Henry VI, Part 1*, *King John*, and *Richard II* are without prose.

That there is more verse in Shakespeare's plays than there is prose reflects the Greek and Roman view that prose was not a suitable medium for literature. The same view held sway in England until into Renaissance times. As Puttenham, writing in 1589, puts it: verse is 'a manner of utterance more eloquent and rethorical then the ordinarie prose.'[48] The 'eloquent versus ordinary' distinction lies behind many of the specific factors which govern when Shakespeare uses verse or prose. Verse is high, sublime, poetic, while prose is low, mundane and ... prosaic. One relevant factor is genre. Verse was considered the correct medium for tragedy, while prose was permissible in the less elevated genre of comedy. Figure 10.1 suggests this. It is why the comedy of *Love's Labour's Lost* stands out among the early works. The top four plays for prose use are all comedies: *The Merry Wives of Windsor, Much Ado About Nothing, Twelfth Night*, and *As You Like It*. Conversely, the plays with little or no prose are tragedies or histories. But genre is certainly not the only factor. Another is the class or status of the speaker. The general rule (followed particularly in the early plays) is that higher status speakers use verse, lower status ones use prose. Hence the Porter in *Macbeth* is one of the few characters to use prose in that play. The princes, lords, kings talk to each other (and even to their spouses) in blank verse. However, after the early period even this condition does not always hold, and we find high-status characters like Rosalind, Henry V, Hamlet, and Lear using prose.

The status not just of the speaker but also of the interlocutor is important. The speech of Prince Hal (in *Henry IV, Parts 1 and 2*) reveals this. When addressing his father and other important personages, he uses blank verse. But a number of scenes in these plays show Prince Hal slumming it in taverns with Falstaff and his cronies. To these 'low-life' characters he uses prose. Similarly Hamlet talks prose with the lowly gravediggers (5.1). What happens in soliloquies, when the interlocutor is oneself? Hamlet uses prose when talking to Rosencranz and Guildenstern (3.2), partly because he disdains the two courtiers. As soon as they exit and Hamlet begins to soliloquize (*'Tis now the very witching time of night*: 3.2.395), he uses blank verse. Falstaff, on the other hand, as a 'low' character, talks to himself in prose – for example in his celebrated soliloquized defence of alcohol: *I had a thousand sons, the first human principle I would teach them should be to forswear thin potations, and to addict themselves to sack* (2H4 4.3.120).

Among the other factors at work is mental state. Madness, for example, is associated with prose. Thus the high-status, king's son, Hamlet drops into prose when feigning madness, and this is also true of another kingly figure – Lear, who mostly talks prose in his madness, verse in his sanity. Similarly, Lady Macbeth, who normally uses blank verse, speaks in prose during the sleepwalking scene (5.1). It is clearly the appropriate medium for nightmares.

Subject matter and mood are also relevant. In *Henry IV, Part 1*, Hotspur and his wife Lady Percy mainly speak blank verse to each other, being characters of high birth. But occasionally they 'break into prose,' particularly when bantering with each other. For example, when Hotspur asks his wife to sing a song in public, she refuses to do it – *in good sooth*, she says. Hotspur picks up on this oath, speaking (at least initially) in prose (3.1.242):

> Heart! you swear like a comfit-maker's wife – 'Not you, in good sooth!,' and 'As true as I live!,' and 'As God shall mend me!,' and 'As sure as day!' – And givest such sarcenet [flimsy] surety for thy oaths ...

Or is it prose? Wright (1988) contains a short but insightful section on prose. He points out that prose may be easy to distinguish from verse on the printed page, with conventions including beginning verse lines with a capital letter. But in performance, he says, 'the most notable aspect of Shakespeare's prose is that it is often hard to distinguish from verse.'[49] One of the ways the listener can distinguish between the two is by the presence of regular iambs, which indicate verse. But prose too can be substantially iambic. Some have argued, Wright notes, that Dickens (possibly under the influence of Shakespeare) has passages of iambic prose, particularly in his early novels.[50] A Shakespearean character often discussed in this respect is Falstaff's flamboyant companion Pistol, who appears in *Henry IV, Part 2*, *Henry V*, and *The Merry Wives of Windsor*. Perhaps he has picked up iambic rhythms from visits to the theatre; he certainly seems to think it attractive to speak prose with verse rhythms (sometimes near-iambs). Wright's example is from *Henry V* where Pistol says (4.1.54): *Tell him I'll knock his leek about his pate upon Saint Davy's day.*

Since prose can be iambic, it is sometimes difficult to hear (as opposed to seeing on the page) whether a passage was intended as verse or prose. The lines of Hotspur and his wife in the passage discussed earlier are a case in point; though some modern editors have these lines in prose, they are in verse in the First Folio. The contrary situation can equally hold. We have already noted that as a comic character, Falstaff seldom speaks verse. One of the occasions when modern editors give him a few lines of blank verse is when he is speaking to a high-bred person: one of the king's sons, Prince John of Lancaster. Here are the lines as they appear in an Arden edition:[51]

> *My lord, I beseech you give me leave to go*
> *Through Gloucestershire, and when you come to court*
> *Stand my good lord, pray, in your good report.*
>
> (2H4 4.3.80)

Not quite iambs but, the Arden editor says, 'the feeling is of verse,' and there is a rhyme. But the First Folio has the passage in prose, without capitals for line-initial *Through* and *Stand*.

Part of the reason why prose can sound like verse is that prose can carry rhythms (it can be 'iambic prose' for example). The other reason is that, as we saw in 10.2, verse can be subject to a large number of variations. In Wright's words: 'Prose may turn iambic, just as verse, with its manifold variant resources, may take a step in the direction of prose.' These two factors together account for Wright's conclusion that 'the division between verse and prose is not so absolute as we are likely to think it.'[52]

To return for the last time to Procrustes and his sorry bed. In his early writings, Shakespeare (like other Tudor writers) tended to 'make the people fit the bed.' That is, characters, ideas, thoughts were made to fit the medium. Those like Wright and Vickers show that, by the end of his career, Shakespeare had learned to 'make the bed fit the people' – the medium was modified where necessary, more adequately to convey what was being said.

Notes

1. Sicherman is quoted in Capell (1970), p. 194.
2. Raleigh (1908), p. 134.
3. Groves (2011), p. 119.
4. Powell (1968), p. 393.
5. Sicherman (1984), p. 190.
6. Wright (1988), p. 103.
7. *Ibid.*, p. 104.
8. Chambers (1930), p. 397.
9. McDonald (2003), p. 80.
10. *Ibid.*, p. 83.
11. Wright (1988), p. 9.
12. *Ibid.*, p. 105. Some of Wright's categories may initially seem uncomfortably overlapping. For example, a 'short-line' may seem similar to a line containing an iamb with an omitted syllable. But the first is not seen as a pentameter. The second is a pentameter, but with a deficient foot.
13. McDonald (2003), p. 85.
14. Wright (1988), p. 137.
15. *Ibid.*, p. 120.
16. *Ibid.*, p. 120.
17. Bowers (1980), p. 81. Cited in Wright (1988), p. 117.
18. Crystal (2008), p. 115.
19. McDonald (2003), p. 84.
20. Wright (1988), p. 141.
21. *Ibid.*, p. 139.
22. Groves (2011), p. 119.
23. *Ibid.*, p. 120.
24. *Ibid.*, p. 122.
25. Furness (1873), p. 144.
26. Groves (2011), p. 127.
27. Abbott (1870), para. 511.
28. Wright (1988), p. 117.
29. Crystal and Crystal (2005), p. 51.
30. Wright (1988), p. 46.
31. *Ibid.*, p. 13.
32. Leech (1969), p. 126.
33. Wright (1988), p. 213.
34. *Ibid.*, p. 213.
35. Rokison (2013), p. 287.
36. Holinshed (1577), p. 405. Cited in Ingham and Ingham (2011), p. 98.
37. *Ibid.*, p. 420. Cited in Ingham and Ingham (2011), p. 99.
38. Ingham and Ingham (2011), p. 108.
39. *Ibid.*, p. 115.
40. Attridge (2014), pp. 348–9.
41. Vickers (1968), p. 332.
42. *Ibid.*, p. 332.
43. *Ibid.*, p. 21.
44. The examples in Table 10.2 are not always Vickers' own.

45 Clemen (1951), chapter 13.
46 Vickers (1968), p. 430.
47 The following discussion about the circumstances in which prose is used is based on these two sources, Vickers and Crystal, as well as various others available, including Seccombe and Allen (1903), which has a section on Shakespeare's use of prose.
48 Puttenham (1869), Chapter 3.
49 Wright (1988), p. 110.
50 See www.librarything.com/topic/11337 for such a claim.
51 Humphreys (2007).
52 Wright (1968), p. 113.

11 Rhetoric

'Maggot ostentation'?

11.1 Rhetoric's bad press

In July 1878, a banquet was given in Knightsbridge for the British politician Benjamin Disraeli, twice Prime Minister of Britain. He used his speech there to attack his rival, William Gladstone, describing him as 'a sophistical rhetorician: inebriated with the exuberance of his own verbosity.' This was not intended as a compliment, and it is an example of the bad press that rhetoric has often received through the ages. Similar associations between rhetoric and floridness, artificiality and lack of sincerity were made in Shakespeare's time. For example, for a good part of *Love's Labour's Lost*, one of the principal characters, Berowne, has used his rhetorical powers in the service of seduction. But in the last scene of the play, when the mood has turned serious, he vows to express his 'wooing mind' with simpler, less flowery, language (5.2.406):

> *Taffeta phrases, silken terms precise,*
> *Three-piled hyperboles, spruce affection,*
> *Figures pedantical – these summer flies*
> *Have blown me full of maggot ostentation.*
> *I do forswear them; and I here protest*
> *By this white glove – how white the hand, God knows! –*
> *Henceforth my wooing mind shall be expressed*
> *In russet yeas and honest kersey noes.*

Kersey is a village in Suffolk, thought to be the origin of kersey cloth, a thick, plain cloth. Hence the adjective came to mean 'plain' or 'unadorned.'

Shakespeare often makes fun of characters whose florid rhetoric has blown them full of 'maggot ostentation.' *Love's Labour's Lost* has several such characters, including Don Armado, the Spanish knight, and Holofernes, the pedantic schoolmaster. Here is what the latter says about the former (5.1.10):

> *His humour is lofty, his discourse peremptory, his tongue filed, his eye ambitious, his gait majestical, and his general behaviour vain, ridiculous, and thrasonical. He is too picked, too spruce, too affected, too odd, as it were, too peregrinate, as I may call it.*

Here part of the comical effect is achieved by the use of rhetorical devices like synonyms (the figure of speech *synonyma* will be discussed in 11.5.4), repetition of phrases, reciting lists. Shakespeare's ear for rhetorical mediocrity is also revealed in the *Pyramus and Thisbe* play which the mechanicals perform in *A Midsummer Night's Dream*. So too in the love sonnets which Orlando deposits on the trees in *As You Like It*; before Rosalind discovers they were written for her by her beloved Orlando, she describes one of them as a *tedious homily of love* (3.2.151).

But despite the bad press – and the ridicule – Shakespeare and Renaissance writers took rhetoric very seriously. Indeed, rhetoric, C. S. Lewis says, 'is the greatest barrier between us and our ancestors … Nearly all our older poetry was written and read by men to whom the distinction between poetry and rhetoric … would have been meaningless.'[1] In recent decades, a number of accounts of Renaissance 'literary language' have appeared, helping us today to surmount the barrier. These include Sonnino (1968), Vickers (1970 and 1971), Colney (1990), Hussey (1992), Ronberg (1992), and Adamson (1999). Even now, in the early twenty-first century, there are still 'firsts' in the area. Thus Adamson et al.'s (2007) collection of papers is described by one reviewer as the 'first modern study specifically devoted to Renaissance figures of speech.'[2] Similarly, Mack (2011) is said by its author to be 'the first comprehensive history of Renaissance rhetoric.'[3]

A number of the studies just mentioned include useful brief histories of rhetoric. Vickers' (1970) authoritative account was one of the first. Others include Sonnino (1968), Vickers (1971), Ronberg (1992), Adamson (1999), and Adamson et al. (2007). A short excursion into this historical territory will help with the 'barrier' C. S. Lewis mentioned.

11.2 Some rhetorical history

For the classical Greeks and Romans, rhetoric was the study of techniques of 'persuasion,' initially in law courts, but soon passing into politics. Rhetoric 'taught you how to win over friends, and either persuade enemies or make them look ridiculous.'[4] The Romans were responsible for disseminating the ideas of rhetoric through their Empire. In mediaeval universities, rhetoric was one element of the introductory liberal arts programme called the 'Trivium'; the word signals a division into three parts, the other two elements being grammar and logic.

The whole notion of 'renaissance,' of course, involved looking back to classical times, and bringing the virtues of those times into the present. John Colet – the humanist and educationalist who in 1509 founded St Paul's School in London – well captures the Renaissance view of European history. He saw it as falling into three stages: the 'Golden Age' of classical civilization, the present day which was striving to recreate that 'Golden Age,' and between the two, the 'Middle Ages,' which he saw as barbaric (he calls it a 'blind world'; more common to us is the term 'dark ages'). The way that Colet, together with the Dutch humanist Desiderius Erasmus, 'strove to recreate the Golden Age' was through a concerted effort to overhaul the educational system, partly by increasing knowledge of Latin, and at the same time 'improving' English in the direction of classical models.[5]

In terms of language (very much the terms in which those like Colet thought), the 'Golden Age' was much associated with the period of Latin history from about 190 to 19 BC. A major figure of that period (his dates were in fact 106–43 BC) was the Roman philosopher Marcus Tullius, commonly known as Cicero, or Tully. Of his several books on rhetoric, most influential in the Renaissance were *De Inventione* (a kind of handbook for orators) and *De Oratore*. Other classical texts popular at that time were the twelve-volume *Institutio Oratoria* by the Hispanic Roman Quintilian (c. 35-c. 100AD), and the anonymous book addressed to one C. Herennius, entitled *Ad Herennium* ('To Herennius'), dated from late 80s BC. Northern Renaissance humanists also produced their own rhetorical handbooks. Most influential was Erasmus' *De Copia*, published in 1512. There were too a good number of English rhetoric texts produced in the period, including Henry Peacham's *The Garden of Eloquence* (1577), and George Puttenham's *The Arte of English Poesie* (1589), both appearing in Shakespeare's lifetime.

According to Mack (2011), 'between 1460 and 1620 more than 800 editions of classical rhetoric texts were printed all over Europe.'[6] The figure confirms that rhetoric, which we tend today to see as a relatively small, self-contained subject, pervaded many areas of Renaissance life. School pupils were made to do rhetorical exericises – writing imaginary speeches that celebrated dead characters might have made, and constructing elaborate arguments for, and then against, stated views (a Ciceronian procedure known as *in utramque partem* – 'from both directions'). Rhetoric's influence really did go far beyond law and politics. It invaded literature also, influencing how speeches in drama and pieces of poetry were constructed. At the head of the invading army was Cicero, whose influence on Elizabethan writing, including Shakespeare, was considerable.

11.3 Ciceronian style

Ronberg (1992) uses a speech from *Hamlet* to investigate the hallmarks of the Ciceronian style in Shakespeare.[7] It comes early in the play (1.4.23), when Hamlet, Horatio, and companions hear sounds of wassailing coming from the palace – a custom, Hamlet feels, *more honoured in the breach than the observance*. He generalizes:

> *So oft it chances in particular men*
> *That – for some vicious mole of nature in them,*
> *As in their birth, wherein they are not guilty,*
> *Since nature cannot choose his origin –*
> *By the o'ergrowth of some complexion,*

Oft breaking down the pales and forts of reason,
Or by some habit that too much o'er-leavens
The form of plausive manners − that these men,
Carrying, I say, the stamp of one defect,
Being nature's livery or fortune's star,
His virtues else, be they as pure as grace,
As infinite as man may undergo,
Shall in the general censure take corruption
From that particular fault.

The speech exemplifies some salient characteristics of the Ciceronian style:[8]

(a) Long sentences. The passage is one sentence, 14 lines long. Ronberg gives an even longer example from Sir Philip Sidney, an author particularly influenced by Cicero. The two opening sentences of Sidney's *Arcadia* are 29 lines long, no less. Another Shakespearean example is Gaunt's celebrated speech from *Richard II*, (2.1.31–68), beginning *This royal throne of kings*. The sentence is 21 lines long.

(b) Hypotaxis (subordination). This shows the influence of Latin syntax. It is a characteristic that leads to the use of conjunctions and prepositions like *provided, providing, considering, during, notwithstanding*, many of which became popular in Renaissance English.[9] The use of *-ing* participial forms in the *Hamlet* passage illustrates: *breaking down, carrying, being*. Notice also the lengthy *that* clause from line 2 until 8; at its end, the *that* is repeated to indicate a return to the main sentence. Then, 'as soon as we are on the main track,' Ronberg says, 'Hamlet highlights the circumstances of the flaw once again in a participial clause (*Carrying … defects*), to which is subordinated another (*His virtues … undergo*) … The concessive clause itself incorporates the comparative clause *as man may* undergo.'[10]

(c) 'Piling up' and 'holding back.' It is common to find the word 'period' used to describe a unit of rhetoric, often spanning a number of sentences. A rhetorical period is, says Adamson (1999: 584), now often thought of as 'a particular type of complex sentence, in which the main clause is completed at, or towards the end of, the construction, having been preceded or interrupted by one or more subordinate clauses.' Our description above of the latter half of *Hamlet*'s speech well captures how clauses 'pile up' in a cluster towards the period's end. It is often then, at the very end, that the main verb is reached, and the sentence/period concluded. There is a 'holding back' till this final moment. In the *Hamlet* passage, the main verb and its clause are the very last words: *take corruption / From that particular fault*. The 'holding back' is even more pronounced in the *Richard II This royal throne of kings* speech mentioned earlier. The sentence's subject is a collection of noun phrases − *this sceptred isle, this other Eden, this blessed plot*. They continue for 19 lines − the sentence has a 19-line subject! The main verb and the rest of the sentence − *Is now leased out … / Like to a tenement or pelting farm* – come in lines 20 and 21. 'Holding back' like this may be seen as a way of creating climax, with the period's sense not being revealed until the very end. An alternative way of creating a final 'climax' is to have the period ending with a summary statement – a role which, as we saw in 10.4, often falls on the final couplet of a sonnet.

(d) 'Turning point.' It is also characteristic of the Ciceronian style for periods to have 'some well-defined turning point, with phrases and clauses tending to mass themselves in parallel formation on both sides of the turning point.'[11] Once again there is an example in the *Hamlet* speech. The first eight lines include a series of clauses on the topic of 'men with vicious moles.' The return to the subject at the end of line 8 (*that these men …*) is the turning point, leading into another series of clauses.

11.4 Beyond Cicero

The chronology and dating of Shakespeare plays is the subject of much scholarly debate. According to one view, *Twelfth Night* was written in 1601, and his next play was *Troilus and Cressida* (1602). If you read these two plays in succession, you cannot but be surprised – even shocked – at the differences between them. There are of course huge differences in their attitudes towards love. But there are also startling stylistic changes. Here are the celebrated lines with which *Twelfth Night* opens, uttered by love-sick Orsino (1.1.1):

> *If music be the food of love, play on,*
> *Give me excess of it, that, surfeiting,*
> *The appetite may sicken, and so die.*
> *That strain again! It had a dying fall.*
> *O, it came o'er my ear like the sweet sound*
> *That breathes upon a bank of violets,*
> *Stealing and giving odour.*

Compare this with a speech from Ulysses in *Troilus and Cressida*. The Trojan Hector has challenged any Greek to single combat. The obvious soldier for the Greeks to put forward is Achilles, but of late he has become proud and lazy. The Greeks therefore decide to nominate Ajax instead:

> *There is no tarrying here; the hart Achilles*
> *Keeps thicket. Please it our great general*
> *To call together all his state of war;*
> *Fresh kings are come to Troy. Tomorrow*
> *We must with all our main of power stand fast,*
> *And here's a lord – come knights from east to west,*
> *And cull their flower, Ajax shall cope the best.*

(TC 2.3.255)

It would be inappropriate to compare these speeches in any detail: Orsino discourses on music and love, while soldier Ulysses is talking to eminent Greek military commanders about war. But the differences in style are dramatic. Ulysses' sentences are 'jerky,' knotty, and a little difficult to follow. Something significant is clearly happening on the stylistic front. What is it?

Right at the beginning of this book, in 1.2, we saw that tastes in prose style were changing at the beginning of the seventeenth century. The Ciceronian rhetoric that we have just been describing was being replaced by less florid styles. This affected the reception that some of Shakespeare's writing received in that century, with criticisms of what Dryden called 'the fury of his fancy.'

The change in rhetorical fashion did not only affect critical views of Shakespeare's language. It is also evident in Shakespeare's own work. At the turn of the sixteenth century, a little under half of Shakespeare's works were still to be written, and could therefore be expected to show some of the stylistic changes that were in the air. *Troilus and Cressida* contains elements of the stylistic change. But it is only really when we reach *Coriolanus*, plus the so-called Romances (*Pericles*, *Cymbeline*, *The Winter's Tale*, *The Tempest*, *The Two Noble Kinsmen*), that the outlines of significant stylistic change are sufficiently delineated for us to speak about 'Shakespeare's late style.'

The anti-Ciceronian styles that emerged at the beginning of the seventeenth century are described in detail by the American academic, Morris Croll, in a paper written in 1929, and reprinted in Watson (1970), a collection entitled *Literary English Since Shakespeare*. A number of the chapters in Watson's collection are relevant to Shakespeare; another one dealing with styles is Barish (1960), which contrasts Shakespeare in his Ciceronian mode with Jonson's use of the 'new' styles. Croll uses the word 'baroque' to describe these new ways of writing, identifying in them characteristics found in other art forms (music and painting) also described as 'baroque.' Croll identifies two writing styles, which he calls the 'curt' and the 'loose.' They were reactions against the proportioned, elegant style of Cicero. Symmetrical, well-balanced sentences were replaced by asymmetrical, uneven ones. The aim was not to express finished, rounded thoughts, but to give the impression of 'the mind at work' – the fits and starts of thought processes: not thoughts themselves, 'but a mind thinking.'[12] The result was a jerky, uneven style, characteristic of half-formed thought, and an absence of anything that was not essential to getting the message across. One particularly vivid description comes from the seventeenth-century British writer John Aubrey. He is describing the Roman rhetorician Seneca, born about 11 years before Cicero died, who is associated by Croll with the curt style. Aubrey quotes the view that Seneca 'writes as a Boare does pisse, *scilicet* by jirkes.'[13]

Croll identifies four main characteristics of the curt style:

- sentences are often short;
- periods tend to start with the point being made (a 'summary'), rather than the Ciceronian preference for working up to a final summary statement. In Croll's words: 'the first member is likely to be a self-contained and

complete statement of the whole idea of the period.' Thereafter follow a succession of other related thoughts. The effect is of 'successive flashes of a jewel or prism';
- there is 'deliberate asymmetry' in the constituent parts of a period. The length of the parts may be unequal, and the focus may shift as the period develops. This stands in contrast to Ciceronian balance and symmetry;
- periods often show the 'omission of syntactic ligatures.' The syntactic links between various parts of the period may be loose, or indeed simply not stated.[14]

Croll's second, 'loose,' style is sometimes also known as the 'libertine style,' since its sources lie not in Seneca, but with the sixteenth- and seventeenth-century European religious free-thinkers known as the Libertines. Loose style sentences need not be short (or 'curt') at all. Indeed, they could be very long, but with the constituent parts loosely joined together. Elements would follow on one from the other in a chain, with one point leading on to the next, in a way which may make the overall coherence of the period obscure. Coordinating (rather than subordinating) conjunctions, like *and*, *but*, and *for* would tend to be used. As in the curt style, constituents were often unbalanced – the sentence subjects may change during the period, and there may be pieces of syntax which make the sense obscure.

Croll is not concerned specifically with Shakespeare, and he does not give Shakespearean examples. The *Troilus and Cressida* speech given earlier contains some of these characteristics. So too do these sentences from *Henry V* (3.7.15). The Dauphin (or is it the Duke of Bourbon? – see 9.2.1) is singing the praises of his horse:

> *When I bestride him, I soar, I am a hawk. He trots the air; the earth sings when he touches it; the basest horn of his hoof is more musical than the pipe of Hermes.*

The opening sentence states the theme. The subsequent parts are 'successive flashes of a jewel or prism.' Notice how the grammatical subjects change as the period develops (*I, he, the earth* etc.). The impression is indeed of thought in process. *Henry V* was written in about 1598–9, and it is in later plays that the clearest examples occur. Here is one from *Measure for Measure*. Lucio is complaining about the Duke's departure, leaving in charge his deputy who has instituted a decree against sexual misadventure (3.2.163):

> *I would the Duke we talk of were returned again. This ungenitured agent will unpeople the province with continency. Sparrows must not build in his house-eaves because they are lecherous. The Duke yet would have dark deeds darkly answered. He would never bring them to light. Would he were returned.*[15]

All four of Croll's points are illustrated in this passage, with 'deliberate asymmetry' shown less in terms of sentence length as in terms of changes in topic.

Note too that the result is a style that is sometimes difficult to understand – a point that is often made about the late plays. It is the 'omission of syntactic ligatures' which chiefly leads to this. In his study of Shakespeare's late style, McDonald (2006) discusses this at length under the title of *asyndeton*, defined by the *OED* as 'a rhetorical figure which omits the conjunction.' He cites a study by Houston (1988) which shows that *Cymbeline* has 78 instances of *asyndeton*, almost twice as many as in *King Lear* and *Antony and Cleopatra*, 'which themselves have more than the earlier tragedies.'[16] One of McDonald's examples is this passage from *Henry VIII*, spoken by the Duke of Buckingham. He has just been arrested for treason, and suspects that Cardinal Wolsey is behind the arrest, having perhaps bribed Buckingham's 'surveyor' (estate manager) to make accusations. Buckingham says (1.1.222):

> *My surveyor is false. The o'er-great Cardinal*
> *Hath showed him gold. My life is spanned already.*
> *I am the shadow of poor Buckingham*

Though the meaning of the speech is clear enough, it lacks conjunctions like 'because' and 'and' – plus perhaps an adverb such as 'consequently' – which would have made the relationships between the parts of this period more explicit. But, McDonald says, the lack of these 'gives the speech a sense of finality, a businesslike gravity: the impression that there is no more to say.'[17]

Croll's characterizations of 'curt' and 'loose' styles do not convince everyone. In his *Francis Bacon and Renaissance Prose* (1968a), Vickers expresses dissatisfaction with the notion that there is one movement (the 'baroque') which guides and makes its presence known in various art forms, including literature and its styles. Croll, Vickers argues, does not base his theories on the 'analysis of the authors concerned,' but on the desire to identify 'so-called "schools".'[18]

McDonald is another who is not convinced. He argues that the characteristics we have associated with that style – convolutions, looseness, curtness, and the rest – are not (as Croll would have) the manifestations of an anti-Ciceronian revolution. They simply reflect the 'narrative amplitude and structural looseness' of the romance genre. *Asyndeton* occurs, for example, because 'in romance fiction generally, the narrative sequence eschews logic. Connectives are suppressed, leaving the plot full of temporal and geographical gaps.'[19] All in all, 'Shakespeare's late style, comprising as it does hundreds of sentences very casually tied together, is recapitulated structurally in the episodic, disjointed unfolding of dramatic romance.'[20]

Vickers is even more critical of McDonald than he is of Croll. In Vickers (2008) he expresses scepticism of the view that individual stylistic features will 'mimic' the overall structure of a play.

> Such analogies between a linguistic element, even a whole sentence, and a long and complex play, are the product of a scholastic approach which

operates at a more abstract level than that of reading a play or seeing it performed, and foregrounds one detail at the expense of the whole.[21]

Though the two targets of Vickers' attacks – Croll and McDonald – differ very much in their theses, for Vickers their approaches have in common that they are indeed thesis-based: motivated more by theories than by analysis of authors and their actual texts.

11.5 Figures of speech

11.5.1 Hendiadys *and* Hamlet

Perhaps, if your attention is not drawn to it, you may not notice it. But once it has been pointed out, there is no missing it. The 'it' is the number of constructions in *Hamlet* which involve items joined together by the word *and*. The usual combinations are 'noun + *and* + noun' or 'adjective + *and* + adjective.' These instances are taken from just the first scene of the play:

with fear and wonder	*that fair and warlike form*	*the sensible and true avouch*
the gross and scope of mine opinion	*this same strict and most observant watch*	*by law and heraldry*
mettle, hot and full	*here and there*	*for food and diet*
this post-haste and rummage	*high and palmy state of Rome*	*did squeak and gibber*
trains of fire and dews of blood	*heaven and earth together*	*our climatures and countrymen*
lofty and shrill-sounding throat	*th'extravagant and erring spirit*	*so hallowed and so gracious*

Some of these constructions are expressions common to the language, and not particularly noteworthy – like *here and there, heaven and earth together*. Others are examples of the rhetorical figure known as *hendiadys*, defined by the OED as one 'in which a single complex idea is expressed by two words connected by a conjunction; e.g. by two substantives with *and* instead of an adjective and substantive.' The figure was well known in Shakespeare's time, and is called by Puttenham, in his 1589 *Arte of English Poesie*, 'the figure of twynnes,' capturing the idea that in *hendiadys* two ideas are yoked together. In 1981, George Wright (he of *Shakespeare's Metrical Art* fame, discussed at length in Chapter 10) published a paper entitled '*Hendiadys* and Hamlet.' The figure, Wright explains, has a good classical pedigree, the term being coined by the Latin grammarian Servius to describe a figure common in *Aeneid*. A common classical example is from Virgil's *Georgics* – the phrase *pateris libamus et auro* – 'we drink from cups and gold.' This is often translated using an adjective + noun – 'we drink from golden cups.'

The significance of Wright's paper is that it exemplifies the kind of in-depth analysis of single rhetorical features that have appeared since the middle of the twentieth century. Shakespeare uses *hendiadys* a lot. Wright gives the numbers: there are about 300 instances in all; 70 per cent occur in plays written between 1599 and 1606; thereafter, says Kermode (2000), Shakespeare's 'enthusiasm for the device was waning.'[22] *Hamlet* has the greatest number – 66 occurrences. As our examples above show, 'noun + noun' is indeed the most common combination (78 per cent in all Shakespeare), but 'adjective + adjective' is also found, and occasionally other parts of speech. The most noteworthy characteristic of *hendiadys* is that often the conjoined elements are of intriguingly dissimilar character. Wright gives many examples. Two are from the *To be, or not to be* soliloquy. In *slings and arrows* (3.1.58) you have an 'instrument for slinging' (*slings*), yoked together with a 'thing slung' (*arrows*). But, notice, a sling does not sling arrows; a sense of symmetry might have led us to expect, Wright says, 'bows and arrows,' or 'slings and bows,' or 'slings and stones,' or 'stones and arrows.' There are other types of relationship differences that distinguish the conjoined parts. Twelve lines after *slings and arrows*, we have *whips and scorns of time* (3.1.70), where a concrete noun is linked to an abstract one. Earlier in the play, the Ghost talks about Hamlet's *knotted and combined locks* (1.5.18). He is not referring to two different kinds of locks, but locks that are 'combined by being knotted.' But when the Ghost says he must return to *sulphurous and tormenting flames* (1.5.3), he means flames that 'torment because they are sulphurous.' Wright explores these and other semantic relations holding between the constituent parts of Shakespearean *hendiadys* examples.[23]

Such unusual yoking of ideas together can lead to difficulties in interpretation. Sometimes a 'noun + noun' sequence may be interpreted by changing one of the nouns into an adjective. We have already seen an example in Virgil's 'we drink from golden cups.' A Shakespearean instance noted by Wright is Hamlet's *youth and observation* (1.5.101) which can be interpreted to mean 'youthful observation.' But when Laertes speaks of *the perfume and suppliance of a minute* (1.3.9), we are dealing with a 'less easily describable relation.'[24] And when Hamlet says Fortinbras' soldiers are going to die *for a fantasy and trick of fame* (4.4.61), he perhaps means (Wright suggests) '"for a deceptive dream of fame." But if we take the words one by one, it is hard to make them and their syntax add up to this meaning.'[25] Wright's conclusion is that *hendiadys* often involves 'a syntactic complexity that seems fathomable only by an intuitional understanding of the way the words interweave their meanings, rather than by painstaking lexical analysis.'[26]

Wright also explores the situations in which Shakespeare uses *hendiadys*. The figure is among those 'formal locutions that estrange the diction from ordinary speech.'[27] Thus, Wright says, it is often associated with a 'high style,' conveying 'elevation, dignity or remoteness from ordinary experience.'[28] So when Goneril rebukes Albany in *King Lear* (1.4.338), she speaks of *this milky gentleness and course of yours*. Her use of *hendiadys* expresses distant contempt for Albany. *Hendiadys* is also associated with ceremonial set pieces: Polonius instructing Reynaldo, Laertes advising Ophelia, 'Hamlet questioning the cosmos or defining poetry.'[29] Another occasion for the figure's use is in plays 'that explore the problematical depths of thought and feeling,' and this helps to explain its occurrence in *Hamlet* and the other major tragedies.[30] This is because *hendiadys* often involves 'an interweaving, indeed a muddling, of meanings, a deliberate violation of clear sense.'[31] In this statement, and elsewhere, Wright is suggesting that it is the subject matter of *Hamlet* that makes the use of *hendiadys* so common in that play.

11.5.2 Figures of speech in Renaissance England

Our rather lengthy look at *hendiadys* has served to show how in the late twentieth century scholarship began to explore Renaissance figures of speech in some detail. *Hendiadys* is of course one of a multitude of such figures, and for many today – as indeed in the Renaissance – these devices are the main stuff of rhetoric. There have over time been many attempts to subject the field to classifications. The main areas covered under the discipline were generally the four set out by Cicero: *dispositio* (structuring the argument), *elocutio* (expressing the argument in suitably rhetorical language), *memoria* (remembering for the purposes of presentation), *pronunciatio* or *actio* (delivering the argument). Various ways of classifying the figures themselves have also have been developed. It is common to distinguish between *schemes* (from Greek 'shapes') and *tropes* ('turns'). *Schemes* are to do with the 'arrangement of words' and involve such figures as repetition, and those related to the balance of sentences. *Tropes* involve a 'transference of a word's meaning,'[32] 'discussing one thing as if it were another, for example by using metaphor.'[33] Some use the term *figure* as an alternative term for *scheme*; others, like Peacham, use it as the umbrella term, so that both *schemes* and *tropes* are 'figures of speech.' We will follow this usage.

Renaissance writers were particularly interested in the practical applications of rhetoric, rather than its theory, and they gave by far the most attention to *elocutio*. Textbooks like Peacham's and Puttenham's (mentioned in 11.2) – and many others – had as a major aim to list figures of speech. 'For Puttenham,' Adamson et al. (2007) say, 'as for most of his contemporaries, literary rhetoric meant *elocutio* and *elocutio* meant figures of speech.'[34] Educated Elizabethans knew their rhetorical figures. Vickers (1971) cites Willcock and Walker, the editors of Puttenham's works, on the topic:

> A well-educated modern reader may confess without shame to momentary confusion between Hypozeuxis and Hypozeugma, but to his Elizabethan prototype the categories of the figures were, like the multiplication tables, a part of his foundations ... We are all aware of the patterning in Elizabethan verse of this period, but we are generally content to name the genus – balance, antithesis, repetition, and so on. The educated Elizabethan could give a name to every species.[35]

Schoolboys were expected to learn scores of rhetorical figures and know about their uses. In *Ad Herennium* there were 65 to learn, while the second edition of Peacham had 200. Puttenham tried to lessen the learning load by giving some figures of speech English names. We have already seen his definition of *hendiadys* as 'the figure of twynnes.' In the same spirit he called *hyperbole*, 'loud liar,' and *ironia*, 'drie mock.' *Zeugma*, where 'a single word is made to refer to two or more words in the sentence' (OED), is called 'single supplie.'

11.5.3 Listing figures of speech

Because of the importance given to figures of speech in the Renaissance, it is not surprising that since the mid-twentieth century there have been various attempts to produce lists of them, sometimes based around Shakespeare's usage. An early list appeared in Sister Miram Joseph's *Shakespeare's Use of the Arts of Language*, dated 1947 and partly reprinted as her 1962 book *Rhetoric in Shakespeare's Time*. Then in 1968, Lee Ann Sonnino published her *Handbook of Sixteenth Century Rhetoric*. The book does not centre round Shakespeare, but it provides a useful foundation for subsequent studies that do. She lists rhetorical figures – about 500 of them – in alphabetical order. For each she provides definitions, taken from both classical and Renaissance authors. There are also examples, not from poetry or drama, but from Renaissance rhetorical handbooks. To help readers find a rhetorical figure whose name they have forgotten, she also gives a 'descriptive index' of figures classified under functions. Two of her functional categories (there are over 35 in all) are: 'figures that amplify the importance of the subject of discourse' and 'figures that exaggerate or diminish.' A third is 'figures which vary the normal syntax,' and under this comes *hendiadys*, or *endiadis* as she calls it. The book also contains lists of recognized Renaissance styles and genres.

The Greek or Latin names of some of Sonnino's figures make them sound more arcane than they in fact are. Thus the very first item on her list is *Abominatio* or, in Greek, *Bdelygmia*. These are obscure names for a common figure: the expression of hatred or abhorrence, including such Elizabethan commonplaces as *Fie upon it*. Lysander's insults to Hermia in *A Midsummer Night's Dream* are more vigorous instances of *bdelygmia*. *Get you gone*, he says to her (3.2.328):

> *you dwarf;*
> *You minimus, of hindering knot-grass made;*
> *You bead, you acorn.*

Most vigorous of all are the utterances of Theresites, the 'deformed and scurrilous Greek' in *Troilus and Cressida*, who seems to exist on a diet of nothing but *bdelygmia*. The multitude of different figures, sometimes with small differences between them, reinforce Willcock and Walker's point (in 11.5.2) about 'genus' and 'species.' *Bdelygmia*, for example, appears on Sonnino's 'descriptive index' under the category ('genus') of 'figures of personal abuse or accusation.' There are nine other figures ('species') on that list. They include *execratio* – 'to curse and abuse a person for things which cannot be proven' – versus *exprobatio* – 'to chastize a proven crime.'

Brian Vickers is a major figure in Renaissance rhetorical studies. We have already mentioned his 1970 book, *Classical Rhetoric in English Poetry*. It was followed the next year by a paper entitled *Shakespeare's Use of Rhetoric*. Both of these publications contain lists of figures of speech. Vickers (1970) argues that there are those who 'accuse rhetoric of providing "rigid", "mechanical" or "sterile" rules or "systems which kill the imagination".'[36] But in fact, he says, 'the figures contain within themselves a whole series of emotional and psychological effects, almost prior to the presence of meaning or argument.'[37] According to him, the 'functional possibilities' of rhetorical figures – their actual uses rather than just their formal characteristics – were also the concern of the English Renaissance rhetoricians. They too were aware that figures of speech served artistic purposes other than simply to ornament. For example, Peacham, in the 1593 version of his *Garden of Eloquence*, contains comments about use in his descriptions of figures. Hence he describes *anaphora* (*epanaphora*) as 'a forme of speech which beginneth diverse members, still with one and the same word.' To this he adds a comment about its use, which is 'chiefly to repeat a word of importance, and effectual signification.' We will give an example from Shakespeare at the end of section 11.5.5.

In his final chapter, Vickers (1970) analyses passages from Sidney, Spenser, Herbert. There is also an analysis of Shakespeare's Sonnet 129 – the one which begins: *Th' expense of spirit in a waste of shame/ Is lust in action*. But given the title of his book, it is understandable that he should not cover Shakespeare in any detail. Not so the 1971 paper, which is all about Shakespeare. For his examples, Vickers chooses to concentrate on schemes because, he says, tropes have been so well-covered elsewhere in the literature. Some of his examples once again illustrate Willcock and Walker's point about *genre* (genus) and *species*. Modern readers are familiar with the genre of 'puns.' But, as Vickers shows, the 'pun genre' has 'pun species' – four main ones in fact. He takes all his examples from *Richard III*:[38]

Paronomasia
'repeats a word similar in sound to one already used.'
Cousins, indeed; any by their uncle cozen'd.

(4.4.222)

Antanaclasis
'repeats a word while shifting from one meaning to another'
Cursed the heart that had the heart to do it!

(1.2.14)

Syllepsis
'uses a word having two different meanings, without repeating it'
Your imprisonment shall not be long;
I will deliver or else lie for you

(1.1.115)

[*Lie* = 'go to prison,' or 'tell lies']

Asteismus
'a word is returned by the answerer with an unlooked-for second meaning'

Brackenbury: With this, my lord, myself have naught to do.
Richard: Naught to do with Mistress Shore? I tell thee, fellow,
              He that doth naught with her, excepting one,
              Were best he do it secretly, alone.
                                        (1.1.98)
[*Naught* could mean 'nothing' or 'immorality']

There have been other, more recent, lists. Ronberg (1992) has a chapter on rhetoric (entitled 'The art of the matter'). It includes a short history, plus a list of tropes and schemes. He acknowledges that lengthy lists of these already exist, so focuses on the important and common ones, providing clear definitions, and examples from the period as a whole and not just Shakespeare. His list is alphabetical.

Adamson (1999) too has a list, and covers a substantial period (the time-span of Lass 1999 in which her chapter appears is 1476–1776: 300 years). Her section on Renaissance figures of speech makes the point that there have been many lengthy lists, and that any brief account of the figures needs to be based on some principle of selection. Thus her list is not alphabetical, but based on a mode of classification which she largely takes from the poet John Hoskins, whose 1599 *Directions for Speech and Style* contains a taxonomy of figures new for its time. Adamson's two main categories are 'figures of varying' and 'figures of amplifying.' 'Varying,' she says, 'achieves its ends but giving a discourse richness and diversity, amplifying gives it intensity and grandeur.'[39] She then has subcategories, looking at either words or phrases; so there is 'varying the word,' 'varying the phrase,' 'amplifying the word,' and 'amplifying the phrase.' Each of these is considered in great detail – in fact there are four further subcategories under 'varying the word.' She has a Shakespearean example in this category: the line *They do not love, that do not show their love* from *The Two Gentlemen of Verona* (1.2.31), where *love* is used both as a verb and a noun. Also under 'varying the word' are various 'species' of the 'genus' pun.

One of the means of amplifying she considers is the use of Latinate and Germanic vocabularies. She has an interesting example from the final scene of *Hamlet*, where the hero (in almost his last speech) urges Horatio not to kill himself. He says (5.2.341):

Absent thee from felicity awhile,
And in this harsh world draw thy breath in pain

Adamson points out that the second line is almost a paraphrase (an 'amplification') of the first. But there is a difference in vocabulary: the first contains

Romance words, *absent* and *felicity*, while the second has predominantly (though not entirely) Germanic vocabulary.

Adamson's list is not the only one in recent times to use principled criteria to categorize figures, but it is one of the few, and her treatment is particularly detailed.

11.5.4 Detailed figure of speech studies

Like Vickers and Adamson, Read (2007) also discusses puns, concentrating on three of the four 'species' that Vickers mentions: *paronomasia, antanaclasia*, and *syllepsis*. She argues that the pun in particular has been subject to the disapproval often (as we have seen) directed at rhetoric in general. Hence Samuel Johnson – whose criticisms of Shakespeare's style we discussed in 2.3 – was particularly disparaging about the effect of that particular 'fatal Cleopatra' on Shakespeare's writing. The use of puns in contexts of high seriousness must have been particularly bewildering to the eighteenth century (a topic that we touched in in 2.4). Read cites Addison's disapprobation that in Shakespeare's tragedies 'nothing is more usual than to see a hero weeping and quibbling for a dozen lines together.'[40] Especially susceptible to the accusation of inappropriate frivolity are 'death-bed puns.' One celebrated example is John of Gaunt's in *Richard II*, where close to death he puns on his name: *Gaunt am I for the grave, gaunt as a grave* (2.1.82). Another is Mercutio's in *Romeo and Juliet*. Fatally wounded, he announces: '*ask for me tomorrow and you shall find me a grave man*' (3.1.98). Read, whose study is entitled 'Puns: serious wordplay,' shows that punning could be put to serious purposes in Renaissance writing. As regards the death bed, she says that 'playing with words at this juncture is a way of exerting control over hostile fate; even at the approach of death, *homo rhetoricus* does not lose his eloquence.'[41]

Read's study appears in an important recent collection – Adamson et al. (2007), entitled *Renaissance Figures of Speech*. As we have seen, there have been occasional studies focusing in detail on single figure of speech – particularly Wright on *hendiadys*. Adamson et al. (2007) combines depth with breadth. Table 11.1 lists the rhetorical figures that are covered, giving definitions. Chapters covering each of these figures are supplemented by a valuable Introduction, plus a final chapter (Poole, 2007) which shows changing attitudes towards rhetoric between classical and Renaissance times.

The Adamson et al. collection picks up a theme of Vickers (1970), that rhetoric is not necessarily mere ornament, but can be used to artistic ends. The Adamson et al. Introduction contains a Shakespearean example of how rhetorical styles reflect character. It compares the funeral speeches of Brutus and Anthony after the assassination of Caesar in *Julius Caesar*. Brutus' speech is full of *compar* (defined in Table 11.1, and the subject of McDonald's chapter in the collection). It is associated with balance, symmetry, and what Hussey (1992) calls 'the reasonable man.' Adamson et al.'s example (also used by Hussey) is from the Brutus funeral speech:

Table 11.1 Figures of Speech covered in Adamson et al. (2007)[42]

Figure, chapter	Definition of figure
Synonymia (Adamson, Chapter 1)	Peacham: 'when … we iterate one thing diverse times' (particularly by the use of synonyms).
Compar/parison (McDonald, Ch. 2)	'An even balance of clauses, syllables, or other elements in a sentence.'
Periodos (Mueller, Ch. 3)	OED definition for 'period' (III,16): 'A grammatically complete sentence, *esp.* one made up of a number of clauses formed into a balanced or rhythmical whole; (more generally) a series of sentences seen as a linguistic unit.'
Puns (Read, Ch. 4)	Discussed in text.
Prosopopoeia (Alexander, Ch. 5)	'A figure of speech by which an inanimate or abstract thing is represented as a person, or as having personal characteristics, esp. the power to think or speak.'
Ekphrasis (Preston, Ch. 6)	'Enlivening of inanimate things with vivid description.'
Hysteron proteron (Parker, Ch. 7)	'the preposterous.' Coles (1677): 'a speaking or doing praeposterously, putting the cart before the horse.' OED: 'A figure of speech in which the word or phrase that should properly come last is put first.'
Paradiastole (Skinner, Ch. 8)	'A figure of speech in which a favourable turn is given to something unfavourable by the use of an expression that conveys only part of the truth.'
Syncrisis (Donaldson, Ch. 9)	'A figure by which diverse or opposite things are compared.'
Testimony (Serjeantson, Ch. 10)	'Personal or documentary evidence or attestation in support of a fact or statement; hence, any form of evidence or proof.'
Hyperbole (Ettenhuber, Ch. 11)	'A figure of speech consisting in exaggerated or extravagant statement.'
Metalepsis (Cummings, Ch. 12)	'Any metaphorical usage resulting from a series or succession of figurative substitutions.'
'the vices of style' (Poole, Ch. 13)	See text

> *As Caesar loved me, I weep for him; as he was fortunate, I rejoice at it; as he was valiant, I honour him; but, as he was ambitious, I slew him. There is tears for his love; joy for his fortune; honour for his valour; and death for his ambition.*
> (3.2.25)

In contrast, Anthony's rhetoric in his *Friends, Romans, countryman* speech (3.2.74) is more audience-focused and more emotional. One of the figures used is *paralepsis* (*OED*: 'the rhetorical figure of emphasizing or drawing attention to something by professing to say little or nothing about it'). This occurs when

Anthony brings up the question of Caesar's testament, but then dismisses the topic (*Which, pardon me, I do not mean to read* (3.2.132). The speech is also full of *apostrophe* (*OED*: 'a figure of speech, by which a speaker or writer suddenly stops in his discourse, and turns to address pointedly some person or thing, either present or absent'). *O judgement!* he says (3.2.106)), *thou art fled to brutish beasts, / And men have lost their reason.*

Kermode (2000) also shows how Shakespeare skilfully links mode of expression to character. Regarding the dramatist's 'most disgusted and disgusting character,' Iago, Kermode says: 'mention of Desdemona having sex is all that is needed to make him talk dirty.'[43] Thus he tells Desdemona's father, Brabantio, that *an old black ram/Is tupping your white ewe* (1.1.89), and a few lines later that *your daughter and the Moor are now making the beast with two backs* (1.1.116). Such apt matching of language and character is also found in relation to more minor parts. Ariel in *The Tempest*, for example, is a non-human character who observes humans from a 'fairy-like' perspective. Kermode draws attention to the way that he describes shipwrecked Ferdinand, *In an odd angle* [corner] *of the isle, and sitting, /His arms in this sad knot* [with folded arms] (1.2.224). 'The small, sympathetic caricature,' Kermode says, 'is a sketch of a mourning human made by one who is merely familiar with the notion that humans feel sorrow and express it in their own ways.'[44]

11.5.5 Development in Shakespeare's use of rhetoric

Is there any development in Shakespeare's use of rhetorical figures? Vickers (1971) argues that there is. In this passage from the early play, *Richard III*, Queen Margaret is listing the evils Queen Elizabeth has suffered as a result of Richard's cruelty. The speech is a series of parallel questions and other constructions:

> *Where is thy husband now? Where be thy brothers?*
> *Where are thy two sons? Wherein dost thou joy?*
> *Who sues and kneels and says, 'God save the Queen'?*
> *Where be the bending peers that flattered thee?*
> *Where be the thronging troops that followed thee?*
> *Decline all this, and see what now thou art:*
> *For happy wife, a most distressed widow;*
> *For joyful mother, one that wails the name;*
> *For one being sued to, one that humbly sues;*
> *For queen, a very caitiff crowned with care;*
> *For she that scorned at me, now scorned of me;*
> *For she being feared of all, now fearing one;*
> *For she commanding all, obeyed of none.*
>
> (4.4.92)

Rhetoric abounds here: the figures Vickers finds in it are *anaphora, epistrophe, isocolon, parisdon, polyptoton,* and *ploce* (a figure mentioned in 2.4). But

'Shakespeare is manipulating the feeling *via* the rhetoric.'⁴⁵ The feeling comes from the rhetoric, rather than the rhetoric coming from the feeling. Vickers contrasts this with a speech from the late play *The Winter's Tale*. There is a list of parallel questions here too, where Leontes enumerates the signs he thinks show that his wife is being unfaithful:

> *Is whispering nothing?*
> *Is leaning cheek to cheek? Is meeting noses?*
> *Kissing with inside lip? Stopping the career*
> *Of laughing with a sigh? – a note infallible*
> *Of breaking honesty. Horsing foot on foot?*
> *Skulking in corners? Wishing clocks more swift?*
> *Hours minutes? Noon midnight?*
>
> (1.2.285)

About this (and other related passages), Vickers says: 'Here Shakespeare is experiencing the feeling from the inside, his intuitive grasp of human experience finding apparently natural outlet in the shapes of rhetoric.'⁴⁶ The rhetoric comes from feeling, rather than feeling from rhetoric.

Leontes' speech continues like this:

> *And all eyes*
> *Blind with the pin and web but theirs, theirs only,*
> *That would unseen be wicked – is this nothing?*
> *Why, then the world and all that's in't is nothing;*
> *The covering sky is nothing; Bohemia nothing;*
> *My wife is nothing; nor nothing have these nothings,*
> *If this be nothing.*

Vickers (1970) uses the whole passage to give a further example of how Peacham concerns himself with the functions of rhetorical figures. The repetition of 'nothing' is an example of *epistrophe*. Peacham describes it in formal terms as a figure 'which endeth diuerse members of clauses still with one and the same word.'⁴⁷ But he adds a note about use, which this passage well illustrates. *Epistrophe*, Peacham says, 'serueth to leaue a word of importance in the ende of a sentence, that it may the longer hold the sound in the mind of the hearer.'⁴⁸

11.6 A rich variety of tools

Ciceronianus ('*The Ciceronian*') was a treatise, written by Erasmus and published in 1528, in which he attacked overuse of the Ciceronian style. One of his arguments is that people should use a wide range of writing styles to reflect what they want to say. Slavishly copying a rhetorician like Cicero without regard to situation would be foolish: 'Would it not be absurd,' he argues, 'for one to write a letter on a matter of business as carefully as Cicero wrote the oration *Pro Milione*?'[49] The message is particularly important for dramatists who deal with a quantity of people with a quantity of things to say.

In this chapter, we have described just three styles – the Ciceronian, the 'curt,' and the 'loose.' But the stylistic choices Shakespeare made use of were very wide. Another worthy of mention is 'euphuism.' It is named after the character Euphues, the hero of John Lyly's 1578 book *Euphues* (sometimes described as the first English novel). The style was popular in Shakespeare's early years. It is elaborate and complex like Cicero's (and indeed Lyly was sometimes described as 'another Tully'). A characteristic of the style is the use of phrases of equal length appearing in succession. The elements in the phrases are balanced and matching, often having the same structure. But structural similarities are offset by the use of antithesis, with ideas often standing in strong contrast to each other. Alliteration is sometimes also used, and there is a predilection for exotic imagery (often taken from natural history). One of the Shakespearean characters who sometimes uses a euphuistic style is Falstaff. Hussey (1992: 72) cites these lines from *Henry IV, Part 1* (2.4.394), which are in fact adapted from a passage in Lyly's *Euphues*:

> *For though the camomile, the more it is trodden on the faster it grows, yet youth, the more it is wasted the sooner it wears.*

Balance, antithesis, and natural history imagery are all present here. Other Shakespearean characters who use euphuism are *Hamlet's* Polonius, and Moth from *Love's Labour's Lost*.

But the styles which have been graced with established titles – like 'Ciceronian' and 'euphuism' are only part of the picture. Hussey (1992) describes the richness of Shakespearean styles in particular detail. He talks about the stylistic features Shakespeare associates with 'the rational man'; the style associated with discussion of 'affairs of state'; and he asks the question whether there is a Shakespearean 'Roman style,' used by characters like Brutus, Coriolanus, and Anthony.

There are also styles of speech associated with individual characters. Pistol (in *Henry IV, Part 2, Henry V, The Merry Wives of Windsor*) has a particularly interesting idiolect, and Hussey devotes a lengthy section to discussion of his style. Its characteristics are the use of: foreign expressions; archaic words; curious word order; alliteration; classical/literary allusions; bombastic phrases. This extract from *Henry V* illustrates all these features. Pistol is arguing Nym, and threatens, in bad French, to cut Nym's throat: *couper la gorge*:

> *'Couple a gorge!'*
> *That is the word. I thee defy again!*
> *O hound of Crete, think'st thou my spouse to get?*
> *No, to the spital go,*
> *And from the powdering tub of infamy*

Fetch forth the lazar kite of Cressid's kind,
Doll Tearsheet she by name, and her espouse.
I have, and I will hold, the quondam Quickly
For the only she; and – pauca, there's enough.
Go to!

(H5 2.1.68)

This chapter has looked in detail at rhetorical figures, but also at styles in a more general sense. In both cases what we find is a rich and complex collection of tools available to Renaissance poets and dramatists. Modern scholarship has helped to show how Shakespeare used them to the full.

Notes

1. Lewis (1954), p. 61. Cited at the front of Vickers (1970).
2. Rhodes (2008).
3. Mack (2011), p. 1.
4. Vickers (1970), p. 34.
5. The account in this paragraph is based on Adamson (1999).
6. Mack (2011), p. 2.
7. Ronberg (1992), p. 112.
8. We here use the accounts particularly of Adamson (1999), Ronberg (1992), and Barish (1960).
9. Ronberg (1992), p. 105.
10. *Ibid.*, pp. 112–13.
11. Barish (1960), p. 117.
12. Croll (1929), p. 87.
13. Dick (1999), p. 186.
14. Quotations from Croll (1929), p. 89.
15. The example is taken from Johnson (2013).
16. McDonald (2006), p. 90.
17. *Ibid.*, p. 90.
18. Vickers (1968a), p. 13.
19. McDonald (2006), p. 90.
20. McDonald *Ibid.*, pp. 38–9.
21. Vickers (2008), p. 6.
22. Kermode (2000), p. 168.
23. Wright (198), p. 182.
24. *Ibid.*, p. 169.
25. *Ibid.*, p. 169.
26. *Ibid.*, p. 172.
27. *Ibid.*, p. 174.
28. *Ibid.*, p. 173.
29. *Ibid.*, p. 174.
30. *Ibid.*, p. 173.
31. *Ibid.*, p. 173.
32. Vickers (1971), p. 394.
33. Adamson et al. ((2007), p. 6.

34 *Ibid.*, p. 5.
35 Willcock and Walker (1970), p. lxxvff. Cited by Vickers (1971), p. 394.
36 Vickers (1970), p. 77.
37 *Ibid.*, p. 79.
38 All quotations are from Vickers (1971), p. 397.
39 Adamson (1999), p. 549.
40 Read (2007), p. 81.
41 *Ibid.*, p. 93.
42 All definitions are taken from the *OED* unless otherwise stated.
43 Kermode (2000), p. 169.
44 *Ibid.*, p. 290.
45 Vickers (1971), p. 403.
46 *Ibid.*, p. 405.
47 Vickers (1970), p. 106.
48 *Ibid.*, p. 43.
49 Scott (1908), p. 86.

12 Where the future lies

12.1 Turning over stones

'There is today,' we announced in 1.1, 'hardly a Shakespearean linguistic stone that remains unturned.' With so much already done, is there any future for Shakespeare language studies? Yes, there is, because as every gardener knows, when stones are turned over, other stones reveal themselves. There is still much turning-over to be done.

For this short chapter, a number of specialists were approached and asked what they felt the future held for Shakespeare language studies. What follows is based on the responses received, from David Crystal, Jonathan Culpeper, Giles Goodland, Jonathan Hope, and Katie Wales.

12.2 Lexis and pronunciation

Many of the respondents' comments relate to Shakespeare's vocabulary, particularly how many neologisms he was responsible for – topics covered in Chapter 5. Goodland takes up the point made in 5.2.2, that what were earlier regarded as Shakespeare neologisms are now being found in earlier works. Section 5.2.2 gives numerous examples. To add one more from Goodland: the 2009 version of the *OED* has the first citation of *obscene* in *Richard II* (4.1.131), where a deed is described as *heinous, black, obscene*. But the current version of the *OED* gives an earlier (1571) first citation in a translation of Plutarch, where 'evil living' is said to be created by *obscene and filthy wordes*. Despite the recent removal of such items from the neologism list, it is still a long one. Some are the kinds of phrase likely to arise in poetic discourse – compounds like *dog-weary*, which occurs in *The Taming of the Shrew* (4.2.60), where Biondello complains: *I have watched so long that I am dog-weary*. Others are formations derived by simply adding an affix, and these are words which you might well expect to be appearing commonly in the language. An example is *characterless*. It still has a Shakespeare first citation from *Troilus and Cressida* (3.2.186), where Cressida talks about a time when *mighty states characterless are grated* [*worn away*] / *To dusty nothing*. Goodland is confident that as more evidence becomes available, earlier citations will continue to be uncovered. Many of these are likely to be from non-literary texts, such as letters, journals, recipe collects, as well as documents like wills. As was mentioned in Chapter 5.2.2, the *OED* has come to realize the importance of such texts to avoid what we called the 'treasure-house syndrome.'

How will newly available data be searched? The point was made in Chapter 5.1 that computers have revolutionized text analysis. The revolution will doubtless continue into the future, and Hope draws attention to the contribution of projects like EEBO. This project has generated large numbers of fully searchable texts, and the number continues to grow. EEBO operates by initially making texts available to participating institutions. At a later stage they become freely available to the public. Phase 1 of the project generated over 25,000 texts. It was completed in 2009, and the texts were made accessible to the public in 2015. The 45,000 texts planned for Phase 2 will be publicly available in 2020. A good number of the total generated texts will be from Shakespeare's time or before, and will provide valuable information about his lexical practices within a historical context.

The task remains to find the means by which this increasing amount of data may be exploited. Hope draws attention to several 'text-mining' facilities that are in the process of being developed. One such facility is known as 'Early Modern Print,' housed at Washington University in St. Louis. There are two main tools. One is the 'N-Gram Browser.' An N-gram is a single word or a short sequence of contiguous words extracted from a text. The user enters a word or phrase, plus a time period, and the browser gives a graph showing its frequency of use over the period – clearly showing periods of greater and lesser use. The second tool is the 'Key Words in Context' facility. When a word is entered (plus a specific time period if wished), the tool lists all uses from the text data, giving full information about the publications where it appears. For each instance of use, the word is shown in a line of context, and this can be extended by a click to a full text. Hope's view is that facilities like this are 'going to revolutionize the study of Shakespeare's language, and our understanding of Early Modern culture.'[1]

In 5.1 we said that the computer had replaced the 'oxcart' as a means of lexical study. But has the oxcart in fact been abandoned? Recently scientists have come to appreciate that there are some ways in which humans are superior to computers as data-collectors. One such way is in recognizing visual patterns. An astronomy project known as 'Planet Hunters' exploits this. Images of data collected by NASA are shown to large numbers of human volunteers who are asked to observe how the brightness of a star changes over time. So far, over 12 million observations have been analysed, providing useful information in the search for the existence of planets outside the solar system. This 'Planet Hunters' project is one of a large number associated with the 'Zooniverse' organization, which has its headquarters at Oxford University and the Adler Planetarium in Chicago. The method of research has become known as 'crowdsourced,' and it involves what are called 'citizen scientists.' Any interested individual who is prepared to put time into contributing to some area of research can become a citizen scientist; no academic qualifications are required. Zooniverse has more than a million registered volunteers, and it oversees multiple projects in areas associated with astronomy, ecology, cell biology, climate science. Humanities are also included, and one project is known as 'Shakespeare's World' – a collaboration between the Folger Shakespeare Library, Zooniverse, and the OED. In the project, citizen scientists are invited to transcribe portions of manuscripts written during Shakespeare's lifetime. In the first phase of the project the focus is on letters and recipes; later other documents like family papers and legal documents will be added. Individuals who wish to help with transcriptions need simply to go to the project's website, where they will be given a manuscript to start transcribing.[2]

Goodland suggests that the project is likely to contribute significantly to our knowledge of lexis during Shakespeare's lifetime, and this will inevitably lead to continuing revision of Shakespeare's neologism list. Crystal has indeed recently completed one such revision, for the third edition of his *Cambridge Encyclopedia of the English Language*. He draws attention to a further issue relevant to the identification of neologisms. The OED's policy regarding Shakespeare dating is to avoid supposed dates of composition or performance, since it frequently cannot be shown whether a specific word was used at those times. The publication dates of quartos are sometimes used, but often the OED simply gives 'a1616' as the date: 'a' being 'ante,' and 1616 being the date of Shakespeare's death. This style is used for all of the 18 plays that first appeared in print in the First Folio of 1623, as well as for other posthumous editions in which quotations, or headwords, appeared for the first time. Such unspecific 'a1616 datings' pose problems for those trying to establish reliable lists of neologisms. Hence Crystal, in his revision of the Shakespeare neologism list for the *Encyclopedia*'s third edition, has had to resort to a separate chronology of the works.

A second feature of Crystal's new neologism list is that he has found it useful to introduce 'levels of confidence,' classifying neologisms according to how certain it is that they were Shakespeare inventions. The criterion Crystal uses is the 'time-gap' between Shakespeare's use and following occurrences. If a word is found soon after its use in Shakespeare, the case for it being a Shakespeare neologism is lessened. One of Crystal's examples is the word *bald-pated*. Its first OED citation is in *Measure for Measure*, where Lucio described Angelo as a *bald-pated, lying rascal* (5.1.349). The play is dated 1604. The next occurrence is in a 1606 work by the dramatist John Day. The proximity of dates makes it likely that the word was in general circulation. Crystal's example of the opposite situation is *undeaf*. John of Gaunt expresses the hope that his death *may yet undeaf his* [Richard's] *ear* (2.1.16). The time-gap between this and the next recorded occurrence suggests that the word was a genuine Shakespeare neologism. Applying the time-gap criterion, Crystal hypothesizes three levels of confidence:

- *Weak* next use (after Shakespeare) in Shakespeare's generation;
- *Moderate* next use in the generation after Shakespeare;
- *Strong* next use later.

At the end of 8.8 we said that 'the study of past pronunciations has a healthy future.' Interest in this area does indeed continue to grow, Crystal says, particularly in the United States. The Baltimore Shakespeare Factory, for example, produces one OP production every year; in 2018 it was *Othello*. 8.8 also mentioned that the scope of OP is likely to extend to authors other than Shakespeare (and composers other than Dowland and Byrd, who have already been performed in OP).

12.3 The theatre, speech acts, and cognitive stylistics

One of the chapters in the 2001 Adamson et al. collection is Peter Lichtenfels, an author who combines the roles of theatre producer and academic. In the chapter, he argues that the theatre can tell us much about Shakespeare's dramatic language; also that the texts themselves provide many clues about how the plays should be performed. He gives a detailed example from the scene in *Richard III* (1.2) where Richard confronts the pallbearers carrying the body of Henry VI. Lichtenfels shows how the text reveals what actions take place, as well as providing information about how the actors should react to the unfolding events. A second person who combines theatrical and academic interests is Rokison. The full title of her 2011 book reveals the same kind of orientation as Lichtenfels, linking the study of Shakespeare's language with theatre practice. The title is *Shakespearean Verse Speaking: Text and Theatre Practice*.

One of the ways in which Katie Wales feels Shakespeare language studies might develop lies in the same direction. It involves looking at 'Shakespeare on the stage rather than on the page.'[3] She has a particular interest in pronouns, as we saw in 7.3 where her work on the *thou/you* distinction was discussed. Wales (2018) is also about pronouns, and she begins by saying that while *thou* and *you* have been well studied, the pronoun *I* has not. Her paper focuses on *I*, and on the rhetorical figure of speech *prosopopoeia*. The *OED* defines this as 'a rhetorical device by which an imaginary, absent, or dead person is represented as speaking or acting.' She looks at *prosopopoeia* in *Hamlet* where the 'imaginary, absent, or dead person' is the Ghost of Hamlet's father. Wales considers in detail at how the Ghost is referred to. Much of the time the pronoun used is *it*, and on one occasion (1.1.21) Marcellus refers to it as *this thing*. The mysterious, ambiguous nature of the Ghost continues through much of Act 1, reaching a climax when the Ghost eventually speaks – and *prosopopoeia* occurs – in the final scene of the Act.

Wales' paper is exploring a rhetorical figure of speech not to do with poetic expression (as many figures of speech are), but related to on-stage communication between characters. 'Shakespeare's language within a theatrical context' is for her an important future direction.

Since the theatre has a central interest in action and performance, it is likely to be informed by speech-act theory, which we discussed in 7.1; indeed, speech acts might be regarded as linguistically framed acts or actions, even 'performances.' The field is, as we noted, a relatively new one within linguistics.

This means that despite the fact that (as Chapter 7 shows) some Shakespearean speech acts have been studied, there is more work to be done. Culpeper is among those who predict future developments in this area.

He feels that future applications in Shakespeare language studies will also come from 'cognitive stylistics' or 'cognitive poetics.' This is 'a field at the interface between linguistics, literary studies and cognitive science – geared to a better understanding and appreciation of the literary text.'[4] The approach was briefly touched on in 5.4, in relation to metaphor. We saw that CMT views metaphors not as devices introduced simply for poetic effect, but as representations profoundly affected by culture, and in turn affecting the way we think. Oncins-Martinez's (2011) study of Shakespeare's sexual language (described in 5.4) shows the approach in practice. So too does an earlier paper by Culpeper (2000). In this, he uses cognitive theories – developed to help understand 'real' people – to analyse a fictional character: Katherina in *The Taming of the Shrew*. Culpeper utilizes psychological theories concerned with issues such as the role of prior knowledge, and the formation of impressions. His resulting character-profile of Katherina is different from some found in the critical literature, where she is regarded as an entirely shrew-like character, who becomes a 'broken woman' as she is 'tamed' – an outcome clearly shown in the Act 5, Scene 3 'obedience speech' where she describes a submissive role for women. Culpeper has her neither as a total shrew, nor as a broken woman; she is decidedly not a 'flat' caricature from a farce. In recent years, cognitive stylistics has become dominant in literary stylistics, and this suggests a growing future role in Shakespeare language studies.

12.4 Envoi

Looking through the contents of this book, it surely cannot be doubted that language studies have contributed considerably to our understanding and appreciation of Shakespeare. It is also a reasonable prediction that this contribution will grow in the future.

But 'ancient grudges' will still doubtless continue to 'break to new mutiny.' In 3.2 we saw how in the nineteenth century, 'scientific' approaches to Shakespeare criticism were the subject of heated debate, fatally dividing the New Shakspeare Society. Fleay was on the 'scientific' side: 'if you cannot weight, measure, number your results …,' he said, 'you must not hope to convince others, or claim the position of an investigator; you are merely a guesser.' The poet Swinburne (whom Furnivall rudely referred to as 'Pigsbrook') took the opposite view, that 'prosaic' counting and measuring contributed little of insight.

For today's Fleays, linguistics may be seen as a way of avoiding being mere guessers, while those of a Swinburnian disposition will perhaps disdain the linguist's counting and measuring tendencies. But the time is ripe, one might argue, to dispense with such polarized views. A concept that might help bring Fleays and Swinburnes together is inter- (or trans-)disciplinariness. At some points in this book we have come across work which set out to break down the barriers of traditional academic disciplines. In 5.5, for example, we encountered the 'transdisciplinary approaches' found in the Ravassat and Culpeper (2011) collection. Perhaps the future of Shakespeare language studies lies here. If so, a major future role of linguistics will be as a contributor: an emerging discipline that combines with other disciplines – both traditional and new – to offer fresh perspectives.

Notes

1 Personal communication. The Early Modern Print project is described at https://earlyprint.wustl.edu. This site gives access to the two facilities discussed.
2 Zooniverse is described at www.zooniverse.org. The Shakespeare's World website – www.shakespearesworld.org/#/ – permits you to begin the process of transcribing a text.
3 Personal communication.
4 Oncins-Martinez (2011), p. 217.

References

Abbott, E. A. (1870). *A Shakespearian Grammar*. Mineola: Dover Publications (1966).
Adamson, S. (1999). 'Literary language.' In Lass (1999), 539–653.
Adamson, S. (2001). 'Understanding Shakespeare's grammar: Studies in small words.' In Adamson et al. (2001), 210–36.
Adamson, S., Alexander, G., and Ettenhuber, K (eds) (2007). *Renaissance Figures of Speech*. Cambridge: Cambridge University Press.
Adamson, S., Hunter, L., Magnusson, L., Thompson, A., and Wales, K. (eds) (2001). *Reading Shakespeare's Dramatic Language*. London: Arden Shakespeare.
Armstrong, E. A. (1946). *Shakespeare's Imagination*. London: Lindsay Drummond.
Atkins, C. D. (2003). 'The application of bibliographical principles to the editing of punctuation in Shakespeare's sonnets.' *Studies in Philology*, 100/4: 493–513.
Attridge, D. (2014). *The Rhythms of English Poetry*. London: Longman.
Austen, Jane (1814). *Mansfield Park*. In Wiltshire, J. (ed) Cambridge: Cambridge University Press (2005).
Austin, J. L. (1962). *How to Do Things with Words*. Oxford: Oxford University Press.
Barber, C. (1981). '"You" and "thou" in Shakespeare's *Richard III*.' In Meredith (1981), 273–89.
Barber, C. (1997). *Early Modern English Revised Edition*. Edinburgh: Edinburgh University Press.
Barish, J. A. (1960). 'Jonson's dramatic prose.' In Watson (1970), 111–55.
Bartlett, J. (1894). *A new and complete concordance or verbal index to words, phrases, and passages in the dramatic works of Shakespeare with a supplementary concordance to the poems*. London: Macmillan and Co. (1927).
Bate, J. (1984). 'Hazlitt's Shakespearean quotations.' *Prose Studies*, 7: 26–37.
Baugh, A. C. and Cable, T. (2013). *A History of the English Language*. 6th Edition. London: Routledge.
Baxter, J. (1980). *Shakespeare's Poetic Styles*. London: Routledge and Kegan Paul.
Bayley, H. (1906). *The Shakespeare Symphony: An Introduction to the Ethics of Elizabethan Drama*. London: Chapman and Hall.
Bentley, G. E. (1945). *Shakespeare and Jonson Vols 1 and 2*. Chicago: University of Chicago Press.
Birch T. (1756). *History of the Royal Society of London*. London.
Blake, N. F. (2002). *A Grammar of Shakespeare's Language*. Basingstoke: Palgrave Macmillan.
Blayney, P. W. M. (1996). 'Introduction to the second edition.' In Hinman (1996), xxvii–xxxvii.
Bloomfield, L. (1933). *Language*. London: Allen and Unwin (1935).
Bolton, W. F. (1992). *Shakespeare's English: Language in the History Plays*. Oxford: Blackwell.
Booth, S. (1969). *An Essay on Shakespeare's Sonnets*. London: Yale University Press.
Bowdler, T. (1843). 'Preface to the First Edition.' In *The Family Shakespeare, 8th Edition*. London: Longman, Brown and Green.

Bowers, F. (1968). *On Editing Shakespeare*. Charlottesville: University Press of Virginia.

Bowers, F. (1980). 'Establishing Shakespeare's text: notes on short lines and the problem of verse division.' *Studies in Bibliography*, 33, 74–130.

Brewer, C. (2007). *Treasure-House of the Language: The Living OED*. London: Yale University Press.

Brewer, C. (2010). 'The use of literary quotations in the *OED*.' *The Review of English Studies*, 61, 93–125.

Brooks, C. (1947). 'The naked babe and the cloak of manliness.' In Brooks, C., *The Well Wrought Urn*. New York: Harcourt Brace Jovanovich, 22–49.

Brook, G. L. (1976). *The Language of Shakespeare*. London: Deutsch.

Brown, A. (1960). 'The rationale of old-spelling editions of the plays of Shakespeare and his contemporaries: a rejoinder.' *Studies in Bibliography*, 13,:69–76.

Brown, J. (1751). 'Essay on ridicule.' In Brown, J., (1767), *Essays on the Characteristics of the Earl of Shaftesbury*. London, 1–107.

Brown, J. R. (1960). 'The rationale of old-spelling editions of the plays of Shakespeare and his contemporaries.' *Studies in Bibliography*, 13: 49–67.

Brown, P. and Levinson, S. C. (1987). *Politeness: Some Universals in Language Usage*. Cambridge: Cambridge University Press.

Brown, R. and Gilman, A. (1960). 'The pronouns of power and solidarity.' In Sebeok (1960), 253–76.

Brown, R. and Gilman, A. (1989). 'Politeness theory and Shakespeare's four major tragedies.' *Language in Society*, 18: 159–212.

Butler, C. (1633). *The English Grammar*. Oxford.

Calvo, C. (1990). *Power Relations and Fool-Master Discourse in Shakespeare. A Discourse Stylistic Approach to Dramatic Dialogue*. Nottingham University PhD thesis. Available online at http://core.ac.uk/download/pdf/99293.pdf.

Capell, E. (1774). 'A brief essay on verse, as of Shakespeare's modelling; its principles, and its construction.' In Capell, E. *Notes and Various Readings to Shakespeare*. London.

Capell, E. (1780). *Notes and Various readings to Shakespeare, Vol. 2*. New York: Burt Franklin (1970).

Carlyle, T. (1841). 'The hero as poet.' In Gray (1906), 76–111.

Cercignani, F. (1981). *Shakespeare's Works and Elizabethan Pronunciation*. Oxford: Clarendon Press.

Chambers, E. K. (1930). *William Shakespeare: A Study of Facts and Problems. Vol. 2*. Oxford: Clarendon Press.

Clemen, W. H. (1951). *The Development of Shakespeare's Imagery*. London: Methuen.

Cole, P. and Morgan, J. (eds) (1975). *Syntax and Semantics: Speech Acts*. New York: Academic Press.

Coles, E. (1677). *An English Dictionary*. Andesite Press (2015).

Collier, J. P. (1842). *Prospectus of the Shakespeare Society*. Shakespeare Society Publication 1.

Collier, J. P. (1882). *Diary*, xxvi. 40–1 Folger Shakespeare Library MS M. a. 40.

Colney, T. M. (1900). *Rhetoric in the European Tradition*. Chicago: University of Chicago Press.

Cooke, W. (1775). *The Elements of Dramatic Criticism*. Extracted in Vickers (1981), 149–51.

Coulthard, M. (1985). *An Introduction to Discourse Analysis*. 2nd Edition. London: Longman.

Cowden Clarke, M. (1864). *The Complete Concordance to Shakspere; being a verbal index to all the passages in the dramatic works of the poet*. London: W. Kent and Co.

Craig, H. (2011). 'Shakespeare's vocabulary: myth and reality.' *Shakespeare Quarterly*, 62/1, 53–74.

Craig, H. and Kinney, A. F. (2009). *Shakespeare, Computers, and the Mystery of Authorship*. Cambridge: Cambridge University Press.

Croll, M. W. (1929). 'The baroque style in prose.' In Watson (1970), 84–110.

Crystal, B. (2012). *Speeches and Scenes Performed as Shakespeare Would Have Heard Them.* London: British Library Publishing.
Crystal, D. (2004). *The Stories of English.* London: Penguin.
Crystal, D. (2005). *Pronouncing Shakespeare.* Cambridge: Cambridge University Press.
Crystal, D. (2008). *Think on my Words.* Cambridge: Cambridge University Press.
Crystal, D. (2008a). *A Dictionary of Linguistics and Phonetics.* Oxford: Wiley Blackwell.
Crystal, D. (2013). 'Early interest in Shakespearean original pronunciation.' *Language and History*, 56/1: 5–17.
Crystal, D. (2015). *Making a Point: The Pernickety Story of English Punctuation.* London: Profile Books.
Crystal, D. (2016). *The Oxford Dictionary of Original Shakespeare Pronunciation.* Oxford: Oxford University Press.
Crystal, D. and Crystal, B. (2002). *Shakespeare's Words.* London: Penguin Books.
Crystal, D. and Crystal, B. (2002a). *Shakespeare's Words.* Online version: www.shakespeareswords.com/.
Crystal, D. and Crystal, B. (2005). *The Shakespeare Miscellany.* London: Penguin Books.
Culpeper, J. (1996). 'Towards an anatomy of impoliteness.' *Journal of Pragmatics*, 25, 349–67.
Culpeper, J. (2011). 'A new kind of dictionary for Shakespeare's plays: an immodest proposal.' In Ravassat and Culpeper (2011), 58–83.
Culpeper, J. (2011a). *Impoliteness: Using Language to Cause Offence.* Cambridge: Cambridge University Press.
Culpeper, J. (2012). 'The dialogue of plays and their contexts from the Early Modern period to the present day.' In Mazzon and Fodde (2012), 21–39.
Culpeper, J. and Kytö, M. (2010). *Early Modern English Dialogues: Spoken Interaction as Writing.* Cambridge: Cambridge University Press.
Daines, S. (1640). *Orthoepia Anglicana.* London.
Decker, C. (2014). 'Shakespeare editions.' In Marshall (2012), 16–38.
De Saussure, F. (1915). *Cours de Linguistique Générale.* Paris: Payot (1964).
Dick, O. L. (ed.) (1999). *Aubrey's Brief Lives.* Boston: Gordino.
Dobson, E. J. (1957). *English Pronunciation: 1500–1700.* Oxford: Oxford University Press.
Dover Wilson, J. (1921). *The Tempest.* Cambridge: Cambridge University Press (1969).
Dover Wilson, J. (1951). 'Preface to Clemen, W. H. *The Development of Shakespeare's Imagery*.' In Clemen (1951), v-vii.
Dryden, J. (1672). *Defence of the Epilogue.* In Scott, W. 1808 *The Works of John Dryden. Vol. 4.* Edinburgh: Ballantyne and Co (1808).
Dryden, J. (1679). 'Preface to Troilus and Cressida.' In The *Dramatick Works of John Dryden. Vol. 5.* London (1717).
Ekwall, E. (1958). 'Review of Dobson's *English Pronunciation*.' *The Review of English Studies*, 9/35: 303–12.
Elam, K. (2008). *Twelfth Night.* The Arden Shakespeare Third Series. London: Methuen Drama.
Ellegård, A. (1953). *The Auxiliary Do. The Establishment and Regulation of its Use in English.* Stockholm: Almqvist and Wiksell.
Elliott, W. and Valenza, R. (2011). 'Shakespeare's vocabulary: did it dwarf all others?.' In Ravassat and Culpeper (2011), 34–57.
Ellis, A. J. (1869–89). *On Early English Pronunciation.* London.
Empson, W. (1930) *Seven Types of Ambiguity. 3rd Edition.* London: Chatto and Windus (1977).
Fanego, T. (1996). 'English in transition 1500–1700: on variation in second person singular pronoun usage.' *Sederi* (Yearbook of the Spanish and Portuguese Society for English Renaissance Studies), 7, 5–15.

Findlay, A. (2014). *Women in Shakespeare*. London: Bloomsbury Publishing.
Firth, C. H. and Rait, R. S. (eds) (1911). *Acts and Ordinances of the Interregnum, 1642–1660*: 'September 1642: order for stage-plays to cease.' London: His Majesty's Stationery Office.
Fischlin, D. and Fortier, M. (eds) (2000). *Adaptations of Shakespeare: A Critical Anthology of Plays from the Seventeenth Century to the Present*. London: Routledge.
Flatter, R. (1948). *Shakespeare's Producing Hand*. London: Heinemann.
Fleay, F. G. (1874). 'On metrical tests as applied to dramatic poetry. Part 1.' *New Shakspere Society's Transactions, Vol I*. London: Trübner and Co.
Fowler, R. (1975). 'Language and the reader: Shakespeare's Sonnet 73.' In Fowler, R. (ed.), *Style and Structure in Literature: Essays in the New Stylistics*. Oxford: Oxford University Press.
Franz, W. (1900). *Shakespeare-Grammatik*. Halle: Niemeyer.
Furness, H. H. (ed.) (1873) *Macbeth*, Vol. 2 of *A New Variorum Edition of Shakespeare, 3rd Edition*. London and Philadelphia: J. B. Lippincott Co.
Furnivall, F. L. (1861). *Transactions of the New Shakspere Society 1875–6*. London: Trübner and Co.
Garner, B. A. (1982). 'Shakespeare's Latinate neologisms.' In Salmon and Burness (1987), 207–28.
Garrick, D. (1769). Advertisement for *An Ode upon Dedicating and Erecting a Statue, to Shakespeare, at Stratford Upon Avon*. Extracted in Vickers (1979), 344–55.
Gentleman, F. (1770). *The Dramatic Censor*. London.
Gentleman, F. (1773). *Bell's Edition of Shakespeare's Plays, As they are now performed at the Theatres Royal in London*. Extracted in Vickers (1981), 89–112.
Gibbons, A. and Macrae, A. (eds) (2018). *Pronouns in Literature*. Basingstoke: Palgrave Macmillan.
Gilbert, A. J. (1997). *Shakespeare's Dramatic Speech*. Lampeter: The Edwin Mellen Press.
Glanvill, J. (1676). 'Anti-fanatical religion and free philosophy.' Essay 7 in *Essays on Several Important Subjects in Philosophy and Religion*. London.
Goodland, G. (2011). '"Strange deliveries": contextualizing Shakespeare's first citations in the OED.' In Ravassat and Culpeper (2011), 8–33.
Görlach, M. (1991). *Introduction to Early Modern English*. Cambridge: Cambridge University Press.
Graham-White, A. (1982). 'Elizabethan punctuation and the actor: "Gammer Gurton's Needle" as a case study.' *Theatre Journal*, 34/1: 96–106.
Graham-White, A. (1995). *Punctuation and Its Dramatic Value in Shakespearean Drama*. Newark: University of Delaware Press.
Graves, R. and Riding, L. (1926). 'A study in original punctuation and spelling.' In Graves, R. (1949), *The Common Asphodel: Collected Essays on Poetry, 1922–1949*. London: Hamish Hamilton, 84–95.
Gray, H. D. (1906). *Thomas Carlyle's On Heroes, Hero-Worship, and the Heroic in History*. New York: Longmans, Green and Co.
Greenwood, G. (1908). *The Shakespeare Problem Restated*. London: John Lane Company.
Greg, W. W. (1942) *The Editorial Problem in Shakespeare*. Oxford: Oxford University Press.
Grice, P. (1975) 'Logic and conversation.' In Cole and Morgan (1975), 41–58.
Groves, P. (2011). 'Shakespeare's 'short' pentameters and the rhythms of dramatic verse.' In Ravassat and Culpeper (2011), 119–38.
Groves, P. (2013). *Rhythm and Meaning in Shakespeare: A Guide for Readers and Actors*. Monash: Monash University Publishing.
Hardy, B. (2008). *Dickens and Creativity*. London: Continuum.
Hassel, R. C. (2015). *Shakespeare's Religious Language*. London: Bloomsbury Publishing.

Heid, U. (2008). 'Corpus linguistics and lexicography.' In Lüdeling and Kytö (2008), 131–53.
Hill, T. H. (1959). 'Elizabethan and Jacobean printers' use of the tilde.' *Notes and Queries*, Feb., 76–7.
Hinman, C. (1963). *The Printing and Proof-Reading of the First Folio of Shakespeare*. Oxford: Clarendon Press.
Hinman, C. (1996). *The Norton Facsimile. The First Folio of Shakespeare. 2nd Edition*. New York: W. W. Norton and Company.
Holinshed, R. (1577). *Chronicles. Vol. 3*. London (1803).
Hollingsworth, M. (2012). 'Shakespeare criticism.' In Marshall (2012), 39–59.
Hope, J. (1994). 'The use of *thou* and *you* in Early Modern spoken English: evidence from depositions in the Durham ecclesiastical court records.' In Kastovsky (1991), 141–52.
Hope, J. (2002). *Shakespeare's Grammar*. London: Arden Shakespeare.
Hope, J. (2010). *Shakespeare and Language*. London: Arden Shakespeare.
Hope, J. (2012). 'Shakespeare and the English language.' In Sergeant and Swan (2012), 83–92.
Houston, J. P. (1988). *Shakespearean Sentences: A Study in Style and Syntax*. Baton Rouge: Louisiana State University Press.
Hussey, S. S. (1992). *The Literary Language of Shakespeare. 2nd Edition*. London: Longman.
Hymes, D. (1972). 'On communicative competence.' In Pride and Holmes (1972), 269–93.
Hughes, J. (ed.) (1715). *The Works of Mr Edmund Spenser with a Glossary Explaining the Old and Obscure Words*. London.
Humphreys, A. R. (ed.) (2007). *The Second Part of King Henry IV*. London: Arden Shakespeare.
Hurd, R. (1748). *The Works of Richard Hurd. Vol. 1*. London (1811).
Ingham, R. and Ingham, M. (2011). 'Subject-verb inversion and iambic rhythm in Shakespeare's dramatic verse.' In Ravassat and Culpeper (2011), 98–118.
Ingleby, C. M. (1861). *A Complete View of the Shakspere Controversy*. London: Nattali and Bond.
Iyengar, S. (2014). *Shakespeare's Medical Language*. London: Bloomsbury Publishing.
Jacobson, M. (2015). 'Learning to colour in *Hamlet*.' In Yachnin (2015), 103–23.
James, P. (2008). *Not Dead Enough*. 2008 London: Pan Macmillan.
Jarka, L. M. (1967). *Imagery in Coriolanus*. Theses, Dissertations, professional Papers. Paper 2643, University of Minnesota.
Jespersen, O. (1907). *John Hart's Pronunciation of English (1569–1570)*. Heidelberg: C. Winter.
Jespersen, O (1932). *Growth and Structure of the English Language. 10th Edition*. Oxford: Basil Blackwell (1982).
Johnson, K. (2013). *Shakespeare's English*. London: Routledge.
Johnson, S. (1751). *The Rambler*, No. 168, 1751. In Lynam, R. (ed.), *The Works of Samuel Johnson. Vol. 2*. London (1825).
Johnson, S. (1755). *A Dictionary of the English Language. 6th Edition*. London (1785).
Johnson, S. (1756). *Proposals for Printing the Dramatick Works of William Shakespeare*. In Raleigh (1908), 1–8.
Johnson, S. (1765). *A Preface to Shakespeare*. In Raleigh (1908), 9–63.
Johnson, S. and Steevens, G (1765). *The Plays of William Shakespeare*. In Becket, A. (ed.), *Shakespeare's Himself Again: The Language of the Poet Asserted*. London (1815).
Jonson, B. (1640). *The English Grammar*. In Waite, A. V. (ed.), New York: Sturgis and Walton (1909).
Jonson, B. (1640a). *Timber; or Discoveries; made upon Men and Matter*. In Herford, C. H., Simpson, P., and Simpson, E. (eds), *The Works of Ben Jonson*. Oxford: Clarendon Press (1947).
Joseph, M. (1947). *Shakespeare's Use of the Arts of Language*. Eastford, CT: Martino Fine Books (2013).

Joseph, M. (1962). *Rhetoric in Shakespeare's Time*. New York: Harcourt, Brace and World.
Jucker, A. H. and Taavitsainen, I. (eds) (2008). *Speech Acts in the History of English*. Amsterdam: John Benjamins.
Kames, Lord (Henry Home) (1762). *Elements of Criticism*. Extracted in Vickers (1976).
Kastovsky, D. (ed.) (1991). *Historical English Syntax*. Berlin: Mouton de Gruyter.
Kastovsky, D. (ed.) (1994). *Studies in Early Modern English*. Berlin: Mouton De Gruyter.
Keenan, E. L. and Ochs, E. (1979). 'Becoming a competent speaker of Malagasy.' In Shopen (1979), 113–58.
Kermode, F. (2000). *Shakespeare's Language*. Harmondsworth: Penguin.
Knight, C. (ed.) (1851). *The Comedies, Histories, Tragedies and Poems of William Shakspere. 2nd Edition. Vol. 2*. London: Charles Knight and Co.
Knight, C. (1873). *Passages of a Working Life during Half a Century. Vol 2*. Cambridge: Cambridge University Press (2014).
Koelb, C. (1979). 'The iambic pentameter revisited.' In Salmon and Burness (1987), 433–41.
Kökeritz, H. (1953). *Shakespeare's Pronunciation*. New Haven: Yale University Press.
Kökeritz, H. (1961). 'Review of Dobson's *English Pronunciation*.' *Language*, 37/1: 150–16.
Kreps, B. I. (2003). 'Review of Sokol, B. J. and Sokol, M. (eds) 2000 *Shakespeare's Legal Language*.' *Shakespeare Quarterly*, 54/3: 310–12.
Lakoff, G. and Johnson, M. (1980). *Metaphors We Live By*. Chicago: University of Chicago Press.
Lass, R. (ed.) (1999). *The Cambridge History of the English Language Vol. III: 1476 to 1776*. Cambridge: Cambridge University Press.
Lass, R. (1999a). 'Introduction.' In Lass (1999), 1–12.
Lass, R. (1999b) 'Phonology and morphology.' In Lass (1999), 56–186.
Leavis, F. R. (1931). 'Review article "Criticism of the Year".' *The Bookman*, 81, Dec. 1931, 180.
Leech, G. (1969). *A Linguistic Guide to English Poetry*. London: Longman.
Levin, Bernard (1983). *Enthusiasms*. London: Coronet Books.
Lewis, C. S. (1954). *English Literature in the Sixteenth Century*. Oxford: Clarendon Press.
Lim, C. S. (1986). 'Dr Johnson's quotation from *Macbeth*.' *Notes and Queries*, Dec, 1986, 518.
Locke, J. (1689). *An Essay Concerning Human Understanding*. Oxford: Clarendon Press (1894).
Lüdeling, A. and Kytö (eds) (2008). *Corpus Linguistics Vol. 1*. Berlin: Mouton de Gruyter.
Lyons, J. (1971). *Introduction to Theoretical Linguistics*. Cambridge: Cambridge University Press.
Macaulay, G. C. (1912). 'Review of C. T. Onions, "A Shakespeare Glossary".' *The Modern Language Review*, 7/4 (Oct. 1912): 559–61.
Mack, P. (2011). *A History of Renaissance Rhetoric 1380–1620*. Oxford: Oxford University Press.
Mallet, D. (1733). *Of Verbal Criticism. An Epistle to Mr. Pope. Occasioned by Theobald's Shakespeare, and Bentley's Milton*. Extracted in Vickers (1975), 21–2.
Malone, E. (1790). *The Plays and Poems of Shakespeare. Preface*. Extracted in Vickers (1981), 521–55.
Malone, E. (1816). 'An Essay on the chronological order of his plays.' In Malone, E. (ed.), *The Works of William Shakespeare. Vol. 1*. London.
Marlowe C. *Dr Faustus* (1592). In Gill, R. (ed.), London: Methuen (2008).
Marshall, G. (2012). *Shakespeare in the Nineteenth Century*. Cambridge: Cambridge University Press.
Mason, J. M. (1785). *Comments on the Last Edition of Shakespeare's Plays*. Dublin.
Mazzon, G. and Fodde, L. (eds) (2012). *Historical Perspectives on Forms of English Dialogue*. Milan: FrancoAngeli.
McDonald, R. (2003). 'Shakespeare's verse.' In Wells and Orlin (2003), 79–92.
McDonald, R. (2006). *Shakespeare's Late Style*. Cambridge: Cambridge University Press.
McEvoy, S. (2006). *Shakespeare: The Basics Second Edition*. London: Routledge.

McKenzie, D. F. (1959). 'Shakespeare's punctuation – a new beginning.' *Review of English Studies*, 10: 361–70.
Meredith, P. (ed.) (1981). *Leeds Studies in English*. 12.
Miller, D. and Leffel, K. (1994). 'The Middle English reanalysis of DO.' *Diachronica*, XI/2: 171–98.
Mulcaster, R. (1582). *The First Part of the Elementary*. Menston: The Scolar Press (1970).
Mulholland, J. (1967). '"Thou" and "you" in Shakespeare: a study in the second person pronoun.' Salmon and Burness (1987), 153–162.
Müller, M. (1861). *Lectures on the Science of Language. Vol. 1*. London: Longman, Green.
Munro, L. (2015). 'Antique/antic: archaism, neologism and the play of Shakespeare's words in *Love's Labour's Lost* and *2Henry IV*.' In Yachnin (2015), 77–101.
Nevalainen, T. (1991). 'Motivated archaism: the use of affirmative periphrastic *do* in Early Modern English liturgical prose.' In Kastovsky (1991), 303–20.
Nevalainen, T. (1999). 'Early Modern English lexis and semantics.' In Lass (1999), 332–458.
Nevalainen, T. (2001). 'Shakespeare's new words.' In Adamson et al. (2001), 237–55.
Nevalainen, T. (2006). *An Introduction to Early Modern English*. Edinburgh: Edinburgh University Press.
Nevalainen, T. and Raumolin-Brunberg, H. (2003). *Historical Sociolinguistics: Language change in Tudor and Stuart England*. London: Pearson Education.
Nowottny, W. (1962). *The Language Poets Use*. London: The Athlone Press.
Noyes, J. B. and Peirce, C. S. (1864). 'Shakespearean pronunciation.' *North American Review*, 98: 342–69.
Nurmi, A. (1996). 'Periphrasitic DO and BE + ING: interconnecting developments?' In Nevalainen and Raumolin-Brunberg (2003), 151–65.
Nurmi, A. (1999). *A Social History of Periphrastic DO*. Mémoires de la Société Néophilologique de Helsinki, 56. Helsinki: Société Néophilologique.
Offor, J. (ed.) (1819). *Annotations Illustrative of the Plays of Shakespeare*. London.
Oncins-Martinez, José (2011). 'Shakespeare's sexual language and metaphor: a cognitive-stylistic approach.' In Ravassat and Culpeper (2011), 215–45.
Onions, C. T. (revised by Eagleson, R. D.) (1986). *A Shakespeare Glossary*. Oxford: Clarendon Press.
Parker, P. L. (1905). *George Fox's Journal* (abridged). London: Ibster and Co Ltd.
Partridge, A. C. (1964). *Orthography in Shakespeare and Elizabethan Drama*. London: Edward Arnold.
Partridge, E. (1947). *Shakespeare's Bawdy. Revised Edition*. London: Routledge and Kegan Paul (1968).
Partridge, A. C. (1949). *A Dictionary of the Underworld*. London: Macmillan.
Paterson, D. (2010). *Reading Shakespeare's Sonnets. A New Commentary*. London: Faber and Faber.
Pollard, A. (1917). *Shakespeare's Fight with the Pirates and the Problems of the Transmission of His Text*. Cambridge: Cambridge University Press.
Poole, W. (2007). 'The vices of style.' In Adamson et al. *Renaissance Figures of Speech* (2011), 237–51.
Pope, A. and Warburton, W. (eds) (1747). *The Works of Shakespear. Vol. 1. Preface*. Dublin.
Post, J. (ed.) (2013). *Oxford Handbook of Shakespeare's Poetry*. Oxford: Oxford University Press.
Powell, R. (1969). 'Review of Brian Vickers *The Artistry of Shakespeare's* prose.' *The Modern Language Review*, 64/2: 393–4.
Pride, J. and Holmes, J. (eds) (1972). *Sociolinguistics. Selected Readings*. Harmondsworth: Penguin.
Puttenham, G. (1589). *The Arte of English Poesie*. In Edward Arber (ed.), Birmingham (1869).
Raleigh, W. (1908). *Johnson on Shakespeare*. Oxford: Oxford University Press.
Ravassat, M. and Culpeper, J. (eds) (2011). *Stylistics and Shakespeare's Language: Transdisciplinary Approaches*. London: Bloomsbury Publishing.

Read, S. (2007). 'Puns: serious wordplay.' In Adamson et al. (2007), 81–94.
Replogle, C. (1973). 'Shakespeare's salutations: a study in stylistic etiquette.' In Salmon and Burness (1987), 101–16.
Rhodes, N. (2008). Review of Adamson, S., Alexander, G., and Ettenhuber, K, 2007 *Renaissance Figures of Speech. The Review of English Studies*, 59/241: 616–7.
Richardson, W (1774). *A Philosophical Analysis and Illustration of Some of Shakespeare's Remarkable Characters*. London.
Rissanen, M. (1985). 'perphrastic "do" in affirmative statements in early American English.' *Journal of English Linguistics*, 18: 163–83.
Rissanen, M. (1999). 'Syntax.' In Lass (1999), 187–331.
Rissannen, M. (1991). 'Spoken language and the history of *DO*-periphrasis.' In Kastovsky (1991), 321–42.
Ritson, J. (1781). *Remarks, critical and illustrative, on the text and notes of the last edition of Shakspeare: The Merchant of Venice*. London.
Ritson, J. (1793). *The English Anthology*. London.
Roderick, R. (1758). 'Remarks on Shakespeare.' In Edwards, T. (1758), *The Canons of Criticism and Glossary. 6th Edition, with Additions*. London, 212–38.
Rokison, A. (2011). *Shakespearean Verse Speaking: Text and Theatre Practice*. Cambridge: Cambridge University Press.
Rokison, A. (2013). 'Shakespeare's dramatic verse line.' In Post (2013), 285–305.
Ronberg, G. (1992). *A Way with Words: The Language of English Renaissance Literature*. London: Arnold.
Rymer, T. (1693). *A Short View of Tragedy*. Menston, Yorkshire: The Scolar Press (1970).
Salmon, Vivian (1970). 'Some functions of Shakespearean word-formation.' In Salmon and Burness (1987), 193–206.
Salmon, V. (1986). 'The spelling and punctuation of Shakespeare's time.' In Wells and Taylor Shakespeare, W. *The complete works: Original-spelling edition* (1986), xlii–lvi.
Salmon, V. (1999). 'Orthography and punctuation.' In Lass (1999), 13–55.
Salmon, V. and Burness, E. (eds) (1987). *Reader in the Language of Shakespearean Drama*. Amsterdam: Benjamins.
Schäfer, J. (1980). *Documentation in the O.E.D.: Shakespeare and Nashe as test cases*. Oxford: Clarendon Press.
Schäfer, J. (1985). 'Review of Cercignani's *Shakespeare's Works and Elizabethan Pronunciation*.' *The Review of English Studies*, 80/2: 419–21.
Schmidt, A. (1874). 'Preface to the first volume of the first edition,' *Shakespeare-lexicon: A Complete Dictionary of All the English Words, Phrases and Constructions in the works of the poet*, Vol. 1. Berlin: Georg Reimer, and New York: G. E. Stechert (1903).
Schoenbaum, S. (1991). *Shakespeare's Lives*. Oxford: Clarendon Press.
Scott, I. (ed.) (1908). *Erasmus's Ciceronianus*. Teachers College, Columbia University, New York.
Sebeok, T. A. (ed.) (1960). *Style in Language*. Cambridge, Mass.: MIT Press.
Sergeant, P. and Swan, J. (eds) (2012). *English in the World: History, Diversity, Change*. Milton Keynes: Open University.
Seccombe, T. and Allen, L. W. (1903). *The Age of Shakespeare*. London: George Bell and Son.
Shea, J. A. (2015). 'Recasting "angling" in *The Winter's Tale*.' In Yachnin (2015), 125–46.
Shipley, J. T. (1977). *In Praise of English: The Growth and Use of Language*. New York: Times Books.
Shopen, T. (ed.) (1979). *Languages and Their Speakers*. Philadelphia: University of Pennsylvania Press.

Sicherman, C. M. (1984). 'Short lines and interpretation: the case of *Julius Caesar.*' *Shakespeare Quarterly*, 35/2: 180–95.
Simpson, P. (1911). *Shakespearean Punctuation*. Oxford: Clarendon Press.
Singer, S. W. (ed.) (1875). *The Dramatic Works of William Shakespeare*. London: George Bell and Sons.
Slater, E. (1988). *The Problem of 'The Reign of King Edward III': A Statistical Approach*. Cambridge: Cambridge University Press.
Smallwood, R. (ed.) (2005). *Players of Shakespeare, Vol 5*. Cambridge: Cambridge University Press.
Sokol, B. J. and Sokol, M. (eds) (2000). *Shakespeare's Legal Language*. London: The Athlone Press.
Sonnino, Lee Ann (1968). *A Handbook of Sixteenth Century Rhetoric*. London: Routledge.
Sorensen, J. (2000). *The Grammar of Empire in Eighteenth-Century British Writing*. Cambridge: Cambridge University Press.
Spencer, C. (1965). *Five Restoration Adaptations of Shakespeare*. Urbana: University of Illinois Press.
Spencer, H (1927). *Shakespeare Improved: The Restoration Versions in Quarto and on the Stage*. New York: Frederick Ungar Publishing Co.
Spevack, M. (1973). *The Harvard Concordance to Shakespeare*, Hildesheim: Georg Olms, and 1980 *A Complete and Systematic Concordance to the Works of Shakespeare, Vols. 1–9*. Evanston, Illinois: Adler's Foreign Books, Inc.
Sprat, T. (1667). *The History of the Royal Society of London*. London.
Spurgeon, C. F. E. (1961). *Shakespeare's Imagery and What it Tells Us*. Cambridge: Cambridge University Press.
Steevens, G. (1773). *Advertisement to the Reader*. London (1778).
Stein, D. (1990). *The Semantics of Syntactic Change: Aspects of the evolution of 'do' in English*. Berlin: Mouton de Gruyter.
Story, W. W. (1891). *Excursions in Art and Letters*. Cambridge: The Riverside Press.
Swan, M. (1995). *Practical English Usage. 2nd Edition*. Oxford: Oxford University Press.
Tanselle, G. T. and Dunbar, F. W. (1962). 'Legal language in *Coriolanus*.' In Salmon and Burness (1987), 255–62.
Tarlinskaja, M. (1983). 'Evolution of Shakespeare's metrical style.' *Poetics*, 12: 567–87.
Taylor, G. (1989). *Reinventing Shakespeare: A Cultural History from the Restoration to the Present*. London: The Hogarth Press.
Theobald, L. (1726). *Shakespeare Restored: or, a specimen of the many errors, as well committed, as unamended, by Mr Pope in his late edition of this poet. designed not only to correct the said edition, but to restore the true reading of Shakespeare in all the editions ever yet published*. London.
Thomas, J. (1995). *Meaning in Interaction: An Introduction to Pragmatics*. London: Longman.
Thompson, A. and Thompson, J. O. (1987). *Shakespeare: Meaning and Metaphor*. Brighton: The Harvester Press.
Traugott, E. C. (1972). *A History of English Syntax*. New York: Holt, Reinhart and Winston.
Treip, M. (1970). *Milton's Punctuation, and Changing English Usage, 1582–1673*. London: Methuen.
Upton J. (1746). *Critical Observations on Shakespeare*. London.
van Noppen, J-P (1983). 'Review of Schäfer, J. 1980 *Documentation in the O.E.D.: Shakespeare and Nashe as test cases*.' Oxford: Clarendon Press. In *Revue Belge de Philologie et D'Histoire*, 61/3: 707–8.
Vickers, B. (1968). *The Artistry of Shakespeare's Prose*. London: Methuen.
Vickers, B. (1968a). *Francis Bacon and Renaissance Prose*. Cambridge: Cambridge University Press.

Vickers, B. (1970). *Classical Rhetoric in English Poetry*. Basingstoke: Macmillan.
Vickers, B. (1971). 'Shakespeare's use of rhetoric.' In Salmon and Burness (1987), 391–406.
Vickers, B. (1974). *Shakespeare: The Critical Heritage, Vol. 1 1623–1692*. London: Routledge and Kegan Paul.
Vickers, B. (ed.) (1975). *Shakespeare. The Critical Heritage. Vol. 3 1733–52*. London: Routledge and Kegan Paul.
Vickers, B. (1976). *Shakespeare. The Critical Heritage. Vol. 4 1753–6*. London: Routledge and Kegan Paul.
Vickers, B. (ed.) (1979). *Shakespeare. The Critical Heritage. Vol. 5 1765–1774*. London: Routledge and Kegan Paul.
Vickers, B. (ed.) (1981). *Shakespeare. The Critical Heritage. Vol. 6 1774–1801*. London: Routledge and Kegan Paul.
Vickers, B. (2005). 'Review of Blake's "A Grammar of Shakespeare's Language".' *The Review of English Studies*, 56/223: 145–7.
Vickers, B. (2008). 'Approaching Shakespeare's late style.' *Early Modern Literary Studies*, 13/3: 1–26.
Viëtor, W. (1906). *A Shakespeare Phonology*. Marburg: Elwert, and London: Nutt.
Wales, K. M. (1983). '*Thou* and *You* in Early Modern English: Brown and Gilman reappraised.' In *Studia Linguistica*, 37: 107–25.
Wales, K. M. (2018). '"I am thy father's spirit": the first-person pronoun and the rhetoric of identity in *Hamlet*.' In Gibbons and Macrae (2018), 15–31.
Ward, A. (1867). 'At the tomb of Shakespeare.' In *Artemus Ward in London*. New York: Carleton and Co.
Warner, R. (1786). *A Letter to David Garrick, Esq. concerning a Glossary to the Plays of Shakespeare*. London.
Warren, M. J. (1987). 'Repunctuation as interpretation in editions of Shakespeare.' In Salmon and Burness (1987), 455–69.
Watson, G. (ed.) (1970). *Literary English since Shakespeare*. Oxford: Oxford University Press.
Webb, D. (1762). *Remarks on the Beauties of Poetry*. London.
Wells, S. (1964). *Thomas Nashe: Selected Works*. London: Routledge.
Wells, S. (1998). *Oxford Dictionary of Shakespeare*. Oxford: Oxford University Press.
Wells, S. and Orlin, L. C. (eds) (2003). *An Oxford Guide to Shakespeare*. Oxford: Oxford University Press.
Wells, S. and Taylor, G. (eds) (1986). *William Shakespeare: The Complete Works. Original- Spelling Edition*. Oxford: Clarendon Press.
Wells, S. and Taylor, G. (eds) (2005). *William Shakespeare: The Oxford Shakespeare. 2nd Edition*. Oxford: Clarendon Press.
Wermser, R. (1976). *Statistische Studien zur Entwicklung des englischen Wortschatzes (Schweizer Anglistische Arbeiten 91)* Bern: Francke.
Willcock, G. and Walker, A. (eds) (1970). In Puttenham, G., *The Arte of Englishe Poesie*. Cambridge: Cambridge University Press.
Williams, G. (1997). *A Glossary of Shakespeare's Sexual Language*. London: The Athlone Press.
Woudhuysen, H. R. (1989). *Samuel Johnson on Shakespeare*. London: Penguin.
Wright, G. T. (1981). 'Hendiadys and *Hamlet*.' *PMLA*, 96/2: 168–93.
Wright, G. T. (1988). *Shakespeare's Metrical Art*. Berkeley: University of California Press.
Wright, G. T. (2001). 'Shakespeare's metre scanned.' In Adamson et al. (2001), 51–70.
Wright, J. (1905). *The English Dialect Dictionary, Vol. 3*. London: Frowde.
Yachnin, P. (ed.) (2015). *Shakespeare's World of Words*. London: Bloomsbury.
Yule, G. (1996). *Pragmatics*. Oxford: Oxford University Press.

Index

Notes: Page numbers in **bold** denote tables.

Abbott, Edwin 48–51
Accademia della Crusca 6
Ad Herennium 176, 184
Adamson, S. 88, 98, **98**, 175, 177, 184, 187–8, **189**, 198
adaptations, of Shakespeare's work 11–18, **12**, 22; capricious language 17–18; clarifications 15–16; condensing long speeches 14; figurative expressions, literalization of 16; grammar corrections 14–15; indecency, elimination of 16–17; offences against decorum, avoidance of 17
adjectives as adverbs 15
The Advancement of Learning (Bacon) 5
affixation 36, 81
ah, uses of **77–8**, 86
alexandrines 44, 154, 166–7
ambiguity 56–8, **59–60**
anapest 166
antedatings 78, 79
Antony and Cleopatra 26, 62, 66, **78**, 81, 136, 147–8, 181
apostrophe 139, 147–8
Armstrong, Edward 62
The Arte of English Poesie (Puttenham) 145, 176
The Artistry of Shakespeare's Prose (Vickers) 154
As You Like It 34, 50, 53, 80, 119, 136, 137, 148, 160–1, 170, 175
Ashtadhyayi (Sanskrit grammar) 67
asyndeton 181
Atkins, C. D. 143
attribution studies 87
Attridge, Derek 154, 165
Aubrey, John 5, 179
Austen, Jane 46
Austin, John 101

Bacon, Francis 5
Baconian Method 5
Barber, C. 110, 111, 112–13
bardolatry 22, 72, 75
Barish, J. A. 179
Bartlett, John 53
Bayley, Harold 74–5
be and *are* 9
Blake, N. F. 94–5, 96–7, 106, 149
blank verse 155–9, 167, 169, 171
Bloomfield, Leonard 67
Bolton, W. F. 74
Booke at Large Booke at Large for the Amendment of Orthographie for English speech (Bullokar) 127
Bowdler, Henrietta Maria 47
Bowdler, Thomas 47
Bowers, Fredson 142
Boyle, Robert 5
brackets 151
Bref Grammar for English (Bullokar) 127
broken-backed IP **156**
Brook, G. L. 121
Brooks, Cleanth 62
Brown, Arthur 135
Brown, John Russell 24, 134–5
Brown, P. 107
Brown, R. 107–9, 110–11
Bullokar, William 127
Burness, E. 80, 81, 84, 97, **97**
Busse, Ulrich 106
Butler, C. 149

caesurae 37, 38, 145, 154, 159–61, 166
Callow, Simon 80
Calvo, C. 113–14
The Cambridge Dover Wilson Shakespeare, Vol 33 (Dover Wilson) 141–2

Cambridge Encyclopedia of the English Language (Crystal) 197
Capell, Edward **27**, 28, 31, 37–8
capital letters 148–9, 171
capping couplet 164–5
Cartwright, William 3
Cataline His Conspiracy (Jonson) 8
Cercignani, Fausto 120, 121, 122, 123–5
Chambers, E. K. 154–5
Chapman, George 46
Charles I, King 3
Charles II, King 4, 5, 11
Chaucer Society 54
chronology of Shakespeare's plays 44–5, **44–5**
Ciceronian style 176–8, 192; 'holding back' 177–8; hypotaxis 177; long sentences 177; 'piling up' 177; 'turning points' 178
Ciceronianus (Ersamus) 191
Civil War 3–4, 5–6
Classical Rhetoric in English Poetry (Vickers) 186
Clemen, Wolfgang 62–4, 83, 164
Cobbett, William 51
Cognitive Metaphor Theory (CMT) 83
cognitive poetics 199
cognitive stylistics 198–9
Colet, John 175–6
Collier, John Payne 42–3
The Comedy of Errors **78**, 106, 123–4, 125, 150–1, 165
comma 149–50
A Complete View of the Shakspere Controversy (Ingleby) 42
compounding 80–1
computers: versus humans 196; use in linguistic research 71
Concordance (Cowden Clarke) 51–2, 73
Concordance to Shakespeare (Spevack) 71, 72, 85
concordances 51–2, 53, 84, 85–6
consonants 129
Cooke, William 24–5
Coriolanus **12**, 26, 43, 84, 95, 112, 162, **168**, 179, 192
Corpus of Early English Correspondence (CEEC) 99
Coulthard, M. 115
couplet 164–5, 166
Cowden Clarke, Mary 51–2, 73
Craig, H. 73–4, 87
Critical Observations on Shakespeare (Upton) 20–1

Croll, Morris 179–81
Cromwell, Oliver 3–4
Crystal, B. 20, 53, 86, 95, 105, 159
Crystal, D. 20, 53, 73, 74, 75, 86, 95, 105, 111, 120, 121–2, 125, 127, 129–30, 131, 133, 137, 139, 142, 145, 146, 147, 149, 154, 157, 159, 169, 197–198
Culpeper, J. **77**, 84, 86–7, 109, 117, 199, 200
curt style 179–80
Cymbeline 21, 27, 45, 66, 81, 129, 148, 151, 164, 179, 181

dactyl 166
dark spots, Shakespeare's *see* faults, Shakespeare's
D'Avenant, William 11–13, 12, 15, 16–17, 25
Davis 82–3
De Copia (Erasmus) 176
De Inventione (Cicero) 176
De Oratore (Cicero) 176
de Saussure, Ferdinand 67
debardolatrification 74
Defence of the Epilogue (Dryden) 8, 9–10
The Development of Shakespeare's Imagery (Clemen) 62
Dickens, Charles 46, 76, 171
dictionaries 84–5, 86–7; Crystal's 2016 *Dictionary* 130–1; *English Dialect Dictionary* 32; Harrap dictionary 95; Johnson's *Dictionary* 29–30; OED *see Oxford English Dictionary (OED)*; Onions' dictionary 95
Dictionary of the English Language (Johnson) 29–30
diphthongs 126–7, 128–9, 140
Directions for Speech and Style (Hoskins) 187
Disraeli, Benjamin 174
distance relationship, and politeness 108
do, and NICE 90–4
Dobson, Eric 120, 122
Dodd, William 22
double comparatives 9
double endings 44
double meanings 64–5
double negatives 50
Dover Wilson, John 62, 141–2, 145, 147
Dr Faustus (Marlowe) 160
'drag' 158
The Dramatic Censor (Gentleman) 21
Dryden, John 4, 6, 7–10, 12, 15, 16, 17, 18, 51
Dyce, Alexander 52

e cummings 56
Eagleson, Robert 66
Early English Books Online (EEBO) project 71, 78
'Early English Books Online Text Creation Partnership' 71–2
Early English Text Society 54
Early Modern English (EModE) 4, 90, 91, 93, 95, 97, 105, 111–12, 137, 148–9; word formation 80
Early Modern Print 196
edication 141
editions 27–9, 46–8; variorum editions 46–7
editors 23–4, 25, 27–9
educational grammar 48–51
Edwards, Thomas 36
Elementarie (Mulcaster) 144
Elizabethan and Victorian English, difference between 49–51
Elizabethan spelling 133
Elliott, W. 71, 73, 74, 75
Ellis, Alexander 120
Empson, William 57–8, 121
end-stopping 160–1, 162–3
Englische Grammatik (Mätzner) 51
The English Grammar (Jonson) 7, 127
English language reform 5–7
English Pronunciation 1500- 1700 (Dobson) 120
The Enimie of Idlenesse (Fulwood) 105
enjambment 161–2
Enthusiasts 5–6
Erasmus, Desiderius 176
Essay Concerning Human Understanding (Locke) 6
Essay on Dramatic Poesy (Dryden) 7, 9
Euphues (Lyly) 192
euphuism 192
Evelyn, John 6
exclamation mark 146–7
eye-rhymes 125

facsimile reprints 134–5
The Family Shakespeare (Bowdler) 47
faults, Shakespeare's 23–4; conformity 24; inappropriacy 25–6; ornamental language in inappropriate situations 24–5; puns 24; rhyme 26–7, 37; word play 24
feminine endings **44**, 155, **156**
figurative expressions 4, 13, 16, 24–5
figures of speech: detailed studies 188–90; *hendiadys* and *Hamlet* 182–4; listing of 185–8; *prosopopoeia* 198; in Renaissance England 184–5
final preposition 9
First Folios, and graphology 137–9
The First Part of the Elementarie (Mulcaster) 128
first recorded use 76
Fischlin, D. 13
Flatter, R. 133–4
Fleay, Frederick Gard 44–5
flouting maxims 114–17
forgery 46–8
Fortier, M. 13
Fox, George 109–10
Francis Bacon and Renaissance Prose (Vickers) 181
French Academy 6
Freud, Sigmund 64
full stop 149–50, 161
Fulwood, William 105
functional shift (conversion) 81–3
Furley, Benjamin 110
Furnivall, Frederick James 43, 45, 46, 54

Gammer Gurton's Needle (Graham-White) 145
Garden of Eloquence (Peacham) 186
The Garden of Eloquence (Peacham) 176
Garner, B. A. 75, 80
gender, and *thou/you* use 110–11
gender differences 101
Gentleman, Francis 21, 23, 26
George of Hanover 4
Gil, Alexander 128
Gilbert, A. J. 116–17
Gilman, A. 107–9, 110–11
Gladstone, William 174
Glanvill, Joseph 6
The Globe 47
Globe Theatre 120, 129, 145
glossaries 31–2, 52, 84, 86
A Glossary of Shakespeare's Sexual Language (Williams) 84, 85
Golden Age 175–6
Goodland, Giles 78–9, 195–6
Graham-White, A. 142, 144, 145–6
grammar: corrections 14–15; educational grammar 48–51; purpose of 101–2; with sociolinguistic dimension 99–101
Grammar (Abbott) 91
graphology 134–6, 137–8; ~ and & 139; *i* and *j* 139; *ie* and *ee* 141; ſ and *s* 138; *u* and *v* 138–9
Graves, Robert 56

214   Index

Great Vowel Shift 122
Greg, Walter 135
Grice, Paul 114
Groves, P. 153, 154, 158

Hamlet 12, **12**, 17, 24, 25, 46, 47, 49, 58, 64–5, 66, 80, 83, 86, 88, 91, 106, 107, 111, 120, 129, 147, 154, 164, **168**, 170, 176–7, 182–4, 187, 192, 198
Handbook of Sixteenth Century Rhetoric (Sonnino) 185
Hanmer, Thomas **27**, 28, 31
Hart, John 126, 127, 144, 145
Hazlitt, William 46
headless IP **156**
The Helsinki Corpus of English Texts 78
hendiadys 182–4
Henry IV, Part 1 31, 39, 47, 61, 106, 111, 114, 117, 169, 170, 192
Henry IV, Part 2 30, 47, 88, 97, 106, 170, 171, 192
Henry V 31, 34, **59**, 64, 84, 121, 129, 136, 137, 147, 149, 170, 171, 180, 192
Henry VI, Part 1 22, 45, 63, 87, 153, 157, 168
Henry VI, Part 2 105
Henry VI, Part 3 15, 148
Henry VIII 29, 30, 36–7, 45, 181
heptameter **156**
Herennius, C. 176
hexameters **156**, 166
Heywood, John 135
Higden, Ranulf 32
Hinman, Charlton 134
his and *its* 8, 9
Historical Sociolinguistics (Nevalainen and Raumolin-Brunberg) 99
Hobbes, Thomas 29
Hooke, Robert 5
Hope, J. 73, 95–7, 101–2, 110, 196
Hoskins, John 187
Houston, J. P. 181
How to Do Things with Words (Austin) 101
Hughes, John 31
Hurd, Richard 35–6, **35–6**
Hussey, S. S. 192
Hymes, D. 99, 104
Hymn of the Nativity (Milton) 34
hyphen 150–1

iambic pentameter (IP) 153–5, 171; departures and deviations 155, **156**
images, Shakespeare's 58–64, 83, 167, **168**
impoliteness 109

inappropriate language 10–11
incomplete lines 44
indecent language 26
individual plays characteristics, identification of 36–7
Ingham, M. 154, 163–4
Ingham, R. 154, 163–4
Ingleby, Clement 42–3
Institutio Oratoria 176
interdisciplinariness 83–4
inverted commas 151
irregular verbs 15
italics 149

James I, King 3
Jespersen, Otto 72, 73, 76, 126
Johnson, Samuel 21, 23, 24, 25–6, **27**, 28, 29–30, 34, 39, 153, 188
'jolt' 158
Jonson, Ben 3, 7–9, 10, 11, 49, 51, 73, 127, 150, 179
Joseph, Sister Miram 185
Jucker, A. H. 106
Julius Caesar 10, 24, 45, 63, 91, 129, 146, 154, 156–7, 188

Käding, Friedrich 71
Kakietek, Piotr 97–8
Kames, Lord 24
Keenan, Edward 102
Kermode, F. 87, 183, 190
King Lear 12, **12**, 15, 22, 29, 37, 38–9, 52, **77**, 81, 83, 105, 106–8, 110, 154–5, 161, 168–9, 181, 183
Kinney, A. F. 87
Knight, Charles 47–8
Kökeritz, Helge 119, 120, 121, 122, 123

Lamb, Mary and Charles 47
'language rules', Shakespeare's 32–5
Latin 52, 176
Latinate neologisms 80
The Law against Lovers (D'Avenant) 12
leaven see mouldy bread
Leavis, F. R. 58
legal language 84
Levin, Bernard 75–6
Levinson, S. C. 107
Lewis, C. S. 175
lexicographers 29
lexicon 52–3, 64–6
lexis 195–8
Lichtenfels, Peter 198

linguistic language changes, historical context 3–7
linguistic vices 4–5
linguistic virtues 4
Literary English Since Shakespeare (Watson) 179
Literature Online (LION) 78
Locke, John 6
Logonomia Anglica (Gil) 128
loose style 180–1
Love's Labour's Lost 25, 44, **44**, 52, 61, 63, 88, 123, 139, 164, 169–70, 174–5, 192
lust 56–7
Lyons, J. 67

Macbeth 11, **12**, 12–13, 15, 17, 25–6, 29–30, 45, 47, 51, 60, 61–2, 63, 94, 96, 107, 109, 113, 116–17, 129, 158, 166, **168**, 170
Mack, P. 176
malapropisms 75
Mallet, David 24
Malone, Edmond 25–6, **27**, 28, 39, 48, 134
Malone Society 134, 135
Mason, John Monck 26–7
Mätzner, Eduard 51
McDonald, R. 154, 155, 181–2, 188
McEvoy, S. 165
McKenzie, D. F. 143
meaning, simplification of 57
Measure for Measure 12, **12**, 15–17, 20, 26, 27, **60**, 85, 97–8, 180, 197
mental state, and prose 169
The Merchant of Venice **12**, 26, 29, 99, 105, 112, 129, 137, 143, 157, 167
'meridian blaze' 21–2
The Merry Wives of Windsor 26, 49–50, 120, 129, 133, 169, 171, 192
metaphors 83–4, 199
Metaphors We Live By (Lakoff and Johnson) 83
metre 37–8, 91, 122, 125–6, 148, 154, 155, 162–5
Middle English (ME) 7, 26
A Midsummer Night's Dream 46, 81, 98, 117, 129, 139, 147, 166, 168–9, 175, 185
Milton, John 34, 73, 162
modern linguistics 67
Modernizing Shakespeare's Spelling (Wells and Taylor) 135
monosyllabic feet 148, **156**

monstrous syntax 7
mood, and prose 169
'mouldy bread' 20–1, 29
Much Ado About Nothing 12, **12**, 48, 61, 64, 75, **78**, 110, 113, 139, 147, 166, **168**, 170
Mulcaster, Richard 127–8, 145
Mulholland, J. 110, 137, 140, 141, 144
Müller, Max 73
Murray, James 54

Nashe, Thomas 77
neologisms 74–80, 195, 197
Nevalainen, T. 80–1, 93, 99–101
A new and complete concordance or verbal index to words, phrases, and passages in the dramatic works of Shakespeare with a supplementary concordance to the poems (Bartlett) 53
New Bibliography 141
'New Criticism' movement 57
New Shakspeare Society (NSS) 43–4, 45–6, 47, 199
Newton, Isaac 5
N-gram 196
NICE 90
non-restrictive clause 14–15, 101
noun phrase 96, 177
Novum Organum (Bacon) 5
Noyes, J. B. 119

occasional spelling 124–5
Ochs, Elinor 102
Old English (OE) 8, 15
old-spelling editions 134–6
On Early English Pronunciation (Ellis) 120
On Editing Shakespeare (Browers) 142
Oncins-Martinez, José 83–4, 199
Onions, Charles Talbot 34, 65–6, 71, 95
original pronunciation (OP): from 1953 till 1981 122; Crystal's 2016 *Dictionary* 130–1; external evidence for 126–9; internal evidence for 122–6; metre 125–6; occasional spelling 124–5; performances 129–30; puns 119–20, 123–4; rationale for studying 121–2; rhymes 125
Original-Spelling edition (Wells and Taylor) 136, 137, 142
original spelling 134–42
Orthoepia Anglicana (Daines) 145
An Orthographie (Hart) 126, 144, 145, 146

Othello 10–11, 13, 32, 65, 66, 73, 75, **77**, 86, 98–9, 107, 115–16, 163, 167, 168, **168**, 198
oxcarts 72, 196
Oxford Dictionary of Shakespeare 85
Oxford English Dictionary (OED) 54, 66, 76, 95, 195, 197; first citations 34, 76–80, 78–9, 195
Oxford English Dictionary (OED) Online 78, 79–80
Oxford University 71
Oxford University Press 135

Positive affirmative (PA) do 91–4, 97, 99; *see also do*, and NICE
Paṇini 67
Partridge, Eric 64–5, 142–3
Paterson, Don 65
Peacham, Henry 176, 184, 186, 191
pecking order, Shakespeare's language in 87–8, 94
Peirce, C. S. 120, 122
Pepys, Samuel 11
Pericles 45
phonaesthetics 121
phonotactics 92
The Pictorial Shakespere (Knight) 47–8
'Planet Hunters' project 196
politeness 107–9, 110; excessive politeness 109; negative politeness 107; and power relationship 107–8; and ranked extremity 108, 109
Pollard, Alfred 141, 144
Polychronicon 31–2
Pope, Alexander 21, 23, **27**, 28, 29, 31, 48
power, and *thou/you* use 110–11
pragmatics 102; implicature 114–17; impoliteness 109; politeness 107–9, 110; pragmatic noise 117; speech acts 104–7; *thou* and *you* 109–14
Pragmatics (Yule) 114
Present-Day English (PDE) 14, 15, 90, 95, 136
The Printing and Proof-Reading of the First Folio of Shakespeare (Hinman) 134
pronunciation 195–8
ProQuestLLC 71
prose 167–71; and verse 171; *see also* verse
prosopopoeia 198
punctuation 48, 160–1; apostrophe 147–8; capital letters 148–9; changes 56–7; comma 149–50; exclamation mark 146–7; full stop 149–50; function of 144–6; heavy punctuation 146; hyphen 150–1; inverted commas and brackets 151; italics 149; light punctuation 146; new age 151; rhetorical and grammatical functions 144–6; semi-colon 149–50; Shakespeare's and compositors' 142–4; twentieth-century studies 141–2; variations 133–4
puns 119–20, **123**, 123–4, 131, 186, 188
Puttenham, George 144–5, 169, 176, 182, 184
Pyramus and Thisbe 117, 175

Ramée, Pierre de la 127
The Rape of Lucrece 50, 58, 165–6
Raumolin-Brunberg, H. 93, 99–101
Ravassat, M. 84, 200
Read, S. 188
Remarks on the Beauties of Poetry (Webb) 37
Renaissance Figures of Speech (Adamson et al.) 188
Replogle, C. 105–6
restoration, of Shakespeare's work 18–19
restrictive clause 14–15
rhetoric 6; anti-Ciceronian styles 178; bad press 174–5; Ciceronian style 176–8, 192; curt style 179–80; development in Shakespeare's use of 190–1; euphuism 192; figures of speech 182–91; history 175–6; loose style 180–1; tools 191–3
Rhetoric in Shakespeare's Time (Joseph) 185
rhetorical flourishes 13
rhyme royal 165–6
rhymes 38, 44, 125
The Rhythms of English Poetry (Attridge) 154
Richard II **12**, 14, 17–18, 32, 61, 153, 158, 163–4, 166–7, 169, 177, 188, 195
Richard III **12**, 16, 24–5, 45, 93, 95, 106, 110–13, 148, **168**, 186, 190, 198
Richardson, William 21–2, 26
Riding, Laura 56
Rissanen, M. 90–1, 92–3
Ritson, Joseph 26, 31
Roderick, Richard 36–7
romantic intimacy, and *thou/you* distinction 112
Romeo and Juliet 22, 47, 49, 61, 63, 80–1, 109, 112, 120, 121, 129–30, 143, 149, 162, 165, 188
Ronberg, G. 176, 187
Rowe, Nicholas **27**
Royal Society 5, 6
Rymer, Thomas 10–11

–'s 7
–s and -th 99–101

Salmon, Vivian 80, 81, 84, 97, **97**, 133, 137, 149
Schäfer, J. 77, 123
schemes and tropes, distinguishing between 184
Schmidt, Alexander 52–3, 77
scientific revolution, and linguistic tastes 4–6
semi-colon 149–50
Seven Types of Ambiguity (Empson) 57–8, **59–60**
Sewell, George 31
sexual references 64–5, 199
Shakespeare and Language (Hope) 101–2
A Shakespeare Glossary (Onions) 66
Shakespeare Online 86
A Shakespeare Phonology (Viëtor) 120
Shakespeare Restored (Theobald) 18, 23–4, 28
Shakespeare Society (SS) 43–4
Shakespearean Punctuation (Simpson) 141
Shakespearean Verse Speaking: Text and Theatre Practice (Rokison) 198
Shakespeare-lexicon: A Complete Dictionary of All the English Words, Phrases and Constructions in the works of the poet (Schmidt) 52–3, 77
Shakespeare's Bawdy (Partridge) 64
Shakespeare's Fight with the Pirates and the Problems of the Transmission of His Text (Pollard) 141
Shakespeare's Grammar (Hope) 95
Shakespeare's Imagery and What it Tells Us (Spurgeon) 58
Shakespeare's Metrical Art (Wright) 154
Shakespeare's Pronunciation (Kökeritz) 120
Shakespeare's Use of Rhetoric (Vickers) 186
Shakespeare's Use of the Arts of Language (Joseph) 185
Shakespeare's Words (Crystal and Crystal) 86
Shakespeare's Works and Elizabethan Pronunciation (Cercignani) 120
'Shakespeare's World' project 197
A Shakespearian Grammar (Abbott) 48–9
'Shakesperfection' 72
Sherlock, Martin 22
Shipley, Joseph 75
short lines **44**, 154–5, **156**, 156–7, 158, 159, 166
Short View of Tragedy (Rymer) 10
Sicherman, C. M. 154
Simpson, Percy 141, 144
singular/plural mismatches 26–7, 49
Sir Thomas More 142
Slater, E. 74
small words 98, **98**

social class 101; and *thou/you* use 110
sociolinguistic dimension, grammar with 99–101
Sokol, B. J. 84–5
Sokol, M. 84–5
solidarity, and *thou/you* use 111
sonnet 165
Sonnino, Lee Ann 185
The Spanish Tragedy (Kyd) 87
speech acts 104–7, 198–9
Speech Acts in the History of English (Jucker and Taavitsainen) 106
spelling: changes 56; double and single consonants 140; and edication 141; final –*e*, presence or absence of a 139–40; and graphology 137–9; *ie* and *y* at the end of words 140–1; old-spelling editions 134–6; Oxford original-spelling edition 136–7; variations 133–4
Spencer, C. 13, **14**
Spevack, Marvin 71, 72, 85
spondees 166
Sprat, Thomas 5, 6
Spurgeon, Caroline Frances Eleanor 58, 60–1, 83
status, and *thou/you* use 111
Steevens, George 25, **27**, 28, **28**
Stubs, John 110
A Study of Shakespeare (Swinburne) 45
subject matter, and prose 169
subject-verb inversion 163–4
superficialities 56
Swinburne, Algernon 45, 46
systemization of language: individual plays characteristics, identification of 36–7; Shakespeare's 'language rules' 32–5; verse 37–8; word formation 35–6, **35–6**

Taavitsainen, I. 106
Tales from Shakespeare (Lamb and Lamb) 47
The Taming of the Shrew 39, 45, 52, 105, 112, 115–16, 124, 155, 160, 195, 199
Tarlinskaja, M. 163
Tate, Nahum 12, 14, 15, 17, 18, 39
Taylor, G. 7, 38, 72, 135, 136–7, 142, 148
The Tempest 11, 12, **12**, 30, 45, 49, 50, 73, 81, 85, 137–8, 141–2, 179, 190
tetrameters 166
theatre 198–9
Theobald, Lewis 18, 21, 23–4, 26, **27**, 28, 29, 48
Thomas, J. 115
Thompson, A. 83, 87

Thompson, J. O. 83, 87
thou and *you* 109–14
Tichborne's Elegy (Tichbourne) 159
Tichbourne, Chidiock 159
Timon of Athens 45, 105
Titus Andronicus 94, 164
Toronto Lexicons of Early Modern English 78
tragedies, and images 64
transmission faults 29
Treip, M. 142
triple endings 155, **156**
Trivium 175
trochee 155, 166
Troilus and Cressida 14, 15, 16, 17, 18, 20, 22, 34, 83, 129, 145, 178, 179, 180, 185, 195
Troilus and Cressida, or Truth found too late, a Tragedy (Dryden) 8, 9, 15
tropes and schemes, distinguishing between 184
Twelfth Night 45, 75, 91, 110, 129, **168**, 170, 178
The Two Gentlemen of Verona 46, 66, 95, 124, 133, 187
The Two Noble Kinsmen 45, 62, 139, 179

University of Michigan 71
Upton, John 20–1, 23, **32–4**, 32–5

Valenza, R. 71, 73, 74, 75
verb phrase 93, 96
verbosity 10, 174
verbs 61, 81–2, 94
verse: blank verse 155–9, 167, 169, 171; caesurae 159–60; couplet 164–5, 166; end-stopping 160–1, 162–3; enjambment 161–2; iambic pentameter 153–5; line types 155–8; and prose 171; rhyme royal 165–6; rhyme scheme 164–7; sonnet 165; subject–verb inversion 163–4; *see also* prose
Vickers, Brian 167–9, 181–2, 184, 186, 190–1
Victorian and Elizabethan English, difference between 49–51
Viëtor, Wilhelm 120
'*vinewed'st leaven*' *see* 'mouldy bread'
vocabulary, Shakespeare's: neologisms 74–80; total size 72–4
vowels 128–9
vulgarity 26

Wales, Katie 112, 114, 198
Walker, A. 184, 185, 186
Warburton, William **27**, 28
Ward, Artemus 141
Warner, Richard 31–2
Warren, M. J. 146
Webb, Daniel 37
Wells, Stanley 77, 85, 135–6, 136–7, 142
West, Michael 71
White, Richard Grant 120, 129
Wilkins, John 6
Willcock, G. 184, 185, 186
William Shakespeare: A study of facts and problems (Chambers) 154–5
Williams, G. 84, 85
The Winter's Tale 25, 44, **44**, 62, 66, 88, 96, 101–2, 147, 158, 161, 164, 179, 191
Wood, Francis 73
word formations 35–6, **35–6**, 80–3
word lists 51; glossaries 31–2; Johnson's *Dictionary* 29–30
Woudhuysen, H. R. 29, 30
Wright, George 154, 155, 161–2, 165–6, 169–70

you see thou and *you*
Yule, G. 114

zeitgeist, expressions of 71–2

For Product Safety Concerns and Information please contact our EU representative GPSR@taylorandfrancis.com
Taylor & Francis Verlag GmbH, Kaufingerstraße 24, 80331 München, Germany

www.ingramcontent.com/pod-product-compliance
Lightning Source LLC
Chambersburg PA
CBHW050533300426
44113CB00012B/2080